WITHDRAWN
UTSA LIBRARIES

THE HOLIDAY MAKERS

THE HOLIDAY MAKERS

Magazines, Advertising, and Mas

Richard K. Popp

Tourism in Postwar America

LOUISIANA STATE UNIVERSITY PRESS ⚜ BATON ROUGE

Published by Louisiana State University Press
Copyright © 2012 by Louisiana State University Press
All rights reserved
Manufactured in the United States of America
FIRST PRINTING

DESIGNER: Mandy McDonald Scallan
TYPEFACE: Whitman
PRINTER: McNaughton & Gunn, Inc.
BINDER: Acme Bookbinding, Inc.

Library of Congress Cataloging-in-Publication Data
Popp, Richard K., 1977–
 The holiday makers : magazines, advertising, and mass tourism in postwar America / Richard K. Popp.
  p. cm.
 Includes bibliographical references and index.
 ISBN 978-0-8071-4284-4 (cloth) — ISBN 978-0-8071-4286-8 (pdf) — ISBN 978-0-8071-4287-5 (epub) — ISBN 978-0-8071-4288-2 (mobi) 1. Tourism—United States—History—20th century. 2. Tourism—Psychological aspects—United States. 3. Advertising—Tourism—United States. 4. Tourism—United States—Marketing. 5. United States—Social life and customs. I. Title.
 G155.U6P68 2012
 659.19'917304918—dc23
                                        2011039647

The paper in this book meets the guidelines for permanence and durability of the Committee on Production Guidelines for Book Longevity of the Council on Library Resources. ∞

CONTENTS

Acknowledgments   vii

INTRODUCTION:
The New Leisure   1

1. THE NEW MOBILITY:
Travel and Leisure in Depression and War   11

2. CREATING *HOLIDAY:*
Market Research, Play, and Magazine Reading   31

3. SELLING VACATIONS:
Tourist Travel, Free Time, and Classlessness   58

4. "THIS IS HOW IT WILL BE WHEN YOU GET THERE":
Destination Profiles and Middlebrow Geography   82

5. CASTING LURES:
Tourism Advertising and the Experiential Ethos   103

6. GOING OFF THE BEATEN PATH:
Authentic Places and the End of an Era   128

EPILOGUE:
From National Folkway to Personal Quest   145

Notes   149
Index   195

ACKNOWLEDGMENTS

Around 2005, I started to think a lot about travel. Like just about everyone else, I'd always enjoyed getting away. But for some reason, vacation travel started to come into view as an interesting cultural phenomenon in ways I'd never considered before. A seminar paper on the history of advertising and consumer culture consigned me to long afternoons at the library that spring, leafing through magazines from the 1930s and 1940s. While I didn't write about it at the time, I was struck by the collision I saw between two eras that had been discrete in my mind: one of steamships, trunks, and porters and another of airliners, suitcases, and flight attendants. What I saw was that these weren't separate eras that butted into each other, but social worlds that overlapped. For decades both shared the same pages and sometimes even the same ads, best illustrated by the early airliners decked out with sleeping berths, cocktail bars, and dance floors. I came away with an indefinable fascination with midcentury tourism culture and a desire to look into it further. When I started to share some of these foggy notions, I was fortunate to be working with a wonderful group of scholars who taught me how to translate my ideas into a vocabulary of concepts, questions, and leads to pursue.

From the start of this project, then, I've owed a great debt to many people, without whom it wouldn't have been possible. Carolyn Kitch was incredibly enthusiastic about the project from first mention. As I sketched it out, played around with different ideas, and explored new angles, Carolyn was always happy to talk or read a new draft. And in the years since her formal duties with this project ended, she's remained its biggest advocate. But beyond that, working with Carolyn shaped how I do research in ways I can't thank her enough for. Her mentorship allowed me to start writing the kind of cultural history that I loved reading but had no idea how to do. Nancy Morris has also been a huge supporter of this project, and her influence has been enormous. Early on in my studies, when I started to pepper our conversations with words like "time" and "space," Nancy told me to go read theorists like David Harvey. All of a sudden things started to come into focus. Beyond the theoretical literature she introduced me to, Nancy trained me to keep my eye on the ball, always holding the "so what" questions in sight.

I also owe much to teachers and colleagues who have read and commented on different versions of this manuscript. Ken Kusmer and Andy Mendelson introduced me to bodies of literature that had a major impact on the shape and intentions of this project. Both also provided very thorough reads and insightful comments on an earlier version of the manuscript. At a late stage in the process, Rachel Hall read the entire book and offered an amazingly helpful set of comments. Jenell Johnson and members of the Hedgehogs dissertation-writing group—Dawn Gilpin, Guillermo Avila-Saavedra, Melissa Lenos, Kelly George, and Heather Muse—also had interesting things to say about different sections along the way. Conversations with Felicia Song, Bob Mann, Anne Osborne, Mike Xenos, and Sue Robinson also helped to shape my thinking on various ideas that made their way into the book. At conferences over the past few years, many others have offered informative comments that have undoubtedly benefited the project. In particular, scholars involved with the American Journalism Historians Association have been enthusiastic friends to this project.

Just as vital to the research behind *The Holiday Makers* are the dedicated archivists and librarians whose efforts make it possible to dive into the past. I owe a great many thanks to dozens of helpful people at Temple University's Paley Library, Louisiana State University's Middleton Library, the Free Library of Philadelphia, the Van Pelt Library at the University of Pennsylvania, the University of Pennsylvania's Rare Book and Manuscript Library, the Harry Ransom Center at the University of Texas at Austin, the Library of Congress's Manuscript Division and Main Reading Room, the John W. Hartman Center for Sales, Advertising & Marketing History at Duke University, the Newberry Library, and the Wisconsin Historical Society. Hyunmee Kang, Kevin Thibodeaux, and Doyle Armitage were also a big help tracking down stray materials from Middleton Library over the past three years. While I was writing this book, my colleagues at the University of Wisconsin–Milwaukee, Louisiana State University, and the Mass Media and Communication doctoral program at Temple University fostered terrific work environments. Working with Alisa Plant and the rest of the team at LSU Press has been a fantastic experience.

Sue Robinson, Tom and Allison Popp, Amy and Ryan Fogarty, Brian Potter and Jamie Schilling, and Ray and Eileen Popp graciously housed and entertained me during research trips. Kelly and Matt Deering, Basil Popp, Mary Lynn Brown, John and Virginia Stec, Aaron and Caroline Hewitt, Alex Cogswell and Jen Hydeman, and Jay and Betsy Brown have offered needed camaraderie along the way, too. A pair of teachers I met years before starting this project, Al Defazio and Matt McAllister, sparked my interest in the world of ideas and encouraged me to take up scholarship at key points in my education. As I've embarked on a career in academia, Matt has remained a tremendous supporter. My parents, Richard and Susan Popp, have always offered unqualified support and encouragement. Their interest in learning about the broader world out there sparked mine. Because of the environment they fostered at home, asking questions like "how" and "why" has always struck me as the natural thing to do. There's no one who has been more supportive, encouraging, and generous along the way than Shannon Popp. More than once, she's made enormous sacrifices so that I could pursue this line of work. I can't thank her enough. She and our boy are the best holiday troupe anyone could ask for, so I dedicate this book to them.

THE HOLIDAY MAKERS

INTRODUCTION
The New Leisure

In 1959, Alfred Hitchcock appeared before movie audiences and asked, "Have you planned your vacation yet?" The occasion was the trailer for the director's newest film, *North by Northwest*. Hitchcock's spy thriller starred Cary Grant as an advertising executive mistaken for a secret agent and drawn into a saga of international intrigue. Like many of Hitchcock's works, the film told the classic story of someone in the wrong place at the wrong time. But what made *North by Northwest* so distinctly a product of the postwar era was the backdrop it played out against—the United States as a vacationscape. On the run through much of the film, Grant skulked around hotels, raced from New York to Chicago aboard the *Twentieth Century Limited*, flew to the Black Hills vacationland, faked his own death in a national park cafeteria, and, most spectacularly, eluded would-be assassins in a mad scramble across the face of Mount Rushmore. Given the film's setting, Hitchcock's trailer was appropriate. The stout director posed as a travel agent surrounded by posters, literature, and maps. He suggested that the audience consider Grant's itinerary when making their summer plans.[1]

North by Northwest's trailer was more than a clever play on the film; it was a distillation of midcentury travel culture. When Hitchcock's film was released in 1959, the United States was nearly a decade and a half into a period of widespread affluence without precedent. Tourism played a unique and pivotal role in this culture of mass consumption. Paid vacation plans had been extended deep into the American labor force, middle- and working-class people had more disposable income than ever, and a vast transportation network spilled out across the globe. With an eye on these developments, many observers saw a new type of society arising—one predicated on a mobile public, unshackled from work's constraints, and free to roam wherever they pleased.

Socially, the notion of a travel boom grew out of the shift toward a Keynesian, consumer-driven economy in the 1930s and 1940s. Vacations occupied important symbolic ground within this economic order. They suggested that industrial modernity's driving dynamism, a finely tuned balance of raw technological power and rational technocratic order, had achieved such precision that it transcended the production of wealth and moved on to producing time. Long enjoyed by the leisure class, vacationing was an unknown practice to most Americans at the turn of the twentieth century. Yet by midcentury, paid leave periods, carved out for the explicit purpose of giving individuals the chance to get away for a while, had become an expectation for white- and blue-collar workers alike. Even if many middle-income people couldn't travel, paid leave at least made it a possibility. Vacations, then, were not only a highly visible part of the Fordist good life that flowed from business, labor, and government's cooperative pursuit of mass consumption but were metaphoric for the expanding life possibilities brought into view by a more equitable economic order.[2]

In terms of workplace perks, paid vacations were an especially attractive accommodation to the business community. For one, they helped shroud the American economic system in an aura of managerial benevolence. But more important, paid leave was thought to be a greater economic stimulant than alternatives like a shorter workweek.[3] Simply put, vacationers spent money. They bought tickets for planes, trains, buses, and ocean liners, or if traveling by car they burned through gasoline and tires. While away, they dined out, stayed in hotels, motels, and campgrounds, bought tickets for amusements, and gobbled up souvenirs. And just as important, they outfitted themselves with the accoutrements of a leisured way of life: sportswear, swimsuits, luggage, cameras, film, skis, camping gear, and much more. In this way, paid vacations carved out blocks of time in which distinct patterns of consumer activity could develop and take hold.[4] A robust tourist trade could have other benefits as well. After World War II, government and industry viewed travel abroad as an alternative form of foreign aid that used the market and private spending to spread capital around a war-ravaged world. The dollars that American tourists toted abroad would in time trickle back to U.S. coffers by way of purchases for tractors, machine heads, Hollywood film rights, and dozens of other exports. Tourism's spending spree had other benefits as well. In terms of Cold War gamesmanship, tourists in foreign lands could showcase the American standard of living and convey a sense of compassion for other parts of the world, often struggling to rebuild or develop industrially. And as an added bonus, the intercultural contact inherent to foreign travel promised to erode prejudice and sow international harmony. It was in this spirit that the European Travel Commission, for instance, could pitch tourism as a "passport to peace" in the late 1940s.[5]

Culturally, the concept of a travel boom grew out of the confluence of three powerful narratives of American national identity. While all to one degree or another were rooted in narrow midcentury assumptions that conflated Americanness with middle-class whiteness, each narrative was prominent in the popular discourse of the day. The first was that an insatiable wanderlust, or will to see what lay over the horizon, was somehow hardwired into Americans. "Why the wanderlust?" the *New York Times Magazine*'s Edith Efron asked of American vacationers in 1946: "Travel is in their blood, in their national heritage."[6] According to this mythology, wanderlust had propelled European colonists over the Atlantic; it had animated cries of manifest destiny as white settlers scattered across the continent; and now with the frontier closed, wanderlust had taken a new form, driving American vacationers to the far corners of the globe.[7] The transformation of wanderlust from the drive to conquer nature to pleasurable excursion belied the influence of a second narrative of American identity: the United States as a land of leisure. According to this story, the nation's work-oriented culture, steeped in a heavy dose of staid Puritanism and Victorian righteousness, crumbled under a joyous new, amusement-centered culture. Theme parks, urban beaches, cinemas, arcades, dance halls, spectator sports, phonographs, tourist camps, and many of the other innovations that arose between the 1890s and 1920s shoved the nation toward a way of life that placed fun atop the cultural hierarchy of needs. Vacation travel was a sure sign that Americans were more comfortable than ever dropping their work to take their leisure. Postwar mass tourism would grow up alongside a new ideal of everyday leisure modeled on the seamless blend of domestic comfort, backyard recreation, and suburban spaciousness embodied by the California ranch home. Within this context, the vacation was a sort of ritual celebration of free time, mobility, and fun.[8]

While the land-of-leisure narrative exaggerated the extent to which earlier eras were devoid of entertainment, the notion that fun was the animating spirit behind a patently American identity would have struck most observers as well off the mark circa 1900. Even Germans thought Americans were a particularly joyless lot. It was the American character, after all, that Max Weber, writing in 1904, identified as the relentlessly driven prototype for the spirit of capitalism. Yet by midcentury, many observers of American life took leisure's primacy, or what some observers called "the New Leisure," as a starting point.[9] "This characteristic edifice of our times," economist Paul F. Douglass wrote of the U.S. amusement economy in 1957, "is as representative of our modern spirit as the Parthenon was an expression of the age of Athens and Amiens Cathedral a symbol of the Gothic concept of thirteenth century Christianity."[10] Sociologists saw deeper changes in the national character as well, citing the emergence of other-directedness and a new "fun morality." As journalist Martha Gellhorn observed while touring the United States in 1947, "I have never seen any country where so many people took so much time off to have fun."[11]

The third narrative told the story of American technology's obliteration of time and space, beginning with the railroad and culminating with commercial flight.[12] "'Those faraway places with strange-sounding names,'" *Cosmopolitan* gushed at the dawn of the jet age, "are becoming as close as the next city." At the core of this narrative was a view of modern technology and infrastructure as a profoundly liberating force, allowing Americans to go wherever they wished. As one industry spokesperson summed up this sentiment in 1957: "Today Americans are the most mobile people the world has ever known."[13] For many observers, mobility was intoxicating because it suggested mastery over the physical environment. Describing his experience aboard the first commercial jetliner in 1952, one writer relayed the comments of a seatmate: "Makes you feel such a god, doesn't it?" Others lauded the nation's "fantastic automobilism," marveling at the integrated network of homes, superhighways, motels, gas stations, and vacation stops that had quickly overlaid the national landscape.[14] Nations continued to pour vast resources into their ocean liners, as well, while the press heaped praise on these totems of technological might. When the S.S. *United States* won the blue ribbon for fastest transatlantic crossing in 1952, the overjoyed passengers danced a conga line around the ship in celebration. Even the railroads still attracted great attention, introducing blistered Plexiglas roofs, or Vista-Domes, to offer passengers a panoramic view of passing scenery.[15] While blue ribbons and Vista-Domes now appear as quaint relics of an earlier era, doomed to irrelevance by cheap gasoline and jet-age airspeeds, they fit into a midcentury narrative of technological progress that broadly equated modernity with movement.[16]

Magazines played a unique role in making and marketing the travel boom. As the main conduit for the seductive travel ads that beckoned consumers to far-off places, they mediated between the vacation industry and the vacationing public, translating the former's market growth imperatives into the latter's desire for a more leisured way of life. Though magazines were challenged by the giant that the television industry was fast growing into, they still occupied a unique storytelling role in postwar American culture. Blending image and text in news reports, narratives, and social commentary, they provided shape to the issues and trends playing out around readers.[17] Further, magazines offered an avenue for imagining a national, middle-class identity, as readers could see what American culture looked like, knowing that millions of unknown peers in distant neighborhoods like their own were doing the same.[18] Every week or month, magazines conjured up an image of a nation on the move, dashing from one vacationland to the next. And as the tourism industry grew larger and its ad budget swelled, publishers became more and more motivated to feature the stories that could connect travel marketers with travel-minded audiences. The Curtis Publishing Company, owners of the *Saturday Evening Post* and *Ladies' Home Journal*, went further than any other business in this regard, starting the slick, jumbo-sized *Holiday* magazine in 1946 to capitalize on the travel boom.

The Holiday Makers explores this confluence of consumerism, tourist travel, and print culture. It argues that magazine publishers and advertisers came to recognize tourism as a unique means of speaking to Americans' civic and consumer desires for a more leisured and mobile way of life during the mid-twentieth century. By the 1940s, vacation travel, or "two weeks with pay," seemed to many to be developing into a folkway of modern American life. The chance to escape the daily grind represented not only a welcome respite but a manifestation of a national will to roam at last realized en masse. The most forward-thinking marketers of the era saw the value represented by these impulses; by equating wanderlust with a whole carefree ethos toward spending, they saw the touristic imagination as something to be cultivated and capitalized on. Their efforts resulted in magazines that came to look like geographic galleries. Setting their appeals against the backdrop of lush vacationscapes, advertisers from regional boosters to swimsuit makers showcased a wider world out there to be consumed by the vast globe-trotting public. Sandwiched between these lures, readers could ponder over the travel profiles and photo-essays furnished by publishers to welcome this booming ad sector.

While the buzz surrounding tourism certainly reflected the aims of marketers, it would be a mistake to see it as a product of their efforts alone. For many Americans, greater mobility and more leisure time were among the most compelling evidence that industrial modernism had ultimately shown itself a life-improving process. In celebrating the travel boom, publishers and advertisers tapped into a whole collection of phenomena that fired the midcentury American imagination: a collective pride in the egalitarianism represented by mass leisure; a sense that perks like longer vacations portended a widening sphere of free time and personal autonomy; a piqued geographic curiosity fired by new technologies that seemed to bring distant places nearer; and internationalist hopes that cross-cultural contact could sow humanitarian understanding. The individuals who produced travel articles were acting on more than pecuniary motives as well. Many were animated by a strong middlebrow impulse to make uplifting culture, in this case the cosmopolitan world of travel, available to mass audiences they assumed yearned for connection to an urbane way of life. Reflecting this middlebrow ethos, magazine editors' notions of tourism owed more to the sightseeing of cultural pilgrimage than the recreational pleasures of the beach or mountain lake.[19] But it was a modernized pilgrimage, as infused by the lighthearted spirit and egalitarian thrust of the time as the educational impulses of old. Easy mobility lay at the heart of this vision. The vacation was essentially the ultimate expression, ritualized in its heightened state, of the fluid movement that characterized industrial modernity—a common thread that ran through everything from the freeways of urban renewal projects to the feedback loops of information theory. Tourist travel allowed Americans to bask in a world made easy to traverse, whisking across continents and oceans while on vacation in the same manner they raced from suburb to city in everyday life.

What appeared on magazine pages, then, reflected this stew of influences, combining marketers' desires for business growth, audiences' desires for leisured mobility, and editors' desires to bring cultural uplift. Although each was integral, marketers ultimately pulled rank, and it was their enterprise—the cultivation of more and more profitable travel markets—that provided the framework into which the others were squeezed. As Theodor Adorno observed, the "need for freedom" at the base of popular leisure "gets functionalized, extended and reproduced by business; what they [audiences] want is forced upon them once again."[20] And in this manner, readers were presented with a picture of travel as filtered through what marketers could surmise about a distinctly middle-class tourist imagination and consumer ethos.

Yet even as tourism was celebrated as a more and more democratic experience, distinction died hard. The dynamics of selling travel encouraged marketers to fall back on status appeals and forge powerful new ways of sorting audiences according to a class-based logic. Tourism's experiential nature lent itself in advertisers' hands to narratives of transformation that pivoted on acts of social transcendence, such as crossing class borders or breaking away from the tourist crowds. Moreover, magazines like *Holiday* and *Sports Illustrated* urged marketers to pursue audiences that, while quantitatively smaller than the mass market, were qualitatively more inclined to splurge. As market researchers embraced this approach, closely training their sights on tastes and dispositions, vacationing showed itself an easy means to differentiate people who had previously been lumped together in the great middle-income market and reorder them hierarchically along lifestyle lines. In terms of tourism, marketers came to see characteristics at the heart of travel, such as a joie de vivre and a longing for authenticity, as an analogue for stylized ways of living built on specialty consumption.[21] By offering a prototype for marketing practices that drew lines connecting leisure pursuits, sociopsychological dispositions, identity formation, and the consumption of experiential services, the postwar selling of travel presaged a postindustrial consumer culture in which the dissolution of the heterogeneous mass market appeared an attractive prospect. Sightseeing travel would by no means go away after the mid-1960s, but its centrality to notions of a unique "American standard of living" and the narratives of democratized leisure at its base were on the wane. Replacing them in the more fractured American culture that followed was a very different, and far less egalitarian, set of meanings.

Charting a roughly chronological path from the 1920s through the mid-1960s, *The Holiday Makers* tells this story across six chapters. Chapters 1 and 2 establish the contexts within which midcentury American tourist culture and its promotion in magazines grew. The first chapter focuses on how notions of American identity, consumerism, leisure, and mobility were woven together between the 1920s and 1940s. The second explores the creation of *Holiday* magazine in the mid-1940s out of a new market research paradigm that considered leisure habits, audience tastes, and broader sociological trends in interaction with one another. Chapter 3 examines how postwar magazines offered shape to touristic mobility as a social phenomenon and suggested narrative frameworks for readers' own imaginative travels. Chapters 4 and 5 explore the production of geographic lures, focusing on how articles and advertisements were constructed as a sort of tourist pedagogy that encouraged particular ways of thinking about place, leisure, and identity. Chapter 6 delves further into this last point and describes how growing concerns about authenticity in travel converged with the business world's growing infatuation with niche marketing to resituate tourism's place in consumer culture. Finally, a brief epilogue considers what the demise of mobility culture—and the free time and geographic curiosity that made it possible—can tell us about affluence, life expectations, and equality in a market-segmented society.

This inquiry ultimately has two overlapping thrusts of investigation—the popular geography of tourism marketing in midcentury magazines (the *Holiday* part of the title) and its cultural production (the *Makers*). As a study of popular geography, the book focuses on the narratives, themes, and images of place and mobility that appeared in magazine pages.[22] The patterns and connections that emerge from such analysis help to illuminate what Edward Said called "structures of attitude and reference"—or how social, cultural, and economic currents intermeshed in ways that lent an aura of naturalness to geographic identities and relationships.[23] In other words, the text and imagery that circulated through mass media helped foster and reinforce commonsense ways of understanding what places were like, how different areas were related to one another, and what it meant to move among those places. But to understand how and why this body of popular geography was produced, it has to be situated within the institutional contexts that yielded it. As Jackson Lears has argued, cultural historians should pay close attention to institutional power not so much because media businesses seek to dominate audiences but because they rationalize cultural production in the same manner that large bureaucracies standardize everything. While some of the productions yielded by this process undoubtedly strike a chord with audiences, they are not audience expressions in themselves.[24] Rather, they are the products of an industry that has gradually assumed the massive, yet still quite specific, task of growing consumer markets by appealing to audience interests. For marketers at midcentury, this meant producing a culture of mass tourism by fueling audience desires to go forth and see the world. As ad executive David Ogilvy explained, selling travel meant turning "dreams into action—transforming potential energy into kinetic energy."[25] And when successful, this alchemy gave rise to a network of globalized service industries that reshaped physical landscapes and the cultural life of communities.[26]

Turning "dreams into action" also merged the geographic imagination and consumer imagination in new ways. As James Cook has argued, "new forms of self-consciousness" have been perhaps the most important outgrowth of the industrialized production of culture as new frameworks for understanding the self and social experience are popularized at the national, and even transnational, level.[27] The magazine industry's efforts at tourism promotion offer a window into this process, showing how the consumer desires associated with a therapeutic service economy began to take shape within the symbolic forms of industrial modernism. Travel ads and articles offered frameworks for imagining what it meant to inhabit a wider world, to break out of everyday life's stultifying routines, to be well traveled, to make contact with others, and to see the places that had long captivated one's imagination. In the same manner, they helped answer questions about what satisfactions to glean from vacation travel: relaxation or stimulation? Education or fun? Refinement or self-actualization? As the answers that marketers suggested subtly shifted over time, we can gradually see a whole touristic sensibility toward social experience, or what Zygmunt Bauman has called the "sensation-gatherer's life," come into focus.[28] Exploring changes in the tourist imagination thus offers insight on how leisure choices, consumption, life experiences, and notions of identity became more tightly fused in the mid-twentieth century.

The lifestyle profiling that grew out of these developments has been the underlying logic to the fractured media landscape of the late twentieth and early twenty-first centuries. Small specialized periodicals, format-specific radio stations, narrowly programmed cable TV networks, and individually tailored Internet applications have allowed media businesses to target more and more specialized groups. As many critics have pointed out, slicing the great audience into successively smaller pieces has chipped away at a shared national culture. It has encouraged groups to see themselves as walled off from those who do not share their interests, tastes, and views. The gated communities that have sprouted up throughout the country offer a physical corollary. In this manner, marketers have encouraged Americans to think about group identity as less the product of a common experience rooted in citizenship than an engrained set of consumer preferences.[29]

Ironically, mass tourism—a phenomenon that in many ways symbolized the full democratization of leisure in consumer society—helped to eventually diminish the presence of free time in American life. By making spending more and more totemic of one's identity, the American standard of living has almost exclusively been redefined around buying power and possessions rather than personal time. One result of this emphasis has been a widening gulf in vacation time between American workers and their peers in other consumer societies. As vacation times continued to rise throughout the Western world in the late twentieth century, they contracted in the United States. Large employers such as DuPont, for instance, began to do away with their longest vacation packages in the 1980s, cutting them from seven weeks to a month.[30] Alone among industrialized nations, American workers are not protected by mandatory vacation laws. Workers in Europe, Australia, and New Zealand all received at least twenty paid vacation days annually in 2007, while the average American worker received only nine. A full quarter of the American workforce was left without even a single day of paid vacation. To compound matters, long commutes and "electronic leashes," such as e-mail and wireless devices, increasingly allow work to invade Americans' already limited free time. Outraged by this trend, an advocacy group has designated October 24 "Take Back Your Time Day" to mark the additional nine weeks per year that Americans spend on the job.[31]

Not surprisingly, Americans, with less time to travel, take far fewer foreign vacations than their peers in other wealthy nations. Although Americans rank second worldwide in spending on foreign tourism, that lofty ranking owes more to the size of the U.S. population than to a robust travel culture. The United States, with a population of nearly 310 million, spent $73.1 billion on international tourism in 2009. In comparison, Germany (82 million) and the United Kingdom (61 million) spent $80.8 billion and $48.5 billion, respectively.[32] Passport figures are notoriously murky, but estimates of the percentage of American citizens holding valid papers in recent years range from about 20 to 33 percent. In comparison, an estimated 70 percent of British citizens hold a valid passport.[33] Many Americans who have gone abroad in recent years can likely relate to the experience of fielding questions from foreign nationals as to why Americans don't travel. In a variation of this conversation, Americans abroad are commended for venturing outside their borders. Such encounters speak to perceptions, whether accurate or not, that Americans are uniquely parochial and indifferent to other cultures: a foreshortened geographic imagination is simply assumed to be part of American culture. Yet in 1957 the travel writer Horace Sutton could casually refer to "the indefatigable American roamer," and Joseph Wechsberg could make the sweeping claim that "everywhere the word tourist has become synonymous with 'American.'"[34]

Exploring postwar vacation culture shows that not so long ago Americans defined their quality of life very differently. They placed much greater weight on leisure time, personal autonomy, and the experiences that both afforded. In many ways, midcentury Americans cleared the way that other industrialized societies would follow. They enjoyed the longest vacations and introduced the notion that quieting one's wanderlust could be a regular part of ordinary people's lives. For some reason, Americans veered off to follow another path— one that left them alone at home.

1 THE NEW MOBILITY
Travel and Leisure in Depression and War

Surveying the state of American leisure in 1940, historian Foster Rhea Dulles described a nation remade by a half-century-long revolution in play as workweeks grew shorter and a massive amusement industry sprang up around Americans of all incomes. Dulles was not alone in this observation. Indeed, it would have been tough for any thoughtful observer not to notice the arcades, movie houses, ballparks, and beach attractions that had filled American communities since the late nineteenth century. Tourism occupied a unique place in this development, serving as almost an exclamation point to arguments about just how democratic leisure had become. Although relatively few Americans could tour extensively at the time, hopeful commentators saw vacation travel following the same groove of democratization recently cut by more modest forms of leisure. So if cheap urban amusements and a relaxed work ethic meant that short blasts of fun were now a fixture in industrial modernity's weekly rhythms, the integration of long stretches of leisure into the annual calendar was the next natural step. As Dulles contended, "The wealthy could make the fashionable tour in 1825, the well-to-do built up the summer resorts of the 1890's, but every Tom, Dick, and Harry toured the country in the 1930s."[1] *Life* echoed his point, trumpeting in 1940 that "more than they ever dreamed they could vacationing Americans travel."[2]

In celebrating tourism's newly egalitarian nature, *Life* and Dulles voiced what was quickly becoming the received wisdom of the day: the United States had become a culture of mass mobility where pleasure travel was a common, and expected, part of life. According to this narrative, vacationing gave flight to a uniquely American wanderlust that, while buried deep in all citizens, had until then been realizable only by the affluent. Mass mobility heralded a new era in which constraints, whether they be distance, time, or budget, could no longer hold Americans' will to move in check. Mobility, in this regard, was part physical and part mental phenomenon. While it described movement through space, it also spoke to a desire to break out of the everyday environment and experience someplace new.

Observers in the world of commerce were no less enamored. As *Business Week* reported, the "far flung travel business—ranging from the nation's biggest banks and railroads to Coney Island hot dog stands and penny arcades"—was an already big industry on the verge of becoming mammoth. Analysts valued the trade at $5.5 billion in 1939 and estimated that the average American spent 7 percent of his or her annual budget on leisure travel, making the trade by some accounts third only to the automobile manufacturing and steel industries.[3] In some parts of the country, tourism had already become what one observer called "the big 'cash crop.'" Considering the depressed economic climate of the 1930s, businessmen were doubly impressed by the trade's resiliency. Like other sectors of the economy, it suffered early in the decade. But unlike most, it rebounded quickly and proved almost immune to the 1937 recession.[4] One part egalitarian social trend and another part economic dynamo, mass tourism was thus emblematic of the booming consumer culture observers hoped would take hold in the 1940s.

Mass tourism grew out of a number of distinct, but interrelated, developments over the interwar years. Americans adopted new ideas about leisure and living standards, while employers made vacations a common benefit. Within this context, tourist travel was redefined as a folkway of consumer culture, or a shared activity that constructed and affirmed group identity. Vacations were a sort of ritualized mobility, providing Americans with a liminal period outside the structures of everyday life to exercise autonomy and see what lay over the horizon.[5] Tourist travel, in turn, tapped into and helped fuel a heightened geographic curiosity that ran throughout popular culture. Radio broadcasts, movies, and photo magazines were like one side of a coin, backed by the era's cars, ships, trains, and planes. Both seemed to render distant places close at hand. The Second World War put a hold on mass tourism, but it also provided a crucial period when American travel culture was codified and augmented in important ways. At home, rations and travel restrictions kept civilians more stationary than they had been in years. These constraints, and the feelings of deprivation they stirred, helped cement a sense of American citizenship defined by consumer amenities like tourist travel. When World War II ended, the resumption of ordinary vacationing was taken as a powerful sign that things were not only getting back to normal but also bringing the culture of mass mobility to full fruition. How the emerging travel culture of the interwar years combined with Americans' experiences during World War II to shape postwar expectations is the subject of this chapter.

Two Weeks with Pay

As Dulles's narrative indicated, tourism was a well-established part of American culture by the 1920s and 1930s. Since colonial times, wealthy elites had visited spas and made Grand Tours of Europe. Upper-middle-class Americans had summered at resorts and trekked to western parks dating from the late nineteenth century. Less affluent Americans had well-worn travel routines as well, taking them to urban beaches, amusement parks, and wilderness areas. But the role of vacationing in American culture would change dramatically between the late 1920s and World War II as shifting employment terms and changing ideas about leisure spurred Americans across income brackets to look at travel in new ways. As historian Cindy Aron notes, it was the Great Depression, of all eras, when leisure travel "became an important component of an acceptable standard of living." While paid vacations were the norm for office workers at the start of the Depression, they were a rare perk for blue-collar employees. "Vacations with Pay," one management journal incredulously asked as late as 1935, "for white collar workers, of course, for wage earners?"[6] That sentiment would quickly appear outdated, however, as one large industry after another granted paid vacations for the first time in the face of a newly empowered labor movement. *Business Week* summed up the development in a 1943 report, commenting that "a few years ago, vacations for most production workers were unusual. Union action has since made them commonplace."[7]

The extension of paid vacations to much of the industrial workforce did not mean that lower-middle- and working-class families suddenly took up tourist travel en masse. Many lacked the extra income for lavish trips or the knowledge of how to plan them, while others simply preferred their traditional excursions. But regardless, democratized vacation plans helped solidify new ideas about work and leisure, holding that just as everyone was entitled to pay in exchange for their labors, they were also entitled to their *own time* in exchange for surrendering long hours to employers. The eight-hours movement of the late nineteenth century made the first beachheads in this struggle. Paid vacations were an important, if long delayed, follow-up victory, offering even greater autonomy by sectioning off a yearly block of time—most commonly two weeks—long enough to live outside the shadow of work.[8]

In popular vernacular, the phrase "two weeks" gave this temporal concept a name, describing both a stretch of time and a social phenomenon. As sociologist Eviatar Zerubavel has argued, calendars, schedules, and other shared temporal units help constitute social identities by placing individuals on the same clock.[9] In the mid-twentieth century, "two weeks" was a distinct way of looking at the annual calendar that helped shape what it meant to be a modern American. Turned into an analogy for tourist travel, phrases like "the annual two weeks with pay" or "your two weeks" spoke to the sense of autonomy that vacations offered. Framed as an annual event, the term suggested a national folkway, performed once a year. And with the possessive "your" attached, it neatly cleaved the calendar into two distinct, if lopsided, spheres of influence—one belonging to the employer and one belonging to the employee. Ethel Romig Fuller channeled this view in a 1939 poem called "Prayer for the Vacations of Young Office Workers":

> Two weeks' vacation, all they have, dear Lord;
> But fourteen precious days, like nuggets mined
> From work, where year-around, they are confined
> To walled routine. The pennies saved up toward
> This meager pinch of hours, means sesame
> For countless beauty-starved young girls and lads.[10]

As a way of understanding time, two weeks encapsulated a sense of control over at least part of one's schedule and with it an ability to transcend mundane routines. Travel industry representatives observed the same trends and recognized them as working in their favor. "Our people are becoming increasingly eager to travel and they won't stay home," adman James Albert Wales wrote in 1938, "even if they have to save and skimp during 50 weeks of the year in order to go places during the two of the vacation period."[11] Wales's use of language like "our people" illustrates the extent to which notions of national identity sat at the base of this temporal outlook. Venturing beyond the long arm of workplace discipline for two weeks of fun was a ritual means of enacting and affirming a defining set of modern American values.

The sense of unfettered mobility symbolized by the "annual two weeks" was reinforced by another accoutrement of what would soon be cast as the American standard of living—automobile ownership. Like tourism, the automobile's origins as a luxury item, coupled with its connotations of individual freedom, made it a powerful status symbol. While some communities had already begun to shape themselves around the car by the 1920s, motoring was still very much viewed through the lens of leisure at the time. In particular, automobiles were thought to be making the thrills of rapid self-directed movement a routine part of life. Robert Lynd and Helen Merrell

Lynd observed in their 1929 study of Muncie, Indiana, that motoring more than any other innovation was "making leisure-time enjoyment a regularly expected part of every day and week rather than an occasional event." Along with regularizing the joys of speedy travel, cars rendered the feelings of spatial mastery that came with exploring new places all the more common an experience. "The automobile," they observed "is extending the radius of those who are allowed vacations with pay and is putting short trips within the reach of some for whom such vacations are still 'not in the dictionary.'"[12]

The pleasures of automobility were seen as highly addictive, sating desires buried deep within Americans as a people. Even in the Depression, car use remained stable. Department of Labor researchers studying family budgets in the mid-1930s labeled motoring "one of the most depression-proof elements" in American life. Families chose to sacrifice clothes, furnishings, and food rather than give up car trips. Between 1920 and 1938, the total yearly mileage racked up by American tourists increased from 67,639,906,000 to 228,775,184,740, with 83 percent via automobile.[13] In turn, this legion of motorists gave rise to a roadside trade that *Fortune* called the biggest continuous marketplace ever established. According to the magazine, auto touring had developed into a national mania: "So God made the American restive. The American in turn and in due time got into the automobile and found it good. . . . It was good because it continually satisfied and at the same time greatly sharpened his hunger for movement. Which is very probably the profoundest and most compelling of American racial hungers. The fact is that the automobile became a hypnosis. The automobile became the opium of the American people."[14]

Along the same lines, the *Saturday Evening Post*'s Anne Cameron characterized her own "wanderitis" as an irrepressible addiction: "I noticed that familiar quiver when I watched the breezes rippling across the fields and disappearing over the hill with a tantalizing air of going places. Then maps began to dance before my eyes after I went to bed, and the attack became acute. My friends shook their head and openly wondered if I'd taken to gasoline again."[15] The notion that travel tapped into a primal wanderlust deep within Americans was a common refrain. The way travel guides and articles described it, tourism represented the same impulse to see what lay over the horizon that had earlier driven European settlers across the Atlantic and pioneers to the shores of the Pacific. Inheriting this instinct, the modern American's answer to the westward trek was the annual vacation. The American Automobile Association (AAA) called this urge to move the "New Mobility," or "a new and more spacious manner of living which has its own speech, its own folkways, its own culture."[16]

The "New Mobility" allowed Americans to release the wanderlust that modern life forced them to suppress. As managers in business and industry recognized, such a spilling of pent-up energies could lead to greater productivity in the workplace. But it could also fend off a general malaise with the new ways of living central to a corporate economy. This view was perhaps best expressed in a 1925 "Save to Travel" ad aimed at young office workers: "Life at home seems dull and prosaic, until the great day when a tour is finally undertaken. Thereafter a new zest is added to life, the unappeased longings disappear and unwonted content blooms in the midst of old routine surroundings, no matter how drab and uninspiring." Vacations were not only an opportunity to blow off steam but also a transformative experience that reanimated the drudgeries of everyday life.[17]

While automobiles were the fastest-growing mode of travel, they were by no means alone in feeding desires for easy mobility. Ocean voyages, railway journeys, and air travel remained relatively exclusive compared with auto touring, but each underwent significant changes that contributed to a sense that modern life was characterized by movement. Transatlantic voyages opened to a broader base in the 1920s, trickling further into the middle classes with the introduction of "tourist third class." The reckless expats who populated novels by Fitzgerald, Hemingway, and others put a face on the growing crowd of Americans who set off across the Atlantic.[18] Railway travel remained much the same as it had since the turn of the century, with most lines marketing vacation sites along their routes. But as the lines replaced their aging, angular stock with streamlined cars in the 1930s, rail travel received a modernist facelift. The sleek aluminum exteriors, designed to evoke the grace and speed of air travel, helped to place the railways—at least visually—within a modern culture of rapid movement.[19]

Aviation, the inspiration for the streamlined look, developed into a glamorous, if sparsely used, mode of travel over the interwar years. Flight pushed the limits of the imagination, introducing a mind-boggling new geographic scale. Distances that took days to cover by ship or rail could now be traversed in less than a day. And flying remained dangerous enough to lend a powerful sense of heroism to those who ventured into the skies. The public's fascination with flight did not equate, however, to a flying public.[20] Despite the low rates of commercial air travel, the airlines came to assume a distinct place in interwar culture, offering a glimpse at a near future that seemed to promise total mobility. As one TWA ad put it, "You simply step aboard, and before you can begin to believe it, *you're there.*" Most wondrous was Pan American Airways, the country's sole international carrier, which seemed to cast a net over the world and draw distant cities ever closer. The airline carefully fostered this image of air-age colossus, calling itself a "chosen instrument." As *Fortune* explained in 1936, "The key to world power is not expansion but compression. The success of the modern state depends on how small it can make itself and the rest of the world. This is the function performed for the U.S. by Pan American Airways. And it is basic."[21]

All together, then, the country's growing transportation base came to symbolize "the New Mobility," and these networks of mass movement were celebrated throughout popular culture. Films such as *Flying Down to Rio* (1933), *Florida Special* (1936), and *It Happened One Night* (1934) placed travel infrastructure in a starring role. Meanwhile, radio programs such as *Grand Central Station* did the same over the airwaves. "As a bullet seeks its target," the announcer proclaimed, "shining rails in every part of our great country are aimed at Grand Central Station, heart of the nation's greatest city. Drawn by the magnetic force of the fantastic metropolis, day and night great trains rush toward the Hudson River."[22] Capitalizing on radio's capacity to stir the imagination, the program conjured an image of streamlined vehicles firing across the landscape, placing the entire nation in quick and easy contact.

Interwar magazines strove to represent this sense of mobility in novel ways, as well, by imploring readers to think about their geographic relationships to other parts of the world as profoundly rearranged. Richard Edes Harrison's air-age cartographs for *Fortune* and *National Geographic* showed midwesterners that they were no farther away from Berlin by way of the Arctic than the East Coast was via the Atlantic. At times, sections and even whole issues of *Fortune* took the form of a guide book, offering lengthy profiles written in an argot that suggested a heightened awareness of place. A special issue on New York City, created to coincide with the 1939 World's Fair, spurred the magazine's most intensive rumination. Opening with a visitors' guide to the city's virtues and vices, it offered what the editors called a "Baedeker of Business in New York."[23] The fair itself was the biggest vacation destination of its time and perhaps the era's most elaborate celebration of mobility. Laden with exhibits like General Motor's Highways and Horizons—an enormous model of a freeway-dominated future—the event was intended to dramatize what organizer Grover Whalen called the "age of super-contact."[24]

John Dos Passos recognized mobility's centrality to modern American identity, filling the pages of his *U.S.A.* trilogy (1937) with characters who crisscrossed the Western Hemisphere in everything from freighters to Pierce Arrow touring cars. Tellingly, the epic story closed with a hitchhiker who stood along the highway, thumbing a ride as cars sped by and planes soared overhead: "The transcontinental passenger thinks contracts, profits, vacationtrips, mighty continent between Atlantic and Pacific, power, wires humming dollars, cities jammed, hills empty, and the indiantrail leading into the wagonroad, the macadamed pike, the concrete skyway; trains, planes; history the billiondollar speedup."[25] As Dos Passos observed, modern transportation constituted both a new type of hyperkinetic society and a line of continuity with the past.

Mass-Merchandising Travel

As the contrast between Dos Passos's stalled hitchhiker and airborne executive indicated, access to the nation's transport networks was by no means universal. Cost remained a formidable barrier as industry players sought to build a mass market for vacation travel. Whereas auto touring was relatively affordable (once individuals owned a car), few Americans were able to finance distant travel via ship, train, or plane, even in the flush times of the 1920s. A vacation's hefty price tag made it an especially deliberated-over part of the household budget, placing it in league with furniture, automobiles, and other major purchases. "In the case of the less affluent travelers, such as stenographers and office clerks," *Printers' Ink* reminded readers, "money spent for vacations is the *one* major expenditure."[26] Travel interests recognized that their product simply cost more than most Americans had available at any given time. Given this predicament, they needed to create ways of not only selling but also financing vacations. "Save to Travel" plans, endorsed by the steamship and railway lines in the mid-1920s, put forward savings accounts as a solution. Just as with Christmas clubs, depositors could stow money away all year and then splurge once vacation time arrived.[27]

Yet disciplined saving was only a partial solution, as it still limited the market to those who could stash away enough savings to finance a trip in full. Looking for an end around, industry experts pressed the need for mass-merchandising techniques, such as extending credit and launching aggressive ad campaigns. "Travel Now—Pay Later" plans were one way of engineering the resources middle-income people needed to travel. In 1932, Cunard Line introduced a "deferred payment plan" aimed at schoolteachers and office workers. By the early 1940s, credit plans had become much more comprehensive, linking railroads, shipping lines, airlines, and banks across the country.[28] Figuring that more vacationers meant more luggage, sportswear, and camera sales, leading department stores, including Marshall Field's, Bullock's, and Wanamaker's, began hosting American Express travel booths in the late 1920s. The New Jersey chain Bamberger's went one step further in 1941, extending store credit for vacation travel.[29]

From the industry's perspective, these tactics could introduce the kinds of rationalized salesmanship that had built mass markets for automobiles and appliances in the 1920s. Don Thomas, the longtime head of Southern California's All-Year Club, for instance, argued that tourism "presents the same opportunity for systematic methods as any commodity business."[30] Mass production metaphors were common in these discussions. Drawing an analogy to the assembly lines at River Rouge, Hiram Motherwell of *Harper's Monthly* suggested the possibility of "a very pleasant 'Ford' trip to Europe for as little as four or five hundred dollars."[31] According to this line of thought, systematically building demand for travel and the means to pay for it could grow markets to a size where holidays were produced with the kinds of efficiencies of scale enjoyed by mass manufacturers.

Along with credit, advertising was seen as the other primary ingredient to mass tourist trade. While nearly all consumer industries relied on extensive advertising by the 1930s, tourism insiders considered it especially important to their business. Heavy advertisers such as the All-Year Club and New England Council insisted that their success was due to an unwavering faith in advertising. Thomas called it "the life blood" of the industry. For these boosters, ads were like a steady call that eventually attracted visitors. Interwar travel advertisements served a number of interrelated purposes. First, they boosted destinations to those readers already accustomed to pleasure travel. Second, advertisements sold the idea of vacationing to the millions of middle-income people for whom it was a new, and sometimes morally dubious, idea. Some worked on breaking the still formidable association between vacations and idleness. Others aimed at persuading novices they had the time and money to join the vacationing set. A long-running objective of the All-Year Club, for instance, was to convince middle-class tourists that two weeks was ample time to cross the country. And third, ads planted a seed in the minds of consumers with little hope of traveling in the near future but who nevertheless looked forward to lighting out someday. As Thomas explained, "Our depression campaigning was not for immediate results, but to build *future desires*."[32]

Within the industry, conventional wisdom was that advertising had kept the field afloat during the hard times of the early Depression. Areas that upped ad spending in the early 1930s, while others slashed theirs, were seen as the earliest beneficiaries of a mid-decade rebound in travel. Some even co-opted economic hardship as a selling tool. As historian Michael Berkowitz has written, Depression-era ads "created a cultural climate in which tourism could become increasingly accepted as a psychic necessity."[33] Many played on economic anxieties: "You're in it! He's in it! We're all in it! What? A rut. The great American rut. Get out of it for a few weeks this summer."[34] Others played up the buyers' market available to those with vacation funds. "When will so few dollars buy this trip again?" asked one steamship cooperative. This kind of persistent advertising, industry watchers agreed, was key to resuscitating the trade. *Business Week* noted in 1934 that "mountain scenery, ocean breezes, and romantic glimpses of foreign cities in full page advertisements have done their business. People are traveling."[35] From this point of view, glossy images and innovative copy stirred Americans' inborn desires to break out of the mundane. Industry thinking was that, pitched broadly at the vast middle-class market and coupled with consumer credit, these campaigns could transform tourism from an idiosyncratic luxury trade to a standard expectation of American life.

Private efforts to transform how vacations were sold worked in tandem with public efforts to foster a mass tourism industry. Over the course of the 1930s, the federal government showed an unprecedented dedication to vacation industry growth—identifying travel as both a social good and an economic good. Governmental programs could sow national pride and unity by cultivating an interest in American places. And they could shepherd industry growth by building the infrastructure needed to reach those places. Federal support for the vacation industry was not altogether new. The national parks had been yoked to tourism interests from their start as railroads and regional boosters lobbied for federal protection of wilderness areas in the late nineteenth century. With the rise of auto tourism during the opening decades of the twentieth century, the scattered handful of early parks was recast as a coherent, constantly expanding system under the National Park Service (NPS) and the parks developed into key sites for celebrating national heritage and identity.[36]

The creation of canonized sights fit into a larger fixation on self-definition in 1930s American culture. Observers of national life, from show business to academia, all sought to stake out the meaning of a distinct American culture rooted in the collective memory of regional folklore, mythology, and traditions.[37] New Deal initiatives—such as the American Guides, the travel series produced by the Federal Writers' Project of the Works Progress Administration (WPA)—also drew on and contributed to this trend. As WPA chief Harry Hopkins explained, the *American Guides* tackled "the ambitious objective of presenting to the American people a portrait of America."[38] The series fully reflected the era's burgeoning tourism culture. Each installment presented a geographic portrait deliberately concerned with fostering national pride and packaged in a framework helpful to auto tourists. Frederick Gutheim, writing for the *Saturday Review of Literature* in 1941, called them "the guides of the motor age." Even the writing style, presented in what he called a "brisk, steady fifty mile an hour pace," mirrored the motorists' perspective. Sections were arranged with travel planning in mind, moving from a general overview, to detailed portraits of cities and regions, to suggested tour itineraries running east–west or north–south along major roadways.[39] A similar project concerned with "introducing Americans to America" was the Farm Security Administration's (FSA) Historical Section's photographic file. Under the direction of Roy Stryker, the FSA built an archive of more than 270,000 prints of distinct American landscapes and archetypes that were farmed out to newspapers, magazines, and photo exhibitions nationwide.[40]

The New Deal's most direct interventions in the tourism industry came with the creation of the Department of the Interior's Civilian Conservation Corps (CCC) and United States Travel Bureau (USTB). The CCC was established early in Roosevelt's first term in an effort to conserve deteriorating forestry and agriculture resources. In the second half of the 1930s, the CCC's mandate expanded to building recreational areas as millions of young men cleared hiking paths and built cabins at hundreds of state parks. Spurred on by local business leaders, the corps' most ambitious project transformed the rural corridor stretching from Virginia's Shenandoah Valley to the Smoky Mountains along the North Carolina–Tennessee border into a major vacationland stocked with two national parks and the Blue Ridge Parkway.[41] The USTB, created in 1937, was an even more direct attempt to bolster the tourist trade, offering research support and spearheading promotional drives, such as 1940's "Travel America Year." The USTB, which operated visitor centers in New York, Washington, D.C., and San Francisco, was also intended to help introduce more Americans to vacationing. Specialized services were made available for groups unaccustomed to travel, including a custom set of publications aimed at African American tourists.[42]

Just as important as the guidance the USTB offered travelers was the signal it sent to the tourist trade. The bureau represented a recognition of tourist travel as a major industry that the state had an interest in nurturing. Industry advocates had pushed for such a commitment for nearly a decade before the bureau's creation. Critics charged that while most other countries operated a national tourist office in New York, there were no such American bureaus in London, Paris, or other world cities.[43] Looking across the Atlantic, they also pointed to the success of public–private partnerships in Italy, France, Germany, and other nations that lured visitors with visa waivers and favorable exchange rates. Over the 1930s, programs ranging from the Popular Front's worker vacation initiatives in France to Nazi Germany's Strength Through Joy saw national governments take a leading role in tourism promotion. While guided by a very different ideology, USTB offices, CCC projects, and WPA guides represented the U.S. government's foray into the tourist trade as a means of growing the economy and achieving select social goals.[44] From the former perspective, a robust tourist trade promised jobs and a highly capitalized travel infrastructure. From the latter, tourist travel allowed Americans to renew their energies, commune with nature, cultivate a sense of national pride, act out a native wanderlust, and broaden their horizons.

The attention heaped on tourism in the late 1930s by leaders in business and government also signaled a shifting technocratic orientation toward services and the role they would play in a modern consumer economy.[45] To be sure, there remained skeptics who clung to nineteenth-century producerist ideals. As one skeptic scoffed in the conservative *American Mercury* in 1930, "The tourist trade has no more right to be called an industry than has the bucolic country fair. Both are amusement enterprises. Both are parasitic rather than productive."[46] Concerted efforts to convince business leaders that tourism was a respectable enterprise, coupled with its resilient growth during hard times, helped make such views appear antiquated.[47] By the early 1940s, tourism occupied a newly important place in the national economy as managerial elites accepted the production and sale of experiences as a plausible alternative to goods.

"Tomorrow We'll Go Places"

The United States' entry into World War II introduced drastic changes to American tourism. During a time when millions entered the armed forces and civilians were expected to make deep sacrifices, an activity traditionally associated with idleness and luxury could not remain unaffected. Sunbathers and sightseers did not fit easily into the image of a nation at war. Yet the popularity of vacationing and the industry's enormous size meant that it could not simply disappear, either. Pleasure travel thus developed into a contentious wartime issue, marked by an amalgam of conflicting messages and irreconcilable ideas. In particular, the war pitted conceptions of vacationing as a social good against notions of vacationing as an economic engine and entitlement. Consumer economists and wartime agencies, such as the Office of Defense Transportation (ODT) and Office of Price Administration (OPA), promoted the former view. They counseled Americans to postpone long-distance trips and seek out nearby options instead. From this perspective, modest trips would exact less of a toll on the nation's transportation resources while still giving vacationers a chance to rest and reenergize for a hard fight. Tourism interests took a similar tack, couching their sales appeals in the patriotic language of "victory vacations" and "civilian furloughs." But some did so in a way that contested calls for sacrifice by pushing on with the industry's long-term agenda to redefine tourist travel as an expectation of American life—in good times or bad. The anxieties and resentments that arose from these contradictory messages shed light on how vacationing was becoming intertwined with ideas about national identity and consumer prerogative. Beyond material plenty, conceptions of American citizenship and the good life were being defined around access to free time and desirable experiences. Mobility, or the sensation of breaking out of the everyday environment, had over the previous two decades developed into the most sharply piqued of these desires.

Although war transformed the economy, it did little to slow the momentum toward democratized vacation plans that had been building since the mid-1930s. Moreover, it accelerated the process as a production boom and labor shortage created an amenable climate for worker demands. With the federal government keeping a lid on wages to control inflation, employees focused their efforts on securing more generous benefits. As a result, industries that had held fast against vacations granted them for the first time, and many other employers lengthened leave periods.[48] Though vacations by definition meant that employees were not working, their recuperative qualities meant that they did not necessarily clash with wartime priorities. Given the heightened strains and stakes of war work, some observers—even within government—suggested that vacations were more important than ever. "Everybody will work longer and harder than ever before," President Roosevelt observed in 1942. "And that means that they ought to have a chance for recreation and for taking their minds off their work even more than before." First Lady Eleanor Roosevelt echoed the president, classifying vacations as "not only a right but an obligation" for wartime Americans.[49]

The question remained, though, of what civilians would do with their time off. Federal bureaucrats encouraged Americans to hold their consumer desires in check and embrace sacrifice as a patriotic duty. Summarizing this view in 1944, economist Hazel Kyrk asserted that "it is an unworthy consumer whose chief question of concern is: How can I avoid the effect of the war upon my family and myself?"[50] Disciplined spending was especially important with regard to leisure. As incomes rose dramatically between 1941 and 1945, many homebound Americans had more disposable income than ever before. With durable goods off the market, consumers plowed their newfound affluence into discretionary spending on movie tickets, sporting events, restaurant meals, liquor, and other amusements.[51] Observers reported entertainment districts in boomtowns like Kansas City crawling with nighttime revelers. As one teenager recalled of wartime Los Angeles: "You could go downtown at two in the morning, it'd be like Saturday. Any time would be Saturday night.

Streets were full of people."[52] Vacations were a natural fit for this pleasure-oriented way of life. But far more than an afternoon at the ballpark or evening at the movies, tourist travel consumed precious resources. Forgoing vacations thus required a measure of self-denial in a climate where leisure had become the main outlet for spending.

To conserve resources but still allow for reinvigorating vacations, family economists recommended "a new pattern of recreation" centered around the home. E. DeAlton and Nell Partridge of the Montclair State Teachers College advised Americans to build "recreation kits" from materials around the house. In lieu of an auto trip, old magazines and a pair of scissors could keep children occupied for hours, while broomsticks came in handy for a game of driveway shuffleboard.[53] Many Americans followed such a program, staying put to work on their homes, tend gardens, and host barbeques. The turn toward home vacations meant a record year for the lawn furniture industry, before the war agencies one by one appropriated its production materials.[54] Although the war agencies favored activities around the home and local communities, most recognized that many Americans were determined to travel. In this case, the best they could do was urge tourists to minimize the strain they put on travel infrastructure. "Vacation at home. If you must 'get away,'" begged ODT head Joseph B. Eastman, "go somewhere near home and begin and end the trip . . . to avoid weekend travel peaks. And don't move around; go to one place and stay there." Some suggested that tourists use public carriers to explore nearby towns. The *Philadelphia Evening Bulletin*, for instance, noted that Camden was just a ferry ride away.[55] The ideal trip, then, was one that didn't involve an automobile and didn't tie up needed space on transcontinental railways.

The many civilians who followed such guidelines, dubbed "priority vacationers," fueled banner years for regional resorts. But still, many Americans clung to prewar vacation habits, taking exception to any constraints on travel. As journalist and Office of War Information (OWI) official Henry Pringle bluntly assessed the situation: "Campaigns against unnecessary travel were less than successful. Americans continued to take vacations, to visit the races, and to make other needless trips."[56] "Chiselers," or ration cheats, found countless ingenious ways around gasoline and tire restrictions. Others ignored ODT pleas by crowding buses and trains. Before long, a lucrative black market sprouted in the ticket trade. All the while, a number of travel businesses continued to advertise, boasting their contributions to the war cause while subtly egging on civilian vacationers. As OPA economists James Maxwell and Margaret Balcom observed, "A babel of voices arose which left citizens unclear as to what was necessary."[57]

When the war's momentum shifted in 1944 as Allied forces drove through

France and island-hopped across the Pacific, business groups began to plan the postwar economy more aggressively, hatching projects and negotiating trade agreements. Postwar planning started early in the tourism industry. North American Travel Organization officials vowed at their 1943 meeting to make the first peace year a "Victory Vacation Year" and commissioned a study to gauge the war's impact on travel infrastructure and consumer sentiments.[58] The New England Council made its own massive study of the postwar vacation market. Other areas created planning boards and worked out postwar ad campaigns. More ambitiously, the Anglo-American Caribbean Commission, a booster group advised by executives from American Express, the Alcoa Steamship Company, and Thomas Cook and Son, outlined plans to totally overhaul the region's tourism infrastructure.[59] Across the Atlantic, the British Travel Association announced an eight-point program in late 1944 to attract postwar tourists. And on the Continent, no sooner could Allied armies liberate a city than American Express opened a new office there.[60] Along with laying the preparatory groundwork, companies developed new products to roll out in peacetime. The Pullman Car Company launched a massive redesign campaign. Railroads across the country developed plans for Vista- and Astra-Domed cars that offered a dazzling view of passing scenery. Others tweaked the minutia of postwar operations. United Airlines carried out extensive market research to guide the interior design of new aircraft, probing consumers' thoughts on seating, legroom, lighting, sleeping berths, cocktails, and dozens of other considerations. The structure of the international airline industry was the biggest issue to resolve. Anticipating a boom, American analysts early on eyed international air routes, along with oil, as the two main points of contention facing allies and foes alike after the war.[61]

As travel businesses laid plans, popular magazines tantalized readers with previews of vacations to come. *Saturday Evening Post* writer Boyden Sparkes predicted "travel potentialities of a revolutionary nature," teasing readers with prospects of flying buses and mass-marketed helicopters. Tapping into popular fascination with air-age spatial scales, flight was central to postwar vacation fantasies. "Any one of the great vacation playgrounds will be actually more accessible than your local picnic ground used to be in the old horse-and-buggy days," Marion White of *Independent Woman* suggested, adding: "Jules Verne might well rise from his grave to brand such statements as mad dreams—but the airplanes of today are proving them sober reality."[62] On the ground, a seemingly endless web of expressways would tie the Americas together. According to Sparkes, beleaguered veterans and war workers could look forward to roaring across these motorways in jeeps and amphibious vehicles developed for warfare but easily converted into pleasure vehicles.[63]

These sorts of dreamy predictions fit into a larger strand of popular discourse that framed the war as a fight for consumer plenty. The spoils of victory, from this perspective, were not so much the defeat of a vicious enemy, or even a ticket home, but a bounty of goods and services bestowed on the nation through the powers of modern industry and free enterprise. Within this context, vacationing was one of the key folkways of "getting and spending" that, as Charles McGovern has argued, was increasingly cast as *the* distinctive feature of American culture.[64] But travel previews also built on the fascination with mobility that pervaded interwar American culture. Sparkes gave voice to this sentiment, explaining that "a considerable part of what we mean when we say 'the American Standard of Living' involves our power to rove and play."[65] In this context, travel was inextricably part of what citizenship meant in a modern industrial society. For certain, vacations entailed access to desirable goods and services. But midcentury tourism also represented a particular outlook toward the physical environment and annual calendar. Part technological feat and part social achievement, "two weeks with pay" meant gliding across a landscape that had for ages anchored ordinary people to lives of unrelenting toil.

F. M. Reck, writing in a 1943 postwar preview for *Better Homes and Gardens*, made an expanded version of this argument:

> Your mind goes back. You think that for five thousand years men struggled for ways to get around. On foot. On horseback. By dugout canoe. In many-oared galleys, with a hundred men sweating in chains to carry a few. Then, in your time and mine, the secret of power was unlocked and men began to ride on rubber, on steel, on cushions of air. Operating in the free climate of individual enterprise and daring, men flung webs of steel rail across the land, built airports, tourist camps, pendulum cars, bedroom cars, air liners, autos and ribbons of concrete. World War II came, and under its impetus we suddenly found ourselves neighbors of the Dane, the Frenchman, the Chinese, and the Boer, and the world was a little place, soon to be within reach of our checkbooks and two-weeks-with-pay.[66]

For Reck, mass mobility was distinctly a product of the nation's entrepreneurial drive. Like many other outlets of commercial speech, the article fused free enterprise with American exceptionalism, prodding readers to view business as the steward of what they valued in culture. But Reck's account also evoked notions of the common weal, identifying American comforts and prosperity as the fruits of communal effort rather than corporate largesse.[67] According to this narrative, American know-how and industriousness tamed the natural world and, in doing so, created an abundant society in which everyone could step outside the shadow of work; even the stenographer's pocketbook could wrangle time and space. Although this narrative greatly overstated middle-income people's travel possibilities, glossed over the immobile conditions of the working poor, and ignored barriers thrown up in front of racial minorities, an unprecedented degree of mobility had spread through American society. And from the vantage point of a humming wartime economy, it looked like vacation travel could become one of the truly common folkways of an affluent industrial society.

For writers like Sparkes and Reck, the war had necessarily bottled up American mobility. But at the same time, by putting new infrastructure into place and accelerating the pace of technological development, the war was incubating a new era of supermobility. "Today," Reck explained, "the bonds we buy are building the highways and skyways that will win the war. Tomorrow, those bonds will pay our way over those highways and skyways to the goals of fun and business. Tomorrow we'll go places." This refrain was a staple of wartime travel advertising. "Tomorrow the World Is Yours!" Martin Aircraft enthused. The Air Transport Association, an industry lobbying group, boasted of the postwar family "with *Everywhere* to go." Featuring a young family casting their gaze upon a globe installed at a sparkling new airport, the ad promised "a couple of hours to the city, which the family never had time to visit before, a brief afternoon to reach the playgrounds of mountain or sea, overnight to the thrilling drama of another hemisphere."[68] According to this narrative, the postwar world would not simply be a continuation of the old but a regenerated version where mass mobility could be realized in full.

"The Brakes Are Off"

Instead of describing a nation that had actually been immobilized, preview articles and advertisements were a reaction to the specter of immobility—a sense that being fenced in somehow violated what it meant to be American. Such fears appear absurd in light of the more than 100,000 Japanese Americans who were actually fenced in at internment camps. Similarly, the inconveniences faced by home-front Americans were incomparable with the horrors faced by civilians and soldiers in war zones. But the great unease that rations and restrictions triggered did speak to a sense of claustrophobia. Even if the war had not straitjacketed civilians, it had bound their movement in significant ways. Throwing off these constraints would be one of the fruits of victory, and many Americans wasted little time in doing so.

Just hours after the Japanese surrender on September 2, 1945, OPA head Chester Bowles broadcast the lifting of gasoline rations. Within hours of the announcement, cars were lined up outside Rocky Mountain National Park. By the following year, the hated ration stickers, still stuck to many cars, entered popular memory as a quaint reminder of wartime sacrifice.[69] For many commentators, the postwar vacation rush, which *Holiday* dubbed "Exodus, 1946," represented a kind of mass catharsis, dispensation, and segue into domestic life. "If this year's escape to the beaches had a certain desperate quality," *Life* observed in a summer 1946 article, "if it brought out bathing suits which obviously had been in moth balls since the early 20's, if the sighs of relief were louder and longer, this was because America had just gone through six straight summers of crisis and everybody needed a rest."[70] According to such accounts, war had forced Americans to repress an inherent will to roam, but the peace allowed it to collectively erupt. As *Better Homes and Gardens* described it, a "5-year-old wanderlust" had been "uncorked at last."[71] Unveiling a regular travel feature in February 1946, *Look* simply declared: "The brakes are off." "We were tied down by our jobs. We could not even get out in the open on Sundays because of gasoline rationing," Secretary of the Interior Harold Ickes explained elsewhere. "Now we want to get moving."[72] Advertisers were happy to echo this line. Promoting "V-W Days" ("Vacations-in-the-West), the Burlington Lines recommended "an interlude of rest after the years of nerve-straining turmoil. A mental and physical lift as we dig into our peacetime work."[73] While the mass catharsis narrative certainly described the experience of many ascetic Americans, it offered a sanitized view of wartime leisure, sans the black markets, chiselers, and civilians perfectly willing to bump a furloughed serviceman.

Along with a mass upwelling of psychic tensions, the 1946 travel boom looked to many observers like a preview of the nation's regenerated spending power. According to this school of thought, consumer desire had built to a bursting point during the war. Press accounts used precisely this kind of language, using metaphors of deluge and invasion to describe travel spending as a spectacular, unstoppable force. *Life* described Florida tourists in 1946 as a "dollar-swollen, postwar torrent." Similarly, *Newsweek* dubbed the summer season "the Gold Rush of '46," reporting that "what would ordinarily be a trickle of travel at the beginning of the vacation season had already swollen to the proportions of a flood."[74] By depicting a booming tourist trade, early accounts picked up a prewar narrative thread that described an emerging culture of mass mobility. Moreover, boom stories solidified an enduring image of the tourism industry as one of consumer capitalism's most dynamic sectors. Part of the windfall enjoyed by the industry derived from a combination of factors unique to 1946. At the end of the war, Americans had accumulated more than $250 billion in savings—a sum six times the gross national income for 1932. The travel industry, in particular, benefited from these lump savings because many goods remained off store shelves while manufacturers retooled their plants for peacetime production. Perhaps most important, transoceanic travel remained heavily restricted as ships and planes moved priority passengers—troops, POWs, and administrators—back and forth. The result was a virtual North American monopoly on tourist travel in 1946.[75]

The landscape that tourists ventured through that year was a tumultuous one, though. Interests that had reluctantly put their agendas on hold during the war were anxious to shape the postwar economy. Central to this debate was the role that New Deal agencies would play going forward. Business leaders looked to have much of the new regulatory system gutted, while unions and consumer groups fought to have it strengthened.[76] This economic feuding had a marked impact on travel. Looming strikes among railway workers and coal miners threatened train service. And with price controls scrapped and millions of Americans eager to splurge on vacations, opportunists adopted a "soak the tourist" strategy. *Holiday* editor J. Frank Beaman wondered why the OPA could not intervene on behalf of vacationers.[77] In Florida, a steep black market remained vibrant for northbound tickets, leaving many passengers stranded. Aside from strikes and price gouging, the sheer volume of tourists stressed the nation's transportation grid. "What 1946 Vacationist Faces: Shortages, Crowds, High Prices" was how *U.S. News and World Report* described the situation.[78] Fearing that much of the state's phenomenal crop of tourists would go home jilted, Florida's state tourist bureau went so far as to run ads warning visitors that they may not be able to find lodging. By the fall, *Life* editorialized that "probably the best and surely the kindest advice that can be given to anybody about to make a trip in the U.S. these days is 'don't. Equipment was never worse, service more expensive and old-fashioned courtesy so scanty as now.'"[79] These problems made vacations a particularly potent symbol of the social and economic frustrations sweeping the nation just after the war. Just as the opportunity for unhindered travel presented itself, price gouging sent rates sky high, strikes threatened services, and travel channels were clogged.

Such stark juxtapositions between expectations and reality produced a swell of cranky consumers convinced they were being cheated of their hard-earned dispensation. "By 1946," historian Meg Jacobs writes, "Americans of all income groups had come to perceive a high standard of affordable living as an entitlement, as their right as patriotic citizens who had suffered through the scarcities of depression and the sacrifices of war."[80] Hiccups in vacation travel, which had been framed as iconic of abundance and consumer freedom, were particularly galling. *Holiday* writer Frederick C. Otham informed hoteliers and restaurateurs in 1946 that "there's a peace on" and no matter how whiskery he appeared, or how windblown his wife, "You will treat us like the Duchess of Windsor and the Duke." Otham warned that he had no patience for excuses about food shortages. "When I order a slab of apple pie (which should be warm and have two crusts) to follow my eggs, the waitress is to say, 'Yes, Sir,' and bring me also, and automatically, another cup of coffee," Otham ranted. "If she titters, she gets that that pie in her face." Reflecting on all the shoddy service he received the previous summer, food and travel writer Duncan Hines suggested a new group, Pet Peevers Unlimited, to rove the country's highways and byways, reporting all the substandard establishments along the way.[81] Otham's and Hines's frustrations illuminate how vacationing had come to be situated within the field of marketplace entitlements that many Americans felt was their due as Americans.

Cartoonist Bill Mauldin lampooned this sense of entitlement in a scene sketched shortly after he returned home from the war. Showing a family of vacationers pulled up to a service station, the father ordered the attendant to "Check th' tires, oil, an' radiator. Wipe the windshield, water th' dog, feed th' canary, take Junior to th' washroom, an' gimme a gallon o' gas."[82] While not all vacationers were so pushy, Mauldin's cartoon suggests how ideas about leisure and travel had been transformed in subtle but important ways by the war experience. The constraints it placed on Americans helped to foster a sense that peace meant not only a return to normalcy but also the start of a new era when comfort and leisure could be expected. Vacations thus became a powerful symbol of what postwar American society was supposed to be like, an image of the nation that, next to material plenty, placed free time and easy mobility at the heart of citizenship.

2 CREATING *HOLIDAY*
Market Research, Play, and Magazine Reading

As World War II drew to a close, businesses in the United States and their backers in government envisioned a coming era of unbound consumer spending.¹ Scanning the horizon for promising markets, researchers at the Curtis Publishing Company zeroed in on travel as an advertising sector ready to skyrocket. The launching of *Holiday*, the magazine Curtis created to capitalize on this bonanza, was a major media industry event and would prove to be the biggest magazine venture of the 1940s—the last decade before magazines were overtaken by television as the dominant national advertising medium. The trade journal *Tide* likened the anticipation surrounding *Holiday*'s release in early 1946 to "the excitement prefacing the first issues of Luce's *Life*," and industry watchers speculated that it matched, or maybe even surpassed, *Life* as the most expensive magazine developed to date.²

Curtis's travel title would never achieve the iconic stature of Luce's photo magazine, but *Holiday* did establish itself as a media industry model during an era of remarkable change. Most important, Curtis's success with *Holiday* helped push the industry toward using research in ways that would ultimately yield a very different view of media products and their audiences. This chapter describes how Curtis created *Holiday* in response to tourism's growing centrality to middle-class American culture. In doing so, it illuminates the early stages of a large-scale shift in the ways that media businesses and marketers thought about audiences, recreation, and consumption. By combining market research and readership studies with sociocultural analysis, and by making research integral to managerial planning, Curtis was at the forefront of a psychographic approach in which media were used to identify specific types of people and define them by their attitudes toward consumption. Leisure—newly anointed in business and academic circles as *the* dynamic force in American life—sat at the heart of this process. According to this argument, Americans' growing orientation toward fun was an enormous marketing opportunity because consumers in the coming years would pour more and more money into the pursuit of pleasure. Leisure content offered magazines a way not only to target specialized audiences but also to reach readers whose notions of identity were especially tied to the purchases they made.[3] Marketers seized upon recreational fields as booming industries and the key to sorting readers who could spend freely from those who could not. Moreover, publishers saw the play spirit at the heart of leisure as an economic resource that could be controlled and brought to market. While publishers undoubtedly overstated their audiences' vulnerability, their boasts spoke to a growing notion that selling experiences, like tourist travel, allowed marketers to tap into an especially therapeutic strand of consumer desire. In tying together disparate ideas about demographics, social trends, leisure, tastes, values, and consumption, Curtis and the publishers who followed it helped redefine magazine reading as a means of prompting audiences to self-identify as particularly acquisitive and desirable types of consumers.

Corralling Consumers

Curtis's market-research activities dated from 1911 when company founder Cyrus Curtis hired schoolteacher Charles Coolidge Parlin to travel the country gathering information on various industries. Curtis's publications, the *Ladies' Home Journal* and *Saturday Evening Post,* had grown quickly over the previous two decades and embodied the rise of mass magazines in American culture. Recognizing the chance to reach a national market of consumers who could absorb the growing glut of mass-produced goods, a number of publishers borrowed the metropolitan newspapers' business model and developed magazines with cheap subscription rates subsidized by advertising revenue. Their magazines—*Ladies' Home Journal, Saturday Evening Post, Munsey's, McClure's,* and *Cosmopolitan*—provided a regular diet of fiction, commentary, news, and commercial messages that offered readers a feeling of inclusion in a national, middle-class culture.[4] Under the development of Louisa Knapp Curtis and then Edward Bok, *Ladies' Home Journal* was the most successful of the early mass magazines, and Curtis looked to expand that success into new ventures. The publisher acquired the *Saturday Evening Post* in 1897, and after a slow start the *Post* grew quickly under editor George Horace Lorimer. By 1910, Curtis's twin publications were two of the largest magazines in the country, reaching more than a million subscribers each.[5]

Curtis recognized that in order to continue growing he would have to expand his advertising base. Hoping to sway the many businessmen still skeptical of advertising's merits, he commissioned Parlin in 1911 to arm his salesmen with market data. Looking back on the hole filled by Curtis's research operation, General Foods executive Ralph Starr Butler explained: "The salesmen could talk ably about their publications, but they had nothing in the way of organized business information to present to their customers, nor were they able to relate the values of what they had to sell to trends and principles in business." Over the next three decades, Parlin's division produced voluminous studies on the makeup of key industries. The division became a national authority on markets thanks to the sheer size, scope, thoroughness, and insight of its reports.[6] *Department Store Lines* (1912), for example, was the product of 1,121 interviews and 37,000 miles of travel. Aside from collecting facts and figures on this massive network of retailers, the report was a sociological treatise on household budgets, gender roles, and consumption. Parlin opened the four-volume study with the statement "Woman is a shopper. Out of that fact has come the modern department store." Echoing the innovative, consumer-oriented theories of University of Pennsylvania economist Simon N. Patten, Parlin declared that "the consumer is king. His preference is law and his whim makes and unmakes merchants, jobbers, and manufacturers." The division followed *Department Store Lines* with equally imposing studies of automobiles, packaged food, radio sets, and dozens of other markets over the next two decades.[7]

Parlin's group was at the vanguard of market research from its start, working out the field's contours as it went along. A handful of ad agencies, business consultants, and professors had carried out market-intelligence projects prior to 1911. But the founding of Curtis's research shop in that year crystallized those scattered activities into an emerging field. Parlin's studies were more ambitious and comprehensive than their predecessors. As the Curtis group was joined by a growing number of followers, it continued to blaze a path, conducting ever larger studies and experimenting with novel modes of inquiry. Research duties ranged from analyzing distribution lines to rifling through Philadelphia garbage cans in search of household brand preferences.[8] In the 1920s, the division increasingly trained its sights on reader demographics, studying income, educational levels, and tastes. Parlin's group set out to show potential advertisers that Curtis's audience was, in the words of historian Douglas Ward, "a buying class . . . defined by the ownership of such things as homes, automobiles, typewriters and telephones, or the availability of electricity or department store charge accounts."[9]

Still more research groups emerged in the 1920s and 1930s as other publishers copied Curtis's operation, advertising agencies added research divisions, A. C. Nielsen and others cropped up to measure broadcast audiences, and the Census Bureau and Department of Commerce developed sophisticated consumer-research arms. Through such efforts, market researchers developed a picture of consumers not as distinct individuals but as abstract, statistical agglomerations of income, educational level, buying habits, and brand preferences; and with increasingly specialized notions of the typical buyer of a certain product in mind, advertisers could target these consumer abstractions through selective media buying.[10] Media companies and ad agencies were evangelical about market research because their growth depended on demonstrating advertising's ability to sync consumer demand with producer output. As Roland Marchand pointed out, advertising men of the era fancied themselves consumption engineers. They believed that their number-crunching acumen and uncanny understanding of the mass mind allowed them to build vast markets out of thin air. But in order to do so, media businesses needed tomes of market-research data. "The manufacturer or distributor is interested in his one product or group of products," Donald M. Hobart, Parlin's successor, wrote in 1950. "The magazine publisher, of necessity, is interested not only in the making and marketing of his own product and services, but also in the marketing activity connected with as many products and product groups as he has advertisers and potential advertisers. He is interested in everything that is sold or can be sold nationally, from steel and heavy industrial equipment to food, fine porcelains and gossamer silks, from automobiles to children's togs, from insurance to transportation."[11]

By the 1940s, some market researchers started to see their field as more than just an advertising tool, expounding its benefits as a general instrument of management, indispensable to developing new products and services. Virgil D. Reed, associate director of research at J. Walter Thompson, championed this approach in a 1947 report in *Printers' Ink*, noting that "market research has just passed through the trying age of adolescence with its acne, changing voice and rebellion against parental dominance. Instead of Mr.—title of manhood—it has added *ing* to its name. In that *ing* lie many of the new horizons and greatly increased usefulness for the guidance of policy and planning."[12] Market*ing*-research proselytizers drew inspiration from forward-thinking manufacturers like Alfred P. Sloan Jr.'s General Motors. Beginning in the 1920s, GM rolled out a diverse line of automobiles aimed at specific markets as an alternative to the one-size-fits-all approach of Ford's Model T. Sloan saw market research as at the very core of his company's phenomenal success, cautioning stockholders in 1931 that "it would be a mistake to think of consumer research as an isolated department. . . . In its broad implications it is more in the nature of an *operating philosophy*, which, to be fully effective, must extend through all phases of a business." Marke*ting* research, instead of just helping to sell products, revealed which products to develop in the first place.[13]

The Curtis Publishing Company again put itself in marketing's vanguard, restructuring its Research Division in 1943 to include marketing, advertising, *and* editorial research. The newly coined Research Department not only gathered commercial data but also oversaw the company's efforts at developing and tweaking its own products—the Curtis magazines. Most businesses were much slower to make this kind of transition. While they made use of studies provided by media companies, the vast majority of manufacturers and service providers conducted almost no research of their own. In 1945, production research expenditures outpaced market research by a fifty-to-one margin.[14] A sweeping study by the National Association of Manufacturers and American Marketing Association in 1947 found that only 11 percent of businesses had market-research divisions of at least one full-time employee or more. And the companies that did embrace market research did so tentatively, appropriating less than one-third of 1 percent of sales revenue toward the activity and oftentimes ignoring the results of their studies.[15]

Curtis's early embrace of the new research paradigm owed much to the company's choice for a replacement after Parlin retired in 1938. Donald M. Hobart was a longtime Curtis employee and early convert to Parlin's market-research gospel. The son of a small-town Ohio shopkeeper, he developed a childhood interest in merchandising that he fleshed out as an economics student at the University of Pennsylvania's Wharton School in the late 1910s. Following a brief stint as a merchandising instructor at Wharton and a number of sales jobs in the rubber industry, Hobart joined Curtis's Commercial Research Division in 1923. He worked as Parlin's assistant for the next five years, absorbing his theories and methods on a number of sprawling industry studies. Eager to reenter the sales world, Hobart transferred to the company's Cleveland office in 1928 to sell ad space for the *Saturday Evening Post*. He remained there for the next ten years before returning to Philadelphia to succeed Parlin.[16]

Hobart's tenure in market research and advertising sales gave him an expansive view of the publishing industry. Like Parlin, and true to his Wharton School background, Hobart approached market research as a science. Also like Parlin, he became a leading figure in the field, serving as president of the American Marketing Association in 1945 and authoring two well-regarded textbooks in the early 1950s.[17] But unlike his mentor, Hobart was more interested in developing scientific media-research methods than issuing voluminous industry reports. Bringing Curtis's editorial-research group under his fold in 1943, Hobart fused the publisher's extensive reader-research program with its market-research operations. This enabled his group to synch the Curtis magazines' editorial strategies with trends in the ad market and larger economy. Hobart would later call his approach "dynamic marketing," or the total synthesis of research, calibrated production, and advertising with management decision making, and touted it as the future of industrial growth.[18]

Curtis's expanded research group quickly came to play a central role in company strategizing. In particular, the group was tasked with identifying "new areas of future operation" in the postwar publishing field, recommending a specialized magazine that could achieve mass circulation. Hobart's findings reflected the shifting landscape of magazine publishing at midcentury. In one regard, mass circulation had been the defining logic of prewar publishing as magazines like *Life* and the *Saturday Evening Post* reached millions of households. But in specializing, Curtis followed what a 1945 *Printers' Ink* editorial called the new, "more sensible premise" behind launching periodicals—"namely that the editorial appeal of the publication should corral readers representing a homogeneous group of consumers."[19] Searching for an area of specialization that could still yield a large audience, Hobart's group tagged travel and recreation as relatively underserved areas and set about assessing the size of those markets.

In the spring of 1945, the department interviewed twenty-five hundred magazine readers of varying incomes on a wide range of vacation topics, probing them on what types of vacation plans they were hatching, when and where they planned to travel, and how they thought they would get there. To the department's delight, the findings overwhelmingly indicated that many Americans planned to make a regular habit out of extensive vacation travel.[20] In the same year, the Research Department also unveiled its massive *Advertising Classification Analysis*—a sprawling study of magazine ad expenditures for more than sixty industries between 1933 and 1945. The report found that spending in "travel and accommodations" had risen from $2,844,000 in 1933 to $5,508,532 by 1941. Other relevant ad markets, such as transportation, cameras, and recreational goods and services, had risen precipitously as well.[21] With these figures likely in mind, the Research Department titled its recreation market forecast *The Golden Opportunity*. Curtis could also draw on its recent study of the aviation industry. With its eye on that booming ad market, the Research Department conducted a large-scale study in 1944 to gauge whether the war had changed Americans' perceptions of flying. Again, the study pointed to explosive growth, concurring with industry reports that predicted a fivefold increase in air travel.[22]

Launching *Holiday*

Research in hand, the department was floored by the potential size of the travel market. As Hobart told his American Marketing Association (AMA) audience in 1946: "What we saw made our mouths water. We saw that postwar America represented a travel and pleasure-hungry market—a market made up of millions of people, who, wary of wartime work and restrictions, would be eager to satisfy that innate urge for fun and relaxation."[23] Informed by narratives of an innate national wanderlust and well aware of the fast-growing network of global travel infrastructure, the Curtis Publishing Company envisioned an emerging culture of mass mobility. But as with most observers, it had difficulty pinning down exactly what constituted the tourist trade—an industry notorious for its lack of self-knowledge. A 1936 *Fortune* poll, seeking to shed some light on the then $3 billion market, lamented that it was "an industry that knows less about itself than any of comparable size." More than ten years later, Florida, a state that earned a third of its revenue from tourist spending, did not even keep an official visitors tally. State officials just eyeballed the total at five million per year.[24]

Much of the difficulty presented by measuring the vacation industry stemmed from what statistician Marion Clawson called "definitional and conceptual problems."[25] In other words, what qualified as vacation spending? Some businesses and governmental services, such as resorts and national parks, were easy to identify as part of the vacation economy. But what about spending on vacation necessities, like swimsuits, sportswear, cameras, and film, that were grouped in with larger consumer-goods sectors? Transportation was the hardest aspect of the travel industry to quantify. As a Twentieth Century Fund report argued in 1955, it is "clear that a substantial share of what consumers pay for automobile upkeep and other forms of transportation is spent for recreational purposes," but exactly what that share amounted to was difficult to ascertain.[26] Passport and visa paperwork helped authorities distinguish between business travelers, migrants, and vacationers on transoceanic voyages and flights. But domestic tourists, who were by far the biggest group of vacationers, could pass from state to state without measure. Along with uncertainty about the size of the traveling public, industry leaders and economic researchers knew very little about how much tourists spent. Government agencies, at the federal and state level, grasped at an idea by developing surveys and other research metrics. Beginning in 1946, the Department of Commerce mandated inbound American and outbound foreign travelers to complete postcards reporting how much they spent and where they spent it. Other research bureaus looked to variables like property values and monthly revenue reports, furnished by hotels, motor courts, tourist homes, resorts, and camps, to create a "recreation index."[27] Despite these local and regional efforts, a comprehensive view of the industry at a national or transnational level remained murky.

What most flummoxed Curtis was how to define the advertising market for travel, which potentially included everything from transportation, lodging, and food to leisurewear, sporting goods, and amusements. Confronted with this question, the Research Department offered a novel solution. Instead of seizing upon a group of goods and services, the department conceptualized the magazine's market in terms of mood. As Hobart explained: "We decided upon a basic concept which was that the Holiday market would rightfully include all goods and services purchased by the consumer in satisfaction of his urge for fun and relaxation; and that the factor which motivates the spending is of primary importance." The "holiday mood" was the "way you feel when you plan for or actually experience the pleasures of travel, recreation, sports or enjoy a hobby."[28] According to Curtis, this mind-set was particularly vulnerable to commercial inducement. As one 1946 trade ad explained, there is "nothing like the HOLIDAY spirit to stir up longings—to spark that spending mood—to make people say, 'That's for me . . . *I want it.*'" A later ad put it more bluntly: "The Holiday mood is a SPENDING MOOD." Recast as a state of mind, *Holiday*'s potential ad market included nearly 10 percent of Americans' expenditures, including everything from travel services to "new suits, hats, shoes and furnishings—new 'holiday wear' for sports, travel, vacation."[29]

Curtis's use of psychologically charged words, such as "mood," "motivate," and "longings," stemmed from an emerging line of marketing thought that focused on probing the nuances of consumer affect and behavior. Researchers working in this area recognized that traditional "nose counting" methods could not account for significant differences between groups that demographically looked very similar. Pollster Elmo Roper, for instance, argued in 1940 that different buying patterns could be attributed to more than just income disparities. He suggested that socioeconomic groups could be better visualized in terms of their "scale-of-living." Roper's measure looked beyond income to take account of whether people could indulge their leisure interests and to whom they looked as peers.[30]

Efforts like Roper's were the products of a growing interdependency between the worlds of academia and industry as the principles of social psychology came to permeate market-research thinking. In the early 1940s, sociologist W. Lloyd Warner and his colleagues at the University of Chicago Business School issued the first of many detailed studies of social stratification in U.S. communities. Warner did not delve into the intricacies of consumer behavior but deeply influenced a number of associates who applied his insights on status and group identity to market research.[31] Building on sociological profiles, researchers identified differences in the psychological motivations that animated buying decisions. Paul Lazarsfeld had encouraged researchers as early as 1935 to view buying motivations through a social-psychological prism but produced little research in this vein himself. At the time, advertisers relied heavily on behaviorist psychological appeals, stoking insecurities and selling the satisfactions associated with a product. But they generally took a one-size-fits all approach. As Lever Brothers executive Robert F. Elder explained to the AMA in 1946, businesses "slugged the market" during the interwar years, hitting an undifferentiated mass with an undifferentiated appeal. "Products, packages and price lines," Elder argued, "were all too often not geared to mesh with the needs, desires, and mental processes of consumers." Taking such considerations into account at management's highest levels, he noted, would open up "paths of least resistance" to selling goods and services.[32] In the tourism industry, the All-Year Club's Don Thomas saw the touristic mentality as one such path. Writing in *Sales Management* in 1941, he advised marketers to understand "the tourist as a state of mind." "When we drop work, and get away from it all," Thomas elaborated, "we are different in our personalities, and in our spending."[33]

Curtis's Research Department, which was plugged directly into the middle of the industry-academy nexus, drew on all these wells of thought. The publisher's *Holiday* strategy may have been especially influenced by researchers like George A. Lundberg, who placed consumer behavior in the context of "the whole culture pattern of any society." In his influential *Leisure: A Suburban Study* (1934), Lundberg, a University of Washington sociologist, stressed that leisure could best be understood as a state of mind. This distinct mode of consciousness set off free time from working life, as well as recuperative activities like eating and sleeping. Elaborating on this concept, Lundberg approvingly quoted philosopher Irwin Edman's dictum that "leisure is an affair of mood and atmosphere rather than simply of the clock. It is not a chronological occurrence but a spiritual state. It is unhurried pleasurable living among one's native enthusiasms."[34] When Curtis tapped Lundberg to deliver the first annual Charles Coolidge Parlin Memorial Lecture in May 1945, Lundberg continued to stress the importance of cultural patterns, explaining that consumption took place within the "habit systems of the group—folkways, customs, mores—which make up the web of life into which an individual is born and which condition his actions just as his physical surroundings condition and restrict his behavior." Taking this dynamic into account, Lundberg argued, media producers could target specific consumer groups by speaking in the idioms of success and prestige that characterized their particular way of life.³⁵ One insight Curtis researchers gleaned from Lundberg was a view of magazine reading as a symbolic act. The department's Wroe Alderson asserted in his introduction to Lundberg's lecture that "the character of magazine reading is in some respects more indicative of standard of living than is money income." Citing research in educational psychology, Alderson argued that it should be possible to identify "the upper-class, pace-setting, influential hub of the village" through their tastes in magazines.³⁶

Curtis's merging of demographics and disposition saw the company forging an early form of psychographic segmentation. Psychographic marketing, as business historian Richard Tedlow has explained, goes beyond the targeting of a specific demographic—for example, high-income versus middle-income families—to zero in on "people with a certain lifestyle and attitude toward life." Tedlow dates this shift to "the Pepsi Generation" campaign geared toward energetic young people in the 1950s and 1960s. Others have placed it with the more and more sophisticated media research turned out by publishers in the late 1950s and the marketing strategies pursued by the fledgling cable television industry in the 1970s.³⁷ While they are correct that the full ramifications of psychographic fragmentation would not be felt for decades, its origins date from World War II–era transformations in magazine research.

By the early 1940s, the magazine industry's regular output of industry overviews, consumer surveys, and readership studies had grown into one of the business world's most important sources of commercial information. Statistician Daniel Starch's much anticipated audience studies, for instance, offered rich bodies of demographic data. Others sought to yield insight into the dynamics of consumer behavior.³⁸ In one example, a *Redbook* study measured the respective influence of husbands and wives on purchasing decisions, finding, for instance, that men decided how much to spend on refrigerators but that women determined the kind and brand selected.³⁹ Although magazine research took many forms, it could almost all be described as quantitative in character. The overriding objective of "nose counting," as some called it, was to sort readers into boxes—defined by well-established categories like sex, class, occupation, region, or rural versus urban residency—and then show advertisers how full those boxes were. Mass magazines pointed to their readers' buying power in aggregate, while the class magazines pointed to it in concentrate. Specialty magazines publicized their ability to reach niche markets, such as sportsmen and science enthusiasts.⁴⁰

What magazine research did not do was connect demographics and brand preferences to larger social trends and cultural patterns. As a *McCall's* manager wrote in a 1936 circulation study, "However similar the readers of a particular magazine may be in their reading habits, it does not follow logically that there must be any similarity in their buying habits." More qualitatively minded research consultants who did try to draw such connections were depicted as novel in the trade press well through the early 1950s.[41] By and large, the publishing industry had yet to transition from market research to market*ing* research.

The Curtis Publishing Company was the exception, though. Its decision to frame *Holiday*'s audience in terms of "mood" reflected nuanced views of the links between disposition, consumption, and identity. *Holiday*'s audience, the publisher claimed, read "with the wide-awake interest of people looking for things they want—What to Do, Where to Go, What to Buy."[42] Using language that suggested an amphetamine more than a magazine, one 1947 ad claimed that "the Holiday *idea* or *mood* . . . is something that gets into peoples' blood— gives them the urge to buy! It's something that changes buying for need into spending for fun!"[43] The magazine continued to equate play with lavish spending throughout the next decade, declaring that "Holiday . . . means pleasure and pleasure means business!"[44]

Curtis sold *Holiday*'s readers as a particular type of person—individuals whose income allowed them to travel *and* whose values led them to spend freely. The Research Department connected these disparate attributes by linking leisure interests with the underlying values that motivated them. Framed in this manner, a vacation represented not only a number of discrete economic transactions but "a need to look beyond the everyday horizon" and "the desire for a fuller life."[45] Perhaps poking fun at the quality monthlies, *Holiday* emphasized that its readers were not wealthy hermits but active, social moderns. BBDO, the agency that handled the magazine's trade campaign, explained that *Holiday* "was designed to reflect the Big Change in our nation to a more pleasurable, more mobile way of life. That's why it is read by the leaders of this big change."[46] Wanting to read about travel, then, suggested a patently modern openness to new places, new things, and new ways of living. And that attitude in turn suggested a general outlook toward life in which consumption and leisure played a dominant role.

The sociologist David Reisman famously described this large-scale reorientation in American culture as the rise of an "other-directed" personality. Reisman and his followers argued that the archetypal personality type of the nineteenth century—"inwardly directed" toward entrenched, independent notions of success and moral standing—had given way in the twentieth century to a more fluid personality type directed at winning the approval of others. This new outlook could be seen in everything from best sellers like Dale Carnegie's *How to Win Friends and Influence People* (1936) to the auto industry's success with planned obsolescence. But the change in personality was nowhere more apparent than in the dominant role that leisure had assumed in adults' lives.[47] Sociologist Martha Wolfenstein dubbed this new fixation "the emergence of fun morality," suggesting that "where formerly there was felt to be the danger that in seeking fun, one might be carried away into the depths of wickedness, today there is a recognizable fear that one may not be able to let go sufficiently, that one may not have enough fun."[48]

The extent to which the new "fun morality" had become dominant by the 1940s can be seen in Curtis's changing policies toward alcohol advertising. For six decades, the publisher had spurned beer and liquor advertisers on moral grounds. As late as 1940, the board of directors voted twenty-five to one to continue this policy. But *Holiday* complicated matters. The magazine's editorial mix clearly offered a natural home for appeals from brewers and distillers. Recognizing this fit, company officials debated lifting the ban during the title's developmental period before ultimately deciding against it. The lure of the spirits market proved too great, though, and management revised the company's bylaws to make an exception for *Holiday* in late 1947.[49]

The publisher's abrupt policy shift signaled more than just capitulation to an enticing ad market. It was also emblematic of Curtis's new conception of magazine readers. As a number of scholars have noted, the *Saturday Evening Post* and *Ladies' Home Journal* offered traditional models of masculinity and femininity rooted in late Victorian ideals of work and family life. Drawing on nineteenth-century archetypes, they conceptualized men and women in terms of productivity—men were responsible for economic production and women for reproducing the moral sanctity of the home.[50] The Curtis magazines' success in attracting advertisers hinged on the notion that they offered outlets into the nation's most enterprising households. Alcohol, from this point of view, threatened the health of the productive, upwardly mobile home. *Holiday* operated from a fundamentally different starting point; its audience was visualized first and foremost as people of leisure. Play was their productive activity because it funneled spending into an exploding leisure economy. Old vices, in this new system, fueled the economy rather than putting a drag on it.[51] This radically different outlook was not lost on Curtis's old guard, who throughout the postwar era saw *Holiday* as an ill fit for the sober old company.[52]

Despite the dismay of its Main Line board members, Curtis's redefinition of the magazine reader was a nearly inevitable outgrowth of the company's allegiance to market research. Following *Holiday*'s launch, the publisher conducted a series of studies to definitively peg the magazine's readers. Along with confirming that it attracted a young, affluent, well-educated, geographically diverse, and active set of readers, research found that they were an especially sociable group. One study reported that 98 percent of newsstand buyers held house parties at least once a month. On top of that, a 1947 study of the recreation field found that food and beverage made up 20 percent of the market, third only to transportation and miscellaneous spending.[53] Given the distinctly festive nature of *Holiday*'s audience and its astounding appetite for beer and liquor, management cast aside the company's teetotaling policies. After the reversal, Curtis began selling *Holiday* readers as "Entertainers Deluxe," calling them "a market of hosts and hostesses—a market of spenders."[54] The company's characterization of these readers as pleasure-oriented, or essentially "other-directed," people crept beyond *Holiday* to its other magazines as well. By 1949 Curtis redefined the once staid *Saturday Evening Post* readership as "an alert active market," always on the lookout for recreational items. Connecting this new image to the *Post*'s rock-ribbed Republican subscriber of yesteryear, Curtis executives pointed to the leadership role they exercised in not only the business and social affairs of their communities but its "recreational life" as well. For the Curtis Publishing Company, the shift toward understanding its audience as "other-directed" was complete.[55]

Operationalizing Fun

When it came time to publish the first issues of *Holiday*, Curtis once again turned to the Research Department. Capturing the "Holiday mood" could not be left to chance or trusted to editorial talent alone. Instead, the magazine's look, feel, tone, and content mix would have to be determined through scientific planning and systematic tinkering. The first task, entrusted to project head J. Frank Beaman, was to create a mock-up to undergo Research Department critique. Curtis's editorial research group, or Public Opinion Division, was started in 1940 to test reader responses to magazine content. When research operations were consolidated in 1943, the group was placed under Hobart's command, renamed the Development Division, and given more of a policy-planning function. As director Herbert C. Ludeke described the division's role, "You might compare it to product research in most firms."[56]

The Development Division relied on four methods of testing reader response to editorial material: traffic studies, surveys, statistical analysis, and experiments. Reader traffic studies involved one-on-one consultations through which a researcher collected detailed feedback on magazine content. Surveys were sent out to solicit similar, but closed-ended, feedback. Statistical studies took the datasets the division accumulated over time and processed them in new combinations. Results were compiled into "'readership expectancy' tables" that Ludeke likened to "the actuarial records of a life insurance company." New editorial ideas could then be fed into a device called the "Predictograph" to compute their likelihood of success. For its experimental research, the division looked to the hard sciences for inspiration. As Ludeke explained: "The controlled experiment is patterned after the guinea pig experiments in biology, in which one set of pigs is inoculated with a serum while another set, called a 'control group,' does not get the serum. . . . In our work the guinea pigs are people and the 'serum' may be some new editorial treatment, the effectiveness of which we can measure by the reaction of the reader."[57]

In developing *Holiday*, the Research Department drew on its full methodological toolbox. Having identified travel as a growing market and underserved area, the department conducted industry studies and data analysis to gauge "tastes and plans for travel." Next, the department drew on reader-response inquiries to shape content and layout. Findings from each round were incorporated into a series of mock-ups, or dummies, that were then circulated internally and externally for feedback. Advertising salesmen shopped it around Madison Avenue, the Circulation Department met with distributors, and the Research Department spoke with potential subscribers. For the audience-response test, Curtis gave copies to carefully screened families, who were in turn asked to treat the magazine as they would any other they bought. The homes were then visited by field workers who compiled data on readers' design tastes, attitudes toward the magazine, and interest in certain types of articles. Interviewers left no stone unturned, probing readers on everything from the amount of color photography they expected to whether they favored "small labels like 'Places to Go' . . . and 'Things to Do' in the margins." To get at attitude, field workers were instructed to ask: "What is your personal opinion of this issue of 'Holiday' as a magazine for yourself? I'd like to have you tell me as fully as possible." The interview guide offered a full page for notes on this question.[58] Results were again turned over to Beaman's editorial group for incorporation into the inaugural issue. Once *Holiday*'s scope, look, and feel were set, its editors scrambled through the winter months to prepare the first issues, with the earliest pressing hitting newsstands in February 1946. Even then, Hobart asserted, "the job of the Research Department had only begun." Every item of every issue would need to be tested to gauge reader response.[59]

With actual readers subscribing and purchasing issues, the department would need to discern a crystal-clear image of *who* those people were. Researchers were delighted to find that charter subscribers and newsstand buyers averaged lofty incomes of $6,308 and $4,679 per year at a time when the median household take was just over $2,700. In both groups, more than 60 percent had attended college, and a combined 70 percent of subscribers were in professional or managerial positions. Enjoying the ample income and vacation packages afforded white-collar workers, almost 100 percent of readers engaged in recreational activities, and 80 percent had traveled abroad at least once in their lives. Research revealed that subscribers were also well scattered geographically. After advertising in *Holiday*'s inaugural issue, boosters in Tennessee were inundated with 7,050 requests for promotional literature. Curtis researchers requested the list of names and were able to dig up addresses for more than 5,500 of those readers, finding that they represented all forty-eight states and a diverse range of communities. Just over half, 54 percent, lived in cities of more than 25,000 people, while the remainder lived in towns of less than 25,000. Curtis seemed intent to craft a magazine with broad national appeal, extending beyond the orbit of the metropolitan centers on the coasts. When the Research Department probed readers on their initial impressions of the magazine, for instance, it chose the urban, but unglamorous, market of Buffalo, New York. Coupled with the department's later inquiries into *Holiday* readers' entertaining habits, the composite picture of the audience suggested the well-educated, socially active strata of professionals in cities big and small across the United States. Curtis was just as happy to reach the young doctor in Terre Haute, or the rising middle manager outside Dallas, as the Upper West Side lawyer. What was important was their outlook on life, leisure, and spending.[60]

The result of such copious study was a magazine that, from editorial formula to captioning style, was fully shaped by market research. Summing up the process, Hobart cast his group's activities as collaborative in nature. "Constant marketing research is measuring all phases of consumer and market reaction," he explained, "so *Holiday* is actually being designed and changed by Mr. and Mrs. America in search of a Holiday."[61] According to Hobart's explanation, research simply allowed the publisher to better meet its readers' expectations. But research offered other benefits that had much more to do with commercial efficiency than reader satisfaction. Art director Don May, paraphrased in a *Printers' Ink* report, frankly admitted that research allowed him to craft pages that could "hold the eye of the reader as long as possible, giving the advertiser all the more time to sell his wares."[62] From this point of view, research was a service the publisher carried out primarily for the sake of advertisers—not readers.

Curtis's extensive research also yielded a distinct image of the relationship between *Holiday* and its readers. By setting the cover price at fifty cents and pursuing Americans with the time, money, and motivation to travel, the company pursued an audience that had traditionally been understood as a "class" market. But *Holiday* was also premised on the notion that the number of people who fit into this group had grown exponentially during the war. As a result, vacation travel would be something new and unfamiliar to much of the audience. Beaman called these readers "the armchair tourist of pre-war days" —a growing public of travelers who would need help acquainting themselves with the vacation possibilities that lay ahead. Belying this paternalistic stance, a trade ad introducing *Holiday* to advertisers described it as "a service magazine. It will combine information with entertainment. It will suggest places to go, things to see, what to take and wear. It will advise of interesting things to do within range of a week-end or afternoon."[63] The notion that *Holiday* provided a service to readers operating on unfamiliar ground gave it a strong "middlebrow" flavor. Middlebrow media—including news digests, book clubs, and popular guides to art, philosophy, world history, and other scholarly topics—sought to introduce the swelling ranks of moderately affluent and moderately educated Americans to a world of "Culture" that elites had previously staked out as their own. Just as the Book-of-the-Month Club allowed members to feel plugged into a circuit of contemporary literary culture, *Holiday* could help readers feel privy to the cosmopolitan world of travel.[64]

Heralding the start of a new era, Beaman announced in the first issue that *Holiday* was "designed for the new postwar world, a world in which recreation will be more important to everyone than ever before." He specifically addressed the novice travelers Curtis hoped to reach, writing that "if you have heard promises in the West Wind, if you have restlessly listened to a train whistle at night, looked longingly at an airplane in flight, or dreamed of being cargoed to far off lands on a passing ship, you will appreciate HOLIDAY. We will provide you with new keys to the doorways of recreation and travel. We will be your scouts into fields of romance and adventure."[65] True to its middlebrow intentions, *Holiday* spoke in a didactic tone during its early run. Lowell Thomas told readers of his favorite places around the globe, "with the hope that they will inspire and stimulate your own thinking about your own holiday." Philip and Phyllis Newill, "a couple of transcontinental motor-trip addicts," gave advice to auto tourists considering transcontinental trips. Their bits of wisdom included resetting your watch upon entering a new time zone if traveling east to west but keeping it set on Eastern Standard Time when traveling west to east. That way motorists could get an early start every morning.[66]

Some readers—those who were not only unaccustomed to but

uncomfortable with the world of play—would need additional help. These holdouts against the new leisure would need to be reformed. The sad truth, former YMCA and USO official Malcolm S. Knowles wrote, was that "most people simply don't know how to play." Fortunately, Knowles argued, this impairment could be corrected and controlled through "basic scientific rules for having fun." The smart pleasure seeker, he explained, struck "a balanced diet in recreation just as he does in nutrition," through planning and scheduling. Maximizing one's "pleasure quotient" would help stave off boredom, loneliness, timidity, jealousy, envy, and even pangs of alienation. Most important, it could reorient individuals toward greater "enjoyment of their purchasing power."[67]

Curtis's overall efforts with *Holiday* are an illuminating example of how a general enchantment with control pervaded midcentury business culture. As Jackson Lears has argued, the ascendance of empirical science and managerial capitalism produced a mind-set that framed modernity's dizzying whirl of social activity as ultimately predictable and thus susceptible to direction from above. This "culture of control" reached new heights with the regimentation of play in midcentury consumer society. As Johann Huizinga and others have observed, play represents the basic desire to immerse oneself in a separate world of games, drama, and activities for the sake of their own intrinsic pleasures, rather than material reward. By untethering lived experience from the material concerns of securing life's basic necessities, play animates the social world with extramundane meaning.[68]

Yet play took on a very different meaning in the hands of Curtis managers. Within a Keynesian context, in which the overall quality of life was measured by economic expansion and household spending, business valued play as a means of keeping workers refreshed and content, while at the same time building enormous leisure industries.[69] Curtis, speaking on behalf of big business, did celebrate mass tourism as a token of American classlessness and at times even portrayed leisure as a healthy way for workers to vent their social frustrations. But the publisher was mainly concerned with fueling leisure industry growth and the spillover effect it had on other economic sectors. By taking "Mr. and Mrs. America"—fledgling world travelers—under its wing and tailoring *Holiday* to suit their fancies, Curtis hoped to convert the excitement surrounding travel, "the holiday mood," into tangible purchases of summer jaunts, sunglasses, suitcases, sportswear, skis, scarves, scotch, and so on.

The play spirit was like a natural resource to the publisher, something that could be capitalized on and turned into private wealth. Like any other resource, it had to be systematically cultivated to yield the greatest return. Research, Curtis believed, offered the solution to this task. Market and audience studies could point toward the right people; actuarial tables let the publisher minimize editorial risk; control experiments allowed the Curtis Publishing Company to hone its stimulus on "guinea-pig" readers. What emerged was a magazine that, from Curtis's perspective, was more of an instrument than text, engineered to attract certain consumers and activate latent qualities within them. Over time, research could also tell the publisher how to fine-tune and recalibrate that instrument. The company clearly slipped into hyperbolic excess at times when promoting its research. But beneath Curtis's overstated rhetoric lay a basic certitude that people and culture were malleable and could be molded by those who wielded the right tools. Or as Hobart put it: "The consumer is predictable and can be influenced in many ways. This, it seems to me, is the basic principle behind all dynamic marketing."[70]

Magazines and the Postwar Media Landscape

Holiday's first issues met with mixed reviews. The Curtis Publishing Company boasted of a strong showing in its public statements, pointing to high circulation figures, an attractive readership, and happy advertisers.[71] The magazine earned rave reviews from retailers, too. Nearly one hundred department stores participated in a program to feature the magazine in their window displays and leisurewear departments. Dallas-based Neiman-Marcus made *Holiday* the centerpiece of a fashion show and national broadcast hosted by radio personalities Ilka Chase, Edgar Guest, and Senator Claghorn. Follow-up campaigns at department stores across the country involved window displays, fashion shows, and such practical giveaways as a "How to Pack Clothes" poster.[72] Outside reviewers were less kind, however, blasting the magazine's cluttered look and jumbled editorial mix. The first issue ran a number of travel profiles, spotlighting the popular vacation cities San Francisco and New Orleans, as well as lesser known spots like Guatemala and the New Jersey Pine Barrens. But the magazine also featured a random potluck of articles about hockey, state flowers, dinghies, ballet, square dancing, oyster shucking, the month of March, and a history of checkerboards. The magazine was colorful, but photos were small and lost in busy layouts. *Time* panned it as "a monthly technicolor mouse." By the summer of 1946, *Holiday* was quickly losing subscribers and news vendors were returning stacks of unsold copies.[73] The magazine's start-up costs had decimated Curtis's first-quarter profits, and rumors abounded that the publisher would soon kill it. But instead, management responded by sacking editor Beaman and his team, replacing them with the staff of the still experimental "Magazine X."[74]

Curtis's "Magazine X," a photo magazine modeled after *Life* and *Look*, had been in development for half a year and was slated for introduction in 1948. The project was headed by Ted Patrick, a former advertising man who had cut a high profile on Madison Avenue in the 1930s. Signing on with Young & Rubicam in 1928, Patrick was known around the industry as a talented, free-spirited copywriter. In the words of contemporary Draper Daniels, Patrick dressed "like a pool-hall hustler or a retired jockey fresh out of a Damon Runyan story." He had a reputation for arriving late, taking extended lunches, mysteriously leaving midday, and yet still managing to win the praise of clients and superiors. Adding to his maverick image, Patrick had been active in the pacifist World Peaceways movement in the mid-1930s, penning many of its antiwar advertisements. The copywriter shed his pacifism during World War II, going to work for the Office of War Information (OWI). At the OWI, he was placed in charge of printed matter as chief of the graphics section, overseeing the magazines *Yank*, *U.S.A.* and *Victory*. Patrick left his government post in 1944 and became a vice president with the New York agency Compton Advertising. That return to the ad industry was short lived, though, and Patrick jumped to Curtis in December 1945.[75]

Patrick took over *Holiday* from Beaman in July 1946, plundering much of his "Magazine X" staff, many of whom were OWI veterans of *Yank* and *Victory*. Ignoring *Holiday*'s sagging sales, Curtis executives attributed the overhaul to "differences on editorial policy." In particular, management felt the magazine suffered from a lack of identity. Under Beaman, *Holiday* proposed to "tell you what you can do if you want to fly over the rainbow on a two or three weeks' vacation, as well as the fun that can be discovered in your own backyard."[76] But Curtis president Walter D. Fuller did not see things the same way, fuming: "I don't want stories about how to cook supper in the backyard or how to save up 50¢ to go to Coney Island. I want articles about . . . what to do and what to see at Yellowstone Park. And in between, articles about what to wear at such places. That's what people want from a magazine called *Holiday*. Even people who can't afford to go to Bermuda want to read about it." Beaman's mistake was that in tailoring *Holiday* to the novice traveler, he lost sight of tourism's powerful class connotations. As *Time* would later comment, "The editors hadn't decided whether they were describing a Roman holiday or a beggar's."[77]

Patrick's job was to recast *Holiday*'s identity. The first Patrick-guided issues hit the newsstands in fall 1946 and quickly righted Curtis's teetering ship. By March 1947, *Holiday*'s circulation was growing quickly, and the once skeptical *Time* noted its "brilliant transformation."[78] The magazine's 605,000 monthly buyers were an all-time high for a fifty-cent magazine. By September 1947, circulation had climbed to over 800,000. Patrick explained the magazine's turnaround by commenting that "we had to get away from the travel-guide idea. We wanted an adult magazine that would tell people more about the world so they could act intelligently when and if they set out to see it."[79] The new editor would turn *Holiday* into a chic, much admired magazine over the next two decades. During Patrick's tenure, readers leafed through issues to find William Faulkner on Mississippi, Jack Kerouac on the Lower East Side, S. J. Perelman travelogues, Arnold Newman portraiture, and Robert Capa photo-essays. The magazine was the original home of celebrated works such as E. B. White's "Here Is New York" (1949) and John Steinbeck's *Travels with Charley* (1962).[80] But even under Patrick's esteemed stewardship, *Holiday* remained subject to Curtis's market-research regiment. As one trade ad assured advertisers in 1949, "We have learned more about our readers and what they want. We have learned how to make this a part of our editorial aims. We have learned how to dig still deeper for knowledge and understanding and, we hope, how better to convey this knowledge and understanding."[81]

Curtis's success with *Holiday* distinguished the company and the publication from other major industry players, whose postwar projects met early demises. Cowles Communications, publisher of *Look*, launched a pair of new magazines, *Flair* and *Quick*, in 1950 after years of planning. *Flair*—a class title that featured experimental print techniques such as foldouts, cover windows, and, dangerously, invisible inks that appeared when a match or lit cigarette was held close to the page—was well reviewed but ultimately couldn't cover production costs. *Quick*, a pint-sized newsmagazine that one critic charged made "the *Reader's Digest* look like *Fortune*," found some initial success but eventually folded shop in 1953 when it also failed to cover costs.[82] Crowell-Collier, publisher of *Collier's*, *Woman's Home Companion*, and *American Magazine*, never even got its major project, "International," off the drawing board.[83]

All were victims of a magazine industry in the late 1940s and early 1950s that on the surface appeared safe but below which swirled hazardous undercurrents. The industry enjoyed a torrent of ad spending that came with the expectation of postwar affluence and pent-up consumer demand.[84] But even as revenues soared, changes were under way. In 1949, overall magazine revenue declined for the first time. Analysts blamed the drop on jitters about a possible recession or flare-up in the developing Cold War. Instead of sinking money into the long-range ad schedules that magazines used, many advertisers preferred to wait and see what would happen on the economic and geopolitical fronts. The pause gave some an opportunity to reevaluate their assumptions and plan new strategies that placed more emphasis on television.[85] But even as billings rebounded, the magazine trade's overall health was wracked by rising production costs that shaved profit margins by as much as 50 percent. Paper had doubled in price since 1940, and publishers faced the additional threat of postage-rate hikes.[86] More troublesome still was that key industries, including toiletries and pharmaceuticals, had almost overnight transferred big portions of their ad budgets away from magazines into television.[87]

Television's meteoric rise over the first half of the 1950s was an enigmatic and ominous development for the magazine industry. As late as 1951, magazines still outdrew television ad revenue by tenfold. But analysts were already certain the newcomer had done irreparable damage to parts of the trade.[88] As Cowles learned in 1950, the market for new titles that dabbled in a range of subjects had disappeared. And as the industry would soon find out, even established general-interest titles were on shaky ground. In 1953, *Collier's* shrank to a biweekly, and it disappeared completely three years later. By mid-decade, television had closed much of the revenue gap and was clearly poised to overtake magazines in the short run.[89]

The biggest problem faced by traditional magazines was that audiences were turning away from reading as a form of entertainment. Television viewing, the do-it-yourself hobby craze, travel, and other activities all eroded recreational reading time. Leo Bogart, research director at McCann-Erickson, observed that TV's "biggest effect on magazines is not that it cuts into advertising, but that it cuts into reading."[90] Many young people who did read magazines were using them in an altogether new way. Instead of providing general reading enjoyment, magazines helped supplement other leisure activities—travel, photography, hunting, hot-rodding, or nearly anything else.[91]

Despite the changes playing out across media, most observers maintained that the industry giants—*Life, Look, Saturday Evening Post,* the popular women's titles, and the newsweeklies—would continue to play a key role in the national marketing system. *Business Week* noted in 1955 "that the ones [magazines] that can deliver to huge mass audiences, will continue to do well in the age of mechanized selling." Observers as sociologically astute as David Potter agreed, still seeing magazines as governed by a logic of bigness and mass appeal.[92] From this perspective, a wide reach was a structural necessity to the nation's economic system. Business simply required mass magazines and vast audiences to drive mass consumption. For these observers, it was unimaginable that a medium so central to consumer society for a half century would fade away. And continuing to see their fortunes as tied to mass readership, publishers feverishly signed up new subscribers, flaunted their status as circulation leaders, and framed their audience to Madison Avenue as the nation's thriving middle-income masses.[93] Others in the industry recognized by the mid-1950s, however, that if they were going to remain competitive with television, they would need to find new ways of selling magazines as a medium.[94]

Solidifying Segmentation

Just as the mass magazines were driving their circulation figures skyward, a growing number of business analysts were becoming less enamored with the broad, middle-class audience. Said one media buyer in 1957, "There's quite a group now that are printing 5-million magazines with each issue and claiming 20-million readers or more. With audiences that big, you are going to people, just people. You can't claim much in the way of distinguishing characteristics for your audience. And you are right up against television—which can play the numbers game better than anybody."[95] Mass, undifferentiated audiences were no longer as appealing to a business world that had begun to question the wisdom of marketing to a heterogeneous mass composed of everyone from junior executives to pipe fitters. Curtis's Donald M. Hobart relayed his doubts about the mass market in his own 1954 Parlin lecture. The research chief argued: "We can no longer afford to scatter our selling efforts, with their mounting costs, equally to all parts of the market without regard to sales and profits. We must practice profitable selling by being selective in our marketing effort."[96] In place of shear volume, what advertisers wanted from magazines was precision. "If you can cater to an interest like boating," industry analyst Bernard Gallagher recommended, "and keep your circulation under or not too far over a million, you may have a flourishing property." By narrowing their editorial range and managing subscription lists, publishers could deliver a definable group of readers.[97]

Business Week saw this new technique as a sea change in magazine publishing, noting in 1954 that "although commercial implications have never been ignored, they play a bigger part today in forming the basic concept of new publications than they did back in the 1920s and 1930s. In the earlier era, the new and important magazines really were new ideas, editorially speaking.... The new magazines of the 1940s and 1950s are not new in the same sense. What's new about them is that they are invented to tap a new leisured, moneyed market." The key was "to find a formula that meets a need in the market." Industry watchers repeatedly held up specialized titles, including *Holiday*, *Playboy*, and *Ebony*, as prototypes for new magazines that could work in the television era.[98]

As more specialized magazines prospered over the decade, industry watchers looked for an explanation—zeroing in on the new place of leisure in American life. *Printers' Ink* called specialty publications "text books of gratifying accomplishment," offering the Riesman-inspired hypothesis that "many young adult consumers no longer found satisfaction in a dedication to job, to the larger family, to religion in the all encompassing sense."[99] David Abrahamson has argued that specialty magazines helped readers define their identities around leisure interests by immersing them in an imagined community of like-minded enthusiasts. Scouring the pages of *Hot Rod* and *Popular Photography*, readers could revel in the minutia and vernaculars that only they and their peers could follow.[100] Publishers could in turn offer the makers of custom tailpipes or darkroom lamps a direct line to their most likely customers. Yet for specialty titles to really prosper, publishers had to convince advertisers that their readers were not only auto or camera enthusiasts but particular types of consumers. "Most of these people," an industry respondent explained, "are spending a great deal of money on their major leisure interest and are willing and able to spend more cash on still other pastime activities."[101] To make that case, they needed research. Publisher Robert "Pete" Petersen, for instance, grew his family of auto magazines into an industry phenomenon over the course of the 1950s. But he had great difficulty attracting nonautomotive advertising until he commissioned market researcher Eugene Gilbert to craft a more expansive view of Petersen's readers. Gilbert argued that advertisers should not see the Petersen audience so much as drag racers but as teenage males whose cars were "badges of maturity." "This makes automotive interests the hot button," Gilbert argued, "for the manufacturer of any product who seeks to reach the 13-to-29 age group." After releasing the report, Petersen quickly netted Winston cigarettes and Catalina sportswear as advertisers.[102]

The task before specialty publishers, then, was to show that their readers were a definable segment but that they were not one dimensional. Whatever activity a magazine covered was less important than the personality traits that it somehow spoke to. Leo Bogart referred to this as a magazine's "character," or "strong collective editorial personality which awakens a response in the readers." Motivational research magnate Ernest Dichter, echoing *Holiday's* trade advertising, called it a magazine's "mood," or the qualities activated in a reader when she or he engaged a text.[103] According to this argument, every magazine, whether it was a mass book or specialty title, tapped into some psychological schema common among its audience. As Bogart explained, "Though all available data show only very slight variations in the audience composition of Collier's and the Post, there are genuine psychological differences which make some people choose to read one rather than the other."[104] Publishers needed to define those intangibles to truly understand readers' buying behaviors and market them to their fullest potential. Bogart and Dichter recommended qualitative research for the job. Bogart thought that textual analysis could decipher a magazine's character. Dichter used depth interviews and association games. Most *Time* readers, for instance, associated the magazine with an abstract painting that "was complex, well organized, orderly, colorful, and most interesting." Jerome Greene, an Alfred Politz Media Studies associate, argued that the newsweeklies in general cultivated a sense of "communicativeness" among readers. Sports magazines, on the other hand, reinforced their readers' inherent "venturesomeness."[105]

The search for psychological traits reflected the changing nature of marketing research. By the mid-1950s, much of the business community's lingering suspicion toward market research had been swept away. "Just before the war," the chairman of the Foote, Cone & Belding agency told *Fortune* in 1957, "our employees were mostly copywriters, artists, and media buyers. Today, we have as many people in research, merchandising, and marketing." McCann-Erickson head Marion Harper Jr. bragged that his firm essentially acted as a surrogate research department for clients.[106] Not only were research divisions growing and gaining clout, but they were becoming more intellectually diverse as well. Bogart observed in a 1963 industry overview that "fifteen years ago, psychologists, sociologists, and anthropologists were almost a curiosity in marketing circles. Today their presence is taken for granted."[107] Motivational research (MR), with its sexually charged psychoanalytic theories, was the public face of this change. Dichter and Pierre Martineau, the leading advocates of MR, were mainstays in the business trade press throughout the 1950s and were profiled in Vance Packard's popular exposé of the ad industry—*The Hidden Persuaders* (1957). While MR fell out of fashion in the 1960s, its attention to psychological characteristics and qualitative methods would remain a bedrock of marketing.[108]

Just as important, but less sensational, was the growing interest in lifestyles. Owing more to anthropology and sociology than psychoanalysis, lifestyle research looked at consumption as a social and cultural activity. Martineau and others active in this area built on W. Lloyd Warner's class stratification research. Its most prophetic advocates argued that over the coming decades Americans would increasingly identify around what they bought. In an early summary of this view, University of Chicago sociologist Nelson Foote asserted that life stylization naturally flowed from mass affluence and leisure. "As wants develop for a wider array of goods and services," Foote's 1954 report argued, "the need for their unification through a satisfying and coherent style of living, based on aesthetic rather than economic criteria, becomes increasingly manifest." It was the marketer's job to assist in this process by teaching consumers how disparate goods and services could be assembled into a coherent whole.¹⁰⁹ Overall, publishers needed to adopt a multifaceted approach—combining demographic parsing, editorial specialization, and a definition of their readership informed by sociological, psychological, and cultural analysis—to compete in the post-television climate. The trick was to bring abstract categorizations, like income level, to life and show the broader significance of an interest in travel, sports, fashion, photography, or any other topic—or as Life Inc. researchers referred to it, craft "living statistics."¹¹⁰

Time Inc. had put all these tactics to use by the time it unveiled *Sports Illustrated* in 1954, the most highly anticipated magazine project since the launch of *Holiday* eight years earlier. *Sports Illustrated* (*SI*), Time's new sports weekly and first new title since *Life* (1936), cost the publisher an estimated three million dollars in research and development before the first issue hit newsstands. And the new title was backed by what *Tide* called the "biggest prepublication promotional campaign in history." Publisher H. H. S. Phillips Jr. explained in the inaugural issue that like Time Inc.'s other magazines, *SI* was a distinct response to the needs of its time—in this case, the sporting world's passage from an "era of isolated contest into a new era of tremendous size, of national and international importance."¹¹¹ From a marketing perspective, *SI* was started to tap into the same affluent, recreationally minded market that *Holiday* was built for. Time, however, hoped to reach these readers through an emphasis on sports rather than travel.¹¹²

The similarities were not lost on industry observers, who noted that *SI* was in many ways modeled after *Holiday*. *Business Week* wrote that "Sports Illustrated is following Holiday in appealing to an upper-income group with the money and leisure for travel." Like Curtis's magazine, *SI* was fundamentally premised on the notion that affluence and mobility were hallmarks of a modern consumer culture. Time was also preoccupied with carefully defining *SI*'s readership. The publisher wanted to attract a "quality circulation" in the hundreds of thousands—"not in the millions"—and instituted control measures to reach that group exclusively. To begin with, Time set unusually lofty cover and subscription prices for a sports magazine, at 25¢ and $7.50, respectively. Both were the highest for any weekly on the market—a point highlighted in the company's trade ads. Time also scrutinized its solicitation lists, sending out promotional material only to select households. "Thus," a message to advertisers explained, "we are attracting . . . members of better income families—families generally with homes in the suburbs—active families with an interest in the whole world of sport." *Tide* explained this circulation strategy in more pedestrian language, noting that it was meant to "screen out the bleacherites."¹¹³

Time Inc.'s trade advertising also sold *SI* in terms of mood, drawing a connection between editorial content, the reader's state of mind, and buying behavior, declaring that *SI*'s "business is pleasure." A trade journal insert personified the link between spending and pleasure through an image of a woman reading *SI*. "Maybe I'll never play as well as she does but I could *look* as well," read a thought bubble over her head, "And not *only* on the golf course . . . and there are those wonderful football games this fall and I'll need . . ." Later *SI* explained to potential advertisers that "sports are a selling theme— that shoppers in a pleasurable, sports-impelled mood will spend money to prolong that mood."[114] Thinking in terms of mood rather than content, Time also adopted a very liberal view of *SI*'s ad market. Golf clubs, fishing rods, and basketballs were not the target. Rather, sports was the proxy for a whole attitude toward goods and services of any type. "It's not just that there are twice as many skiers as there were a few years ago," one company executive explained. "It's a new focus on living—a re-orientation of how people look at their lives. Sport has come to determine where we live, how we live, where we buy." Illustrating this point, publisher Harry Phillips recounted an impromptu conversation with two shoe salesmen aboard a train. According to Phillips, they thought *SI* "was the greatest thing to hit the men's shoe business in years."[115] Making the sports magazines an outlet for shoe ads instead of baseball mitts and chewing tobacco required that the magazine reach the right people. Assistant publisher Richard L. Neale, in a 1956 speech to the AMA, summed up the logic behind this approach: "The argument for specialized magazines goes beyond the introduction of new productions. . . . The argument can be simply stated; it is that some people are more important than others, first as customers, secondly, in their influence on other people."[116]

The dictum that "some people were more important than others" gelled with the new paradigm in mass communication research that emphasized the personal influence of "opinion leaders." According to this line of thought, media messages were most powerful when they were funneled through audience members understood to be authorities in their communities.[117] It also fit with the leading edge of market research, which cast a skeptical eye on the mass market. The great import of magazines like *Holiday* and *Sports Illustrated* was that they set in motion the close partnering of intense research with content specialization, yielding new ways of thinking about readers and media audiences in general. In this regard, the move toward psychographics and lifestyle marketing did not spring so much from the margins of the industry but from the two giants—Curtis and Time—stationed at its center. Segmentation was as much a product of corporate rationality as entrepreneurial creativity. It emerged as the media industry's biggest businesses learned how to leverage a sophisticated body of research into more and more efficient means of controlling markets. Despite *Holiday*'s and *SI*'s early setbacks, both ultimately proved an affirmation of the business world's control culture,[118] showing that, if handled correctly, the emerging ethos of "pleasure" and "fun" could be systematically rationalized and made a fount of economic productivity. Following this approach, magazine reading was turned into a sort of litmus test that could pinpoint especially potent strains of consumer behavior. And with those qualitative differences on display, marketers could forget about the bleacherites and Coney Island crowd to better focus their efforts on a free-spending professional class.

3 SELLING VACATIONS
Tourist Travel, Free Time, and Classlessness

In the summer of 1946, twelve friends from Canton, Ohio, calling themselves the Kitty Kat Klub, embarked on a three-week train journey across the American West. To pay for the trip, the six middle-class couples had saved for more than ten years, selling magazine subscriptions and sacrificing other purchases. One couple contributed what they had set aside for silver flatware. For most, it was their first journey outside the Midwest. A day at the Grand Canyon was the most anticipated stop for club member Walt Zagray. "I just want to see the thing. Just look at it," he explained. "You can understand that, can't you?" Zagray's wife, Ida, viewed the trip as an opportunity for self-improvement, figuring it "ought to make us better parents in the sense that maybe we'll be a bit more interesting to our children." The episode's sentimental nature attracted the attention of magazines, newspapers, radio programs, and tourism industry boosters, each of which seized upon the group as emblematic of the postwar travel boom. As *Holiday* characterized it, the journey represented "a very special dream . . . not a spectacular dream because they are not spectacular people—simply the fulfillment of an earnest wish to see the country." At the end of the journey, the Santa Fe railroad gave the Ohio club a dollar to start their next kitty. Five years later the pot was full again, and the Kitty Kats were off—this time to Europe. And again, the press covered their exploits and celebrated them as a uniquely American development.[1]

Narratives like the Kitty Kats' were pervasive in postwar consumer magazines. While the names, places, and details changed, they all told the story of the nation's transformation into a mobile, classless society. It was a story of national identity that picked up where prewar celebrations had left off. But situated within the very different setting left in the wake of the Second World War, the story took on new inflections and carried new implications.

Singularly among industrialized nations, the United States had been spared the infrastructural devastation of war, its economy emerged at full tilt, and its citizens found their pocketbooks stuffed with disposable income. Although many observers worried that the nation's galloping prosperity would screech to a halt as businesses transitioned back to peacetime operations, the failure of any real downturn to materialize led many to surmise that economic growth would go on indefinitely, raising living standards ever higher.[2] Postwar, the United States would play a very different role in geopolitical affairs as well, abandoning the isolationism of the interwar years to embrace an explicitly internationalist foreign policy. After plunging into a Cold War contest with the Soviet Union for influence over a global landscape rocked by war and anticolonial struggles, the United States built extensive diplomatic, economic, and intelligence networks, intended to advance the interests of American-style capitalism and democracy. Technologically, the United States also found itself in more intense contact with the rest of the world as wartime strides in aviation, coupled with a frenzy of infrastructure building, made the air age's collapsed spatial scales far more a reality than ever before.[3]

Just as important, American political culture looked very different in the immediate postwar era than it had when the war began. The populist, progressive spirit that had driven New Deal reforms through the early 1940s had waned. Gone were the public culture projects of groups like the WPA, CCC, and USTB. By the late in the decade, big business's prolonged campaign to counter the regulatory state, slow the momentum of organized labor, and recast free enterprise in a more benevolent light had started to yield important legislative victories like the Taft-Hartley Act.[4] The wildfire growth, often fueled by white flight, of suburbs along the fringes of American cities; the emergence of a sprawling, suburban Sun Belt; and the automobile's continued ascendance in American culture gave a more conservative tint to popular notions of leisure as well. Urban, public amusements lost much of their prominence as private activities carried out in living rooms, woodshops, and backyard patios moved to the forefront. While not everyone moved to the suburbs and adopted a privatized way of life, the image advanced in consumer magazines largely painted it that way.[5]

The meanings of leisure, tourism, and mobility were given a nationalistic bent in this changing environment, used as evidence of American culture's exceptional nature. According to many social observers, mass affluence meant that tourist travel, once the ultimate symbol of leisure-class privilege, had become a semiannual activity in the lives of all but the very poorest citizens. Winter and summer vacations would punctuate Americans' already leisured lives, as the workweek contracted to thirty-five hours and eventually twenty-eight. With all this spare time and money, members of the great middle-income majority, encompassing the middle and working classes, would be free to develop their cultural interests in a manner once exclusive to the affluent.[6] For those interested in travel—and it was assumed that all Americans nursed a desire to see the world—middle-income people would no longer have to make due with a few days at the shore. Rather, typists who had long fantasized about crossing the Atlantic in grand style and auto mechanics who pined to take their families to the tropical beaches they had passed through in wartime would be able to make good on those dreams. The cheaper fares enabled by mass tourism's economies of scale and the speedy travel times delivered by new transport technologies would make these once unheard-of possibilities a regular part of Americans' annual calendars.

This rosy picture was at least how managerial elites in business and government, along with the media commentators who shared their perspective, saw things playing out in the late 1940s and 1950s. The focus of this chapter is to examine how such an image was sketched in popular magazines and how narratives of touristic mobility were enlisted into conversations about leisure, living standards, and the American economic system. Committed to the causes of economic expansion, both for their own enterprises and for American business more generally, and animated by a paternal impulse for cultural uplift, magazine publishers, editors, and writers saw mass tourism as a sort of wonder drug. Economically, it offered a powerful engine for growth. Socially, it provided lived proof of egalitarianism. And culturally, it allowed Americans to broaden their horizons and develop a more cosmopolitan sensibility. As pleasant as this picture of postwar tourism appeared, it bore only a passing resemblance to the role vacation travel played in most Americans' lives. Market studies, often paid for by magazine publishers themselves, indicated as much, showing that lavish vacations were far from a sociologically universal experience. For African Americans and other racial minorities, the vacation boom provided damning evidence that even as class disparities seemed to be leveling out, institutionalized bigotry kept them consigned to second-class status. Instead of mirroring social reality, then, travel boom narratives offered a guide to the culture of easy mobility that marketers hoped the nation would develop into. They suggested what it meant, in social terms, to rove across the fun-filled vacationlands put on display in travel ads and destination profiles. At the same time, they offered interpretive frameworks for understanding what a big trip would mean on the day when that long-anticipated event arrived. By making the travel boom into a story of mass affluence, leisure, and mobility, magazines offered ways of thinking about citizenship in a society in which consumer longings for meaningful experience could seemingly be realized.

Realizing Pipedreams

Much of the poignancy behind narratives like the Kitty Kats' hinged on the long wait and hard work that presaged them. The theme of delayed gratification was a common one in travel boom articles. "'Well John, we've waited for this a long time, haven't we?'" a woman remarked to her husband in a 1947 *American Magazine* article as the aging couple waited on the tarmac, set to embark on a South American tour. "They had—all of their married life," author Tom Bernard explained. "Just two weeks before, the last of their 5 children had been married and, at last, they were going to splurge grandly on the vacation they'd promised themselves for more than 30 years."[7] The story and others like it framed vacations as long-held fantasies, or pipedreams, that individuals were at last able to realize. "The myth that all or even most traveling Americans are rich is a complete myth," John Steinbeck asserted in a 1956 *Holiday* piece. "The great majority have saved and stinted for this time." The author explained, "It isn't easy but they feel their lives will never be complete until they have traveled."[8] The theme of long-deferred travel fantasies surfaced in other places as well. The popular radio program *Welcome Travelers* revolved around it. Broadcast out of Chicago and hosted by entertainer Tommy Bartlett, the show featured guests chosen by scouts who combed the city's airport, train stations, and bus depots in search of "little human-interest vignettes." A *Welcome Travelers* specialty and audience favorite was the hard-luck story. "Innumerable visitors to the program," magazine writer Hubert Kelly explained in a profile of the show, "testify to having remained in one place for years, grubbing and saving to support a child or an invalid relative. To such people the journey they are making usually is the most important and dramatic event of their lives." One typical guest had for many years cared for her crippled husband, a motorcycle cop maimed on the job. Unbeknownst to her, his former colleagues had taken up a collection to send her on a vacation—her first. "At last," Kelly wrote, "the victim of circumstances is taking a trip after a long, dull life of unrecognized sacrifice."[9]

Welcome Travelers, along with similar programs like *Queen for a Day*, tapped into the audience's sense of empathy and charity. But it also drew on the great significance a vacation held for the many people for whom it was an exceedingly rare or altogether new opportunity. In this way, class, although not always addressed explicitly, was at the heart of pipedream stories. They told the story of nation in which ordinary people were given the chance to enjoy privileges they had long known about but had never been able to indulge in themselves. "I had dreamed of seeing Paris since 1924, but I thought it was one of those dreams which never could come true," a California woman reminisced upon returning home from the City of Lights in 1949.[10] Mass vacation travel, especially abroad, was thus powerful evidence that a new age of egalitarian leisure had dawned. According to this narrative, folkways and customs were not carved up by class in the United States. Rather, people from all walks of life shared the same experiences in a modern, industrial democracy. Irwin Shaw, writing for *Holiday* in 1951, reeled off a long list of American types he spotted on his international travels, all "mingled in happy, solvent democracy."[11] In this new era, it was simply an outmoded notion that sightseeing travel was a class privilege, commentators argued. "Globetrotting," *Life* explained in 1949, "is no longer the privilege of the well-to-do; the butchers and bakers and students and farmers now far outnumber and outspend the merchant chiefs." *Ebony* made essentially the same assertion, noting that "no longer is vacationing limited to the well-heeled Negro top-income group.... Today the steno and cabbie, the stockyards butcher and steel puddler take a couple of weeks out of town too."[12] Travel advertising plucked at the same heartstrings. The Matson transpacific line, for instance, enticed *Holiday* readers in 1948 by suggesting: "Ahead lies a dream you've always had more glorious than you ever dreamed it." In the passenger liner trade, the pipedream angle remained a powerful one, even as the market for transoceanic voyages was drying up fast. The psychological consulting firm Social Research, Inc. advised clients in the mid-1960s to remember that the bulk of the market "*associates ship travel with 'scrimping and saving' for the day when they can afford the trip abroad.... It becomes a major event; it is something people expect to do once in a lifetime, or on rare, special occasions.*"[13]

Refracted through the lens of fantasy and social mobility, travel settings could be seen as enchanted spaces where cross-class encounters played out with regularity. Pan American head Juan Trippe described his airline's transatlantic flights as a place where New Jersey mechanics could rub elbows with international business leaders. Elaborating on this point, he relayed an account of a globe-trotting "$3000-a-year Brooklyn postal employee" who booked a flight around the world. High above the Atlantic, the postman struck up a conversation with a friendly seatmate who just happened to be the Turkish ambassador to the United States. The dignitary proceeded to host him in Istanbul. Further along on his journey, the postal worker was treated to a rooftop garden party and personal tour of Calcutta by a wealthy merchant.[14] A major vacation thus acted as an initiation into what had until recently been an exclusive club. It seemed to offer the possibility of magically dissolving class lines. Many commentators took this to mean that if travel had been a preserve of the upper classes, then the fact that so many people were vacationing must herald the coming of a classless society. "In no other country," *Holiday*'s Carl Biemiller wrote in 1952, "has material civilization reached the point where more than half of the people can slip the shackles of normal employment and be paid while they play."[15]

"Slipping the shackles" meant that Americans exercised greater authority over their own time than any other people. Paid vacations, which continued to rise over the postwar years, cleared a spot in the annual schedule for people to go where they pleased. The Department of Labor estimated in 1950 that between 36 million and 38 million of the nation's 44 million salary and wage workers received paid vacations, or three times as many as before the war. By the following year, the Bureau of Labor Statistics could point to cities, such as Denver, where nearly everyone with at least two years on the job received paid vacations.[16] Even more than before the war, vacation periods were becoming engrained in the temporal rhythms that structured American calendars. "Two weeks" remained the vernacular term for this concept, and it was established enough by 1954 that *Look* could simply refer to "the Great American Two Weeks." Moreover, midcentury Americans understood this window of time as a brief, but annually recurring, opportunity for personal autonomy. Scoffing at a psychiatrist who questioned the psychic benefits of vacationing, a J. W. Wanamaker's employee newsletter in 1951 suggested that the doctor observe "our Wanamaker friends working like bees all winter while they sing 'It won't be long till the skies are blue and the trees are green and I long for a long vacation.' And off they'll go, rejoicing like larks, into 'imaginary worlds' for two enchanted weeks." Even those who couldn't get away still spoke in the same temporal idiom. Thus rocker Eddie Cochran could sneer, "I'm gonna take two weeks, gonna have a fine vacation" in his 1958 hit "Summertime Blues" before threatening to "take my problem to the United Nations."[17]

According to many, though, "two weeks" would soon appear woefully antiquated. The National Industrial Conference Board reported in 1946 that 17 percent of salaried workers and 8 percent of wage earners enjoyed three weeks off. Five years later, those totals had risen to 42 and 44 percent. Economist George Soule cited this steady climb as evidence that Americans desired more and more control over their lives. "Leisure, then," Soule wrote in 1957, "is time not sold; time not to be used at the direction of others; but rather time during which the individual is, or may be, master of his own living."[18] Such sentiments were captured in the remarks of a Wanamaker's sales worker who had just returned home from a summer tour through Europe in 1955.

Describing the sense of autonomy she felt while away, Mary Ranieri explained, "It was simply wonderful. You feel so free. You can get up when you like, lunch when you like, relax all you want to, and all the fun you have seems different because it is with pleasant strangers and you know that the next day you're going to be free all day too, and it's all such a luxurious feeling."[19] Aware of the great appeal of long stretches of free time, some companies even began experimenting with year-long vacations. *Holiday* profiled a Chicago advertising firm that gave employees twelve months off on a rotating basis to travel the world. In the blue-collar fields, members of the International Brotherhood of Electrical Workers at a Chicago plant negotiated a full year's vacation for those with ten years of service.[20] While yearlong vacations remained an oddity, they were the exception that proved the rule. They suggested that in the near future the "twelve-month sabbatical" might join well-established and distinctly American temporalities like "two weeks with pay." But more than that, stories that highlighted the temporal aspects of vacationing identified American society as one that afforded individuals unique control over that most precious resource: time.

Selling Vacations and the American System

As paid vacations were extended deeper into the labor force, they undoubtedly opened up opportunities for many people to make the first significant trip of their lives. But because vacationing often spoke to long-held fantasies, it also offered managerial and government elites a valuable chip to play in public debates about the role and power of capital in a modern industrial democracy. In particular, charitable vacation plans and democratized travel habits offered a way to celebrate managerial benevolence and the progressive achievements of what businesspeople called the American system. Recognizing the contributions vacations could make to worker morale, some employers helped organize and even subsidize employee travel. Wanamaker's, for instance, offered its "store family" complimentary use of the travel agency housed in the department store's main gallery. Similarly, RCA sponsored short trips to New York and Atlantic City in the mid-1950s.[21] In arranging worthwhile leisure for employees, Wanamaker's and RCA followed in a tradition of managerial paternalism that dated from the employee outings organized by turn-of-the-century business leaders. Aside from the recreational opportunities they provided, the programs helped broker friendlier relations between managers and workers.[22] And as vacationing assumed an increasingly central role in notions of "the good life," employer involvement was sometimes taken to more elaborate heights.

In 1953, *Fortune* and a number of other press outlets profiled a group of one hundred General Electric workers who, with the assistance of a human resources manager, embarked from Fort Wayne on a TWA "Sky Tourist" jaunt through Europe. Over three weeks, the package tour took them to London, Amsterdam, Cologne, Lucerne, Milan, Rome, Paris, Nice, and a few other stops. *Fortune* duly noted that while the employees made only about sixty dollars a week, their vacation would spare no expense, with stays at the Waldorf Astoria and other elite hotels. To prepare for the adventure, the workers received French language lessons, as well as tutorials on proper dress and comportment. Pan Am was so interested in the trip that it dispatched an executive to study the Indiana club. Around the same time, a specialized travel agency set up shop to handle discount, employer-arranged European vacations.[23] Press coverage of such activities continued over the rest of the decade. In 1957, *Life* profiled an all-expenses-paid trip the pharmaceutical maker A. H. Robins Company offered employees. Closing its plant for a week, the Richmond manufacturer paid forty thousand dollars to send 132 workers to Havana. "I'd forgotten what fun life could be," one secretary reported about the vacation, her first in ten years. A photograph showed a raucous crowd of employees joyously hoisting their sombrero-capped boss into the air.[24] Acts like Robins's were as incredibly generous as they were exceedingly rare. They attracted press attention in part because of their novelty. But they also offered an avenue for magazines to tell a certain kind of story about workplace relations in the United States. Stories of employer benevolence depicted a nation free of industrial exploitation. Far from wringing every last drop of life out of employees, managers were their leisure-time patrons, subsidizing workers' footloose frolics around the globe. In the face of such incredible largesse, who could question the merits of free enterprise?

The Advertising Council, looking to stifle just those sorts of questions, also recognized the rhetorical value of growing vacation time in the group's late 1940s and 1950s efforts to sell the public on "the American System."[25] The campaign's overriding purpose, according to chief Evans Clark, was to explain "why, in spite of its shortcomings, the American economic system has given us the highest standard of living and the greatest freedom in the world." *Printers' Ink* previewed the highly anticipated campaign by noting that it would "undoubtedly stress increased income, lower working hours and more leisure afforded workers."[26] Serving as the centerpiece of the effort was a free booklet called *The Miracle of America*—a folksy manifesto that framed Americans' rising standards of living as the fruit of free enterprise. Digested in *Look* and promoted in Ad Council advertising, the booklet featured images of vacationing families and promised that international tourism would soon become commonplace for all Americans.[27]

In the mid-1950s, the council launched a follow-up campaign, this time branding the U.S. economy as the "People's Capitalism." The fourteen-member committee included figures from the academic and business communities. Among representatives of the publishing world were *Holiday*'s Ted Patrick and Time Inc.'s Roy Larsen. In the words of Yale University's Edmund W. Sinnot, the moderator of a November 1956 roundtable, the "People's Capitalism" was meant to correct the general public's antiquated ideas about capitalism and socialism. Echoing the crux of the American System campaign, the roundtable came to a consensus that what "contributes most to make American capitalism a people's capitalism is the very wide participation in a high standard of living," bringing forth "a dynamic classless society."[28] The notion that Americans universally enjoyed once exclusive activities, like vacationing, was instrumental to the campaign. "At one time," historian and roundtable member David Potter observed, "leisure more than anything else was the badge of the privileged class, while the working man labored from sun to sun. Now, if we have attained a fairly equitable distribution of income, we have reached an absolutely egalitarian distribution of leisure." At a second roundtable in 1957 Potter elaborated: "The availability of an economic surplus above the necessities of life has meant the possession of books, magazines, musical instruments, cameras, sporting equipment, tools for home craftsmanship, and unparalleled opportunities for travel."[29]

Democratized leisure, according to the "People's Capitalism" roundtable, not only eradicated privilege but also dissolved class differences. Sylvester "Pat" Weaver, former NBC programming executive and broadcast industry consultant, argued that "in the status society, each social group may retain all its own distinguishing traits of speech, dress, and so forth, as do the cockneys of London or peasant populations in many areas. But in a society that seeks to be classless, there must be a social principle of interchangeable parts . . . certain peculiarities of dress, speech and even habit must be minimized . . . uniformity in these matters is necessary, and it is the job of the mass media to see that everybody knows how to speak the same language, wear the same kind of clothes and interchange in any group."[30] As Weaver outlined it, mass media could assist greatly in the larger modernist project of demolishing all barriers, whether they be physical or social, that stood in the way of a fluid, smooth-functioning social world. *How American Buying Habits Change*, a 1959 Department of Labor retrospective, noted precisely these types of changes. The report argued that working-class leisure had come to mirror that of middle- and upper-income groups rather than reflect a "distinctively 'working-class'" character. "Short drives to cool off on a hot summer evening, the Sunday trip into the country, and the vacation tour," the report explained, "rapidly replaced or supplemented such forms of recreational activity as trolley rides, strolling in the park, or bicycling." Such statements evidenced a widely shared view among elites that mass affluence would inevitably lead to a mass refinement of working- and lower-middle-class aesthetics.[31] Once exposed to the world of sightseeing travel, novice vacationers would transcend their parochial, class-situated identities and emerge as part of a sophisticated, international community. Or put another way, the department-store girls who toured London or hiked the Grand Canyon were sure to forget all about places like Coney Island.

The roundtable's commentary reflected the consensus that had formed around Keynesian economics by midcentury. According to this school of thought, policymakers could manipulate macroeconomic forces, including government and consumer spending, to drive economic growth. The process was cyclical. A higher standard of living meant more consumer spending, which in turn grew new industries, which in turn created a more robust economy and an even higher standard of living. As Curtis researchers explained in 1947, applying this school of thought to the tourist trade, "The expenditures of visitors result in immediate and direct benefits to many businesses. Equally important, however, are the secondary or indirect benefits which tourist expenditures provide the community. Additional employment is provided for many workers, which means larger payrolls and this in turn means greater purchasing power for every type of business in the community."[32] Leisure industries were a near perfect fit for Keynesian economic models because most had been relatively small, offering ample room for growth. Economists Dero A. Saunders and Sanford S. Parker argued along these lines in a 1954 *Fortune* article, suggesting that leisure, and travel in particular, might be the single most dynamic force in the new economy. "Extra leisure time," suggested the pair, "tends to result in extra leisure spending. Thus the entire leisure market may eventually become the dynamic component of the whole American economy for while consumer appetites for necessities may become sated, where is the limit to the market for pleasure?"[33] The economists' query echoed the rhetoric of publishers like Curtis and Time Inc. All ventured that Americans' seemingly insatiable appetite for fun, combined with their growing affluence and free time, equated to recreational fields that would expand ad infinitum.

Report after report reached the same conclusion—the standardization of paid vacations, higher pay, and a relatively stable economy had transformed tourism from a sizable industry that catered to the affluent into one of the nation's largest, serving the masses.[34] Over the period, analysts added a variable or two, whether it be pent-up demand or the looming threat of war, to help explain spikes in growth. But no matter what the contingencies from year to year, tourism was painted as a permanent, ever expanding fixture in the national economy.[35] The industry's explosive growth was thus a story in and of itself in narratives that continued to characterize travel spending in terms of a deluge or frenzy. In just the first half of the 1950s, *Newsweek* alone ran stories bearing headlines such as "The Vacation Business Is Booming As Never Before," "Americans on the Move," "Americans Hit the Open Road," "Big Rush to the Sun," "Booming Winter Travel," "America on the Go," "Destination: Everywhere," and "Money for Fun."[36] Translating Keynesianism into everyday language, the magazine explained that "Tillie the Toiler's dream is a sizable and growing asset to the American Economy." *Business Week* suggested that Florida's vacation market could be used as a bellwether of the nation's overall economic well-being, offering "almost an index of the public's ability—and willingness—to spend freely." By illustrating how a rising standard of living begets an even higher standard of living, travel boom narratives fed a larger story about the nation's economic might and the unheard of prosperity it yielded.[37]

As Christopher Endy has noted, policymakers and business leaders saw middle-class tourists abroad as potential testaments to the American economic system. American telephone operators and linemen touring the Louvre offered a strong rebuttal to European critics of capitalism on the left and American commercial culture on the right.[38] This instrumental flaunting of American wealth and free time extended to media produced for foreign audiences as well. The United States Information Agency (USIA) recognized the propaganda value in what Potter called "unparalleled opportunities for travel" when it resumed publication in 1956 of a photo magazine for Soviet readers—*Amerika Illustrated;* a photograph of a child at the beach appeared on the cover of the first issue, while inside, stories focused on American vacation habits and sportswear. Similarly, USIA tapped *Sports Illustrated* to build a photo exhibit for display at more than one hundred international bureaus. The photos were intended to show how recreational habits contribute to Americans' "free way of life."[39]

Market studies conducted for the travel industry, however, painted a very different picture of American vacation habits than the one presented by government agencies and consumer magazines. Travel surveys, commissioned by many of the trade's biggest players in the late 1950s and early 1960s, consistently indicated that the vacation market was nowhere near as sociologically diverse as the conventional wisdom suggested. In its inaugural 1956 study, the University of Michigan's Survey Research Center (SRC) found that extensive vacation travel was still well beyond the economic reach of most Americans. Money was by far the biggest obstacle, with 62 percent of participants reporting that travel was simply "too expensive."⁴⁰ Many suggested that despite their inability to afford a major vacation, it was something that they very much longed for. A lower-middle-class cook from Los Angeles reported, "I'd like a trip around the world to see other countries but I haven't the money. . . . I'd travel all the time if I did." Some had less grandiose plans but were still unable to afford the trip. "We'd like to go to Wisconsin," the wife of a solidly middle-class bureaucrat in Indiana reported, "but my teeth need fixing so the money has to go there." The second biggest obstacle, an inability to leave one's job or business (18 percent), also indicated that American workplace policies were not as benevolent as they were often made out to be.⁴¹ As one well-to-do Philadelphia secretary lamented, "We would like to see the U.S. but don't have the time. If you only have two weeks you can't go far . . . guess you can't have your cake and eat it too." For some it was a combination of factors. "We'd like to go to Florida, California and Virginia just to see the country," a middle-income New York City garment cutter explained, "but I only have two weeks vacation. After I retire we can get about more. Of course, there's the question of money." A low-income farmer from South Dakota was even less optimistic: "We'd like to go to the Black Hills but the kids are too small, we don't have enough money, car won't run, I can't get away from the farm . . . guess that's enough reasons."⁴²

In a follow-up report in 1958, the SRC found that there was a wide gulf between the trips that respondents would like to take and what they could realistically plan for. When the participants were asked about their dream destination, 39 percent chose a European destination, 12 percent chose an Asian, African, Australian, Middle Eastern, or South American locale, and 9 percent chose Hawaii. But when they were asked, "If I could pick the way to spend my vacation this year," a question designed to probe actual travel plans, the number who saw Europe as a realistic option fell to 3 percent, other continents to a total of 1 percent, and Hawaii to 2 percent. The biggest determining factor as to where respondents actually went was not where they fantasized about but where they could find free lodging.⁴³ Said the wife of a poor South Dakota farmer, "If we have relatives we visit them so we don't have to pay for a motel." Even more affluent respondents looked for people to stay with. "We go mostly where our relatives are," an upper-income railroad employee noted. Researchers also found that income was still very much a determining factor in whether families would vacation at all. Seventy percent of families that brought in more than $7,500 per year had vacation plans. But only 23 percent of families with incomes below the $3,000 mark thought they could get away.⁴⁴

After gearing his British Travel Association (BTA) campaign at a mass market for three years, advertising executive David Ogilvy was struck by the same conclusion when he viewed his group's research findings. Writing to an associate in 1955, Ogilvy noted that 33 percent of people from the United States traveling to Europe each year were naturalized citizens visiting relatives in their homeland. On top of that, a significant number were resident aliens doing the same. He estimated that the number of "real Americans," by which he must have meant native-born citizens, traveling to Europe was "only about 200,000." "What a *tiny* minority," Ogilvy lamented.[45] By the end of the 1950s, Ogilvy and company had modified their ideas about the market but still saw it as very small. "The two or three million people who will in the next six years visit Europe for the first time," an Ogilvy, Benson, & Mather account representative wrote, "will be very similar to those who have already visited." He identified them as essentially those consumers who had recently vaulted into the upper strata of the middle class. Ogilvy agreed with this view, writing that "the new travelers to Britain must come from the margins of the old market, rather than from some wholly new and untapped universe."[46]

What explains the glaring disparity between the picture of a frenetically mobile nation painted in magazines and the relatively static public that market researchers found? Part of the explanation was that magazine writers and editors seized on the most sensational aspects of American vacations habits but not the most representative. The working- and middle-class globe-trotters profiled in popular magazines were part of a very small minority who made good on pipedreams. But instead of presenting these tourists as extraordinary, magazines presented them as the harbingers of a new norm in American society—the spectacular vacation for all. A more realistic image would have followed vacationers on an auto trip to visit relatives or take in some of the local attractions. This type of story, while it appeared from time to time, lacked the pizzazz of a postman or hatcheck girl making the Grand Tour. On top of that, magazine writers and editors would have a far more difficult time making the average penny-pinching vacation symbolic of a concept like classlessness. The highly selective image they did present dovetailed with the interests of the tourism industry and governmental and business elites. Travel industry leaders hoped to convince more and more people that grand vacations were a realistic option—something they themselves could splurge on. For their part, businessmen and government bureaucrats saw leisure as a vital economic engine. But in addition, they recognized that mass tourism was compelling evidence of the good life offered up by the American economic system. Directed at audiences at home and abroad, mass tourism played an important role in the rhetorical campaign to sell free enterprise to a public that had become increasingly skeptical about unfettered capitalism in recent decades.

Chesapeake & Ohio Railroad president Robert R. Young nicely summarized the hegemonic prospects of a mass tourist trade in a 1946 interview with *Printers' Ink*. "Never before," Young argued, "have people had so much time and money to spend. A great transportation machine with all of its advantages and pleasure, education and culture, is as good insurance against discontent in time of peace as it is against defeat in time of war." More critically, Biff Loman, the angry young man of Arthur Miller's *Death of a Salesman* (1949), recognized it as well. "It's a measly manner of existence," he railed, "To suffer fifty weeks of the year for the sake of a two-week vacation."[47]

"Yankee Wanderlust"

Beyond the good life, the travel boom narrative's ideological lens brought another American political value into focus: the sense of individual freedom that mobility suggested. These two phenomena were in many ways inextricable. Both located American exceptionalism in the ideology of free enterprise and the unencumbered actor. People who did not face irrational, arbitrary constraints, the theory held, would logically come together to create the most robust markets. But the politically inflected narratives that surrounded travel also spoke to the prospects of renewal, at both the individual and social level, that movement enabled. Voicing this sentiment in 1961, the scholar John A. Kouwenhoven explained, "A democracy, by definition, must promise people opportunity to improve their standards of living, to develop their individual potentialities, to rise in the social scale, and so on; and that promise has the double effect of putting a premium on all kinds of mobility . . . and of requiring the rejection of any fixed system."[48] The travel boom was thus a ritual celebration of social fluidity and reinvention. Again, this narrative of national identity set the United States apart from other nations, but in this case it contrasted open societies with totalitarian regimes. *Holiday*, in a 1952 report, called the travel boom "the greatest mass mobility, the greatest incidence of people on the move in the history of the world." "Usually such phenomena have grim roots," explained the editors. "But this mobility which now fills the roads, and skies, and waters of the United States is happy and beneficent."[49] On *Holiday*'s tenth anniversary in 1956, the magazine suggested that the vacation boom represented nothing less than an altogether new epoch, calling it "the age of Mobile Man—Man gifted, for the first time in history, with leisure and the means to enjoy distance on a global scale as well as those pleasures of mind and body which only yesterday were limited to those of great wealth."[50] Paraphrasing Juan Trippe, *Saturday Review* editor William D. Patterson declared it the age of "Everyman Everywhere, unimpeded by geographical barriers." *Newsweek* summarized Americans' eagerness to travel in 1954 by quoting Robert Louis Stevenson: "I travel not to go anywhere, but to go. I travel for travel's sake. The great affair is to move." *Look* used the same quote three years later.[51]

Just as before the war, commentators saw American desires to travel as deeply rooted in national folkways. Arthur W. Baum, a writer for the *Saturday Evening Post*, called this yearn to get up and go a "national tic" and "ingrained restlessness." *Look*, over the course of six years, called it "Yankee Wanderlust" and "a 'don't fence me in' feeling," declaring that "we Americans are the world's most travel-hungry people."[52] John Steinbeck called it the urge to be elsewhere. "Could it be that Americans are a restless people, a mobile people, never satisfied with where they are as a matter of selection?" he asked. "Every one of us, except the Negroes forced here as slaves, are descended from the restless ones." Revisiting the history of tourist travel in 1966, historian Foster Rhea Dulles again situated modern-day vacationing within the grand narrative of Turner's frontier thesis. The "secretaries, clerks, tradesmen, shopkeepers, salespeople, skilled workers, and farmers" dashing across the Atlantic were inheritors of the same "restlessness" that impelled settlers across the continent.[53]

Many others saw the same psychic impulse alive and well in vacation travel. "In all of us, including those of us who have never traveled anywhere," *American Magazine* publisher James MacPherrin wrote in 1954, "there is a deep-seated yearning to know more about America and the world we live in. Perhaps we inherited this feeling from our ancestors. America was not created by 'stay-at-homes.'" John Kord Lagemann, writing a two-part piece on the American road for *Collier's* in 1949, framed it in the same terms: "Today, by automobile as by ox team and prairie schooner, this crossing of the 42d parallel through three hour zones, over mountains, plains and desert, past countless changes of accent and outlook, remains one of the greatest of all American experiences." And for Lagemann, crossing the country activated deep, buried instincts. "Opinions vary about just where the West begins. But don't give it a thought," he advised. "Even if this is the first trip, you'll recognize it from what you overheard as a child in the strum of a banjo or the hoot of a distant locomotive in the night."[54] *On the Road*'s Sal Paradise, Kerouac's self-styled protagonist, recognized the same irresistible call personified in travel companion Dean Moriarty: "It was wildly yea-saying overburst of American joy; it was Western, the wind, an ode from the Plains, something new, long a-coming."[55] Normative concepts like "the age of Mobile Man" and "Everyman Everywhere" were presented as the inevitable result of this national wanderlust; if a desire to roam was simply a part of what it meant to be American, then a government that was "of the people and by the people" would naturally respect and foster those desires.

The spirit of wanderlust, according to some accounts, was even reflected in American sportswear. "Play clothes are made for freedom," *Holiday* fashion editor Toni Robin wrote in 1952, "and they are free themselves from the strict and arbitrary rules of any small group of designers dictating a new style must." Not only did the loose fits, light fabrics, and brilliant hues lend themselves to the outdoors and play, but they also threw off the burden of European high couture. Robin pointed to the praise heaped on the American sportswear industry by designer Edward Molyneux as though he were a modern-day Tocqueville. "Just as sports clothes in England reflect the sobriety of the English countryside," Molyneux suggested, "so your American play and leisure clothes are really exciting in their color, their variety, their utter ease and the honesty with which they interpret the sunshine and bright colors of your resorts." With its casual designs and free-flowing fabrics, Robin suggested, sportswear was emblematic of a distinct American essence. "The look," she explained, "is made up of many parts—of youthfulness, of energy, of exuberance, of much time devoted to leisure and to fun, and perhaps even of some irresponsibility."[56]

Capriciousness was a theme taken up in other forms as well. *Life* profiled an American Automobile Association (AAA) employee who traveled around the United States in 1949, visiting small towns named for European cities. One tour through Pennsylvania and New York netted him London, Belfast, Rome, Milan, Athens, Moscow, Odessa, Naples, Cadiz, Warsaw, Riga, Venice, Paris, Berne, Berlin, Vienna, Copenhagen, Lisbon, Madrid, and Amsterdam. Another traveler profiled by *Life,* John Nichols, was photographed striking a headstand in front of every state capitol building. The following year, Nichols crossed the country again. This time he posed in front of state road markers with a local culinary specialty in hand. In Manhattan, Nichols posed with a Manhattan. In Texas, he feasted on a bowl of chili.[57] These articles were in part novelty stories. But they also spoke to the sheer joy of being able to go where one pleased on nothing more than a whim. Within the broader vacation boom context, the stories pointed out that the freedom to play, or derive pleasure out of life as a worthy pursuit in and of itself, was a distinct aspect of American culture. The capriciousness at the heart of irreverent mobility and colorful sportswear reflected play in its purest form, imbuing culture with a larger animating spirit: fun. When much of the world was embroiled in painful reconstruction and violent political struggle, fun for its own sake could be made into a powerful testament to the American system.

Some observers explicitly connected mobility, wanderlust, and fun with ideological significance. *Holiday*, for instance, called the Kitty Kat Klub's excursions evidence of a distinctively American "right to be restless and mobile." Freedom to travel was taken as metaphoric of the ability to cross political borders without obstruction. "In my traveling and talking," said Harry Dooley, founder of a national chain of sightseeing tours, "I keep coming up against one great fact about America that makes it unique in the world. That is our freedom to travel thousands of miles from home to wherever we wish, whenever we wish. We can hop into our car, or get a train, bus, or plane—and light out! Sometimes we forget that outside of North America not even one per cent of the people on this globe have that same freedom. . . . Most of them can't even go 100 miles from home without getting some bureaucrat's permission." Or worse, travel could spark memories of misery and death. Forced migrations, not vacations, were the touchstone in this case. "Travel, to most people of the world," *Holiday*'s Roger Angell observed in 1950, "is still an undreamed of luxury or an unspeakable horror."[58]

Within this ideological context, anything that hampered the freedom to pass freely across borders was taken as a mark of authoritarianism. In a 1946 *Saturday Evening Post* article, Sir William P. Hildred, director general of the International Air Transport Association, railed against the sea of red tape that travelers were forced to wade through, describing passports and visas as "instruments of despotism and oppression." Along the same lines, *Holiday* announced a crusade toward "the elimination of this paper spaghetti." Former vice president Henry Wallace applauded the magazine's "crusade," calling it a "much needed reform."[59] Wallace and others' aversion to red tape stemmed less from its aggravations than its potential to foil the utopian hopes they attached to foreign travel. From this perspective, tourism could play a major role in safeguarding peace. The intercultural contact at its heart was a cleansing agent for the parochial ignorance and dehumanizing hatreds that spawned war.

Given Ted Patrick's background in antiwar movements, *Holiday*'s dedication to tourism as a force for peace in the world was not surprising. Concepts like the "Age of Mobile Man," as well as the *Saturday Review*'s "Everyman Everywhere," were strongly rooted in the notion that world travel was creating an altogether new type of global community. *Holiday* cautioned against thinking about travel as "escape," encouraging readers to view it instead in terms of "international neighborliness." In the same vein, the *Saturday Review* celebrated an emerging "world community" and approvingly cited Juan Trippe's thesis that the "air tourist" could nullify the threat of nuclear Armageddon. Sightseeing was as much an exercise in global citizenship as a form of pleasure, no less vital to peace than staying abreast of news and current affairs.[60] Both magazines voiced an internationalist ethos that cut through the culture of industrial modernity after the war, surfacing in everything from the United Nations, to International Style architecture, to Edward Steichen's *Family of Man*, to State Department–sponsored jazz tours, to the globe-trotting novels of James Michener. Ideologically, it grew from a combination of Popular Front social justice ideals and "American Century" notions of U.S. global leadership, as well as the natural, if sometimes fleeting, aversion to war experienced by those who suffered through its carnage.[61] Similarly, it was rooted a high-modern faith in order, or an unmitigated sense that the social world and global landscape could be technologically synced and technocratically managed. Finally, it derived from the prospect of mass mobility—especially air travel. The feeling that everyone the world over was in closer contact, especially after a war hatched out of fanatic nationalism, made sentiments of human universalism particularly appealing.[62]

The most influential treatment of the utopian possibilities of air travel came in Wendell Willkie's *One World* (1943). The Republican candidate for president in 1940 penned his popular treatise after flying around the globe during World War II. Willkie saw flight as metaphoric of the startling new interdependence among people worldwide and argued that only a strong international body could preserve peace, human rights, and capitalism. The title itself, *One World*, spoke to the new perspective opened up by air travel—seeing the earth as a single object from above. "When I say that peace must be planned on a world basis," Willkie pleaded, "I mean quite literally that it must embrace the earth. Continents and oceans are plainly only parts of a whole, seen as I have seen them, from the air." Willkie was by no means alone. Flight, as historian David Nye has argued, was widely cited as "the acme of human achievement" and set off waves of breathless paeans.[63]

Radio playwright Norman Corwin, himself the recipient of the Wendell Willkie Foundation's One World Flight Award, described a cross-country flight in ecstatic tones for a 1946 *Holiday* piece.[64] He urged readers to "unfasten your belt aloft, open your eyes, close your mouth, and see your country through the eye of an eagle, a migrating goose, a low-flying angel." Like the romantic tourists of the nineteenth century who when struck by a breathtaking landscape recited the poems of Shelley or Byron, Corwin summoned the words of Walt Whitman:

> The earth expanding righthand and lefthand,
> The picture alive, every part in its best light . . .
> I inhale great draughts of space;
> The East and West are mine, and the North and South are mine.[65]

Walker Evans, in a 1954 *Fortune* photo-essay, took the same poetic tone, writing, "Height—aeronautical altitude—is like sudden wealth. It buys detachment and new perspective, with some lies thrown into the bargain." Advertisements struck the same rapturous tone. The aviation firm Douglas, which was marketing its DC-8s to the airlines in the late 1950s, explained about jet travel: "You sense a detached peacefulness, feeling of majesty with sun and moon, often seen hanging in the sky together."[66]

Tourism was a way to operationalize the One World philosophy. In terms of U.S. global leadership, American tourists could advertise "the American standard of living," while their dollars helped rebuild foreign economies. And in doing so, they could represent the United States as a compassionate ally in a direct, personal way. For those doing the traveling, intercultural contact could broaden their outlook and make them better citizens of the world. *Holiday* saw the industry as rife with possibilities for promoting international camaraderie. Even the roadmaps given out at American gas stations offered a path to global consciousness. "For the present we can attest first-hand to the One World influence of the road map," the magazine noted in 1951. The editorial described a young girl who, upon seeing a European roadmap, remarked how similar it looked to one of the United States. "Perhaps, she unwittingly put her finger on one of the special charms of maps. . . . They speak a universal language. Tunisian, Pennsylvanian, Spaniard and Swede can all meet in understanding of a well-made chart."[67]

With tourist mobility identified as an instrument of goodwill, checks on personal movement were framed as not only unwise but oftentimes sinister. Over and over, Americans' freedom to travel was contrasted with the restrictions encountered in the Communist world. *Look* correspondent William Atwood, for instance, detailed his tour through Eastern Europe in a 1958 travelogue called "One Way to See the Biggest Prison in the World." Similarly, the author of a *Reader's Digest* Russian travelogue contended that "the visitor to the Soviet Union becomes a prisoner of InTourist . . . as soon as he sets foot on Soviet soil." Not surprisingly, the fiercely ideological *Reader's Digest* ran a string of articles denigrating Soviet tourism.[68] The humorless guides who carefully handled western visitors, and, more ominously, the shadowy figures who tailed closely behind them, were also fixtures of guidebook profiles of Communist countries. Temple Fielding, author of the era's most popular travel guides, described even moderate socialist states, such as Yugoslavia, in Orwellian terms. Such accounts presented Communist-bloc citizens as prisoners shackled by the ever present eye of the police state. For Atwood, tourism presented the most realistic and effective means of liberating these individuals. "I'd like to see thousands of Americans take the kind of trip we did," Atwood explained, "making friends with people, talking back to Communists, reminding the System's prisoners that their wardens are not all powerful." American tourists, according to this view, could be the delivery device for the United States' most effective "weapons." "One is the idea of freedom," Atwood wrote, "another is our standard of living, a third is fun." *Holiday*, in a more measured account of Soviet travel, also suggested that the nation's "controlled dribble of tourism" could mark the beginning of political reforms.[69]

Holiday's relatively straightforward account was the exception. In most articles, travel in the Communist world was a foil that made American mobility all the more extraordinary. Perhaps this is why the Berlin Wall became such a potent symbol of totalitarianism after its erection in 1961. Almost right away, the wall became a must-see attraction among American tourists.[70] As a symbol of the travel restraints put in place by the German Democratic Republic, an especially dogmatic regime, the wall could be seen as a sort of monument to the Western world's mobility. Moreover, it offered critics concrete evidence, in the most literal sense, that the Communist world subscribed to a very different set of values—rejecting individual liberty, joyousness, and international harmony in favor of control, ideological weight, and global dominance. Most articles did not consider what the *New Republic* in 1955 called "the US Counterpart to the Iron Curtain," or State Department prohibitions on travel to Eastern-bloc countries and China. Nor did they consider the hundreds of Americans, most famously Paul Robeson, denied passports for voicing dissent. Nor did they consider the restrictions placed on foreign travelers to and within the United States. "Among free nations," historian Henry Steele Commager noted in 1958, "our barriers to travel are the most formidable. . . . And alone of the free nations of the West we put serious restrictions on the freedom of travel of our citizens." Almost entirely ignored in popular consumer magazines, these "right to travel" issues commanded ongoing coverage in the intellectual journals.[71]

Perhaps most problematic for narratives of mobility and political freedom were the United States' decidedly despotic allies. Few articles discussed the possibility that touristic freedoms to visit and explore a nation might not always equate to political freedom within those lands. Spain was a particularly difficult matter in this regard. As relations warmed between the Franco regime and the United States after World War II, the Spanish government cultivated a thriving tourist trade. Writing in the *Nation* in 1947, Horace Sutton noted that the country eagerly wooed American tourists at the same time it clamped down on American foreign correspondents. Despite Franco's authoritarianism, magazine profiles, along with popular guides like Fielding's, praised the country as a rustically charming option for bargain hunters.[72] South Africa was another heavily promoted destination throughout the late 1940s and 1950s. While *Holiday* ran a damning indictment in 1959, the country was more typically presented as part of the free world and a desirable vacation spot just at the time the ruling Afrikaners were instituting apartheid.[73]

Finding Jim-Crow-Free Oases

Americans did not need to look outside their borders, however, to see that mobility was no guarantor of political freedom. African Americans found confirmation in the resorts, hotels, motels, and restaurants that shut them out in every region of the United States. "Summer resorts," *Ebony* reported in 1947, "maintain the color line perhaps more rigidly than any other American institution. From Palm Springs, California to Palm Beach, Florida extends a vast stretch of 'caucasian only' and 'Restricted Clientele' signs on vacation spots."[74] Confronted by such signs, African Americans were forced to restrict their vacationing to tolerant areas, drive long distances between friendly hotels and restaurants, or even sleep in their car. When African Americans did come face to face with bigots, it was an especially galling experience on vacation. Often times, the encounters played out in front of family members and always during a period when individuals had set out to enjoy themselves. While African Americans were not the only group to face travel discrimination, rampant white fears of contact with black bodies meant that they met the most entrenched obstacles and were left with the fewest vacation options. As a 1947 *New Republic* profile of travel agencies noted, "Jews can be sent to what are known in the travel agent's lexicon as 'mixed places,' but where can Negroes be sent? Practically all travel bureaus are unable to deal with them."[75]

The Jim Crow discrimination that confronted black travelers went practically unmentioned in mainstream popular magazines but was treated at length in *Ebony*. By directing African American vacationers to sites and establishments where they were less likely to face prejudice, *Ebony* supplemented specialized travel literature like the *Green Book* and *Travelguide*, offering a resource to readers who wanted to participate in the vacation boom without facing the indignity of slammed doors, hateful stares, and venomous epithets. And in doing so, vacation articles provided a means of pointing to the persisting injustices African Americans were subject to nationwide, even as income-based disparities had started to even out. W. T. Lhamon has argued that mobility was an especially powerful concept to African Americans seeking social change. Set within the 1950s' "deliberately speeding" aesthetic, mobility represented the power to bust through the strictures of segregation.[76] *Ebony* made Black Americans' restricted mobility metaphoric for their second-class citizenship. African Americans may not have been legally barred from traveling where they pleased, the magazine argued, but their lack of access to the infrastructure that facilitated mass tourism amounted to a de facto restriction.

One 1947 feature praised YWCA camps as bastions of racial tolerance. "Instead of the usual 'No Negroes Allowed' signs," *Ebony* reported, "the YWCA camp sports a 'no bigots allowed' slogan and no one comes who is unwilling to live with Negroes, Japanese, or Jews." Photos pictured whites, blacks, and Asians sunbathing, canoeing, and playing together lakeside. The article pointed out not only that the camps fostered racial diversity but also that their cross-class clientele ranged from domestics to professionals. After the police chief of Miami Beach extended an invitation to African American tourists in 1950, an article spotlighted "no-Jim-Crow-travel" options in the area, including the black-owned and operated S.S. *Booker T. Washington*.[77] As was the case with the aptly named ship, *Ebony*'s travel coverage often doubled as an opportunity to celebrate black enterprise while also making the point that white-owned establishments actively rejected a viable market of African American tourists.

Given that black vacationers encountered prejudice from South Carolina to Southern California, foreign travel was portrayed as a particularly liberating experience. Leaving behind the nation that instituted and upheld Jim Crow, African Americans could, according to this narrative, cast off the shackles of racial prejudice.[78] An art student who had just taken a summer tour of Europe was described as "returning from Jim Crow–free Italy and France." France, in particular, had long been viewed as a refuge where African Americans could expect to be treated as equals. But *Ebony* pointed out that black Americans were shown more dignified treatment than they could expect at home in many other nations. Mexico, for instance, was "a Racial Oasis South of Dixie."[79] "To vacation bound Negro tourists anxious for a winter escape not only from snow and ice but also from U.S. racial discrimination," a 1951 article advised: "Nearest Jim-Crow-free oasis can be found in the West Indies." Some Caribbean Islands were more tolerant than others, however, the article was sure to note. It recommended the Virgin Islands, Haiti, and Martinique, while reporting that resorts in Cuba, Puerto Rico, Bermuda, Jamaica, Trinidad, and the Bahamas were all infected with white bigotry. "'Nassau,' says the official travel folder, 'is a resort for the discriminating.' Just how discriminating is soon made known to Negro visitors," *Ebony* reported in 1953.[80]

Oftentimes, *Ebony*'s profiles of racially tolerant spots allowed it to highlight the overall dearth of such places. The magazine pointed to the hypocrisy inherent in ideological celebrations of the vacation boom by highlighting how little of the nation's leisure infrastructure was open to African Americans. One article cited the findings of a mid-1940s study indicating that just one out of one hundred eastern resorts would accept a reservation from an African American. In 1949, the magazine conducted its own study of ski resorts, finding that of 161 resorts contacted, 71 ignored their solicitation, 35 rejected African Americans outright, 8 were closing, 4 could not provide a definitive answer, and 4 would allow them to use the slopes but not the hotel. Thirty-four resorts responded that they would accommodate black vacationers. But most of them did so begrudgingly, opening their doors only out of legal obligation. In a reply *Ebony* cited as typical, the Timberline Lodge on Oregon's Mount Hood explained that "Negroes in the past have not found Timberline Lodge conducive to their own entertainment but since it is a government property there are certainly no objections if they wish to be our guest." In the end, the report could endorse only thirteen that wholeheartedly accepted black guests.[81] Over the course of the early 1950s, *Ebony* reported modest gains for black tourists. The 1953 vacation guide noted an increase in resorts accepting reservations from African Americans. Although some proprietors did so in response to legal pressure, others awoke to a growing market or simply had a change of heart. One Long Island resort owner was quoted: "Negroes can fight wars for us. Why can't we take them into our homes, hotels, and vacation resorts?" While *Ebony* made note of such businesses, it emphasized that they were still anomalies. A report on black-owned motels, for instance, expressed pride in a number of expensive, new establishments but pointed out that they were few and far between. "In 1955," the article noted, "3,500 white motels would put up dogs, but less than 50 unhesitatingly said they would house Negroes."[82]

Letters indicated that readers appreciated the magazine's travel guidance. One reader noted that he learned to ski during the Second World War and was delighted to find the list of racially tolerant winter resorts. A Memphis woman was especially appreciative of the motel guide. Having just made a cross-country journey, she explained that "on our way it was very hard for us because we weren't aware of all the motels they have for Negroes. We were just lucky enough to find two places to spend the night without being insulted. We hated to inquire at the various ones we did see because of fear of being insulted. This article will help us a lot . . . because we will know just where to go and know they'll admit us."[83] Her poignant description vividly illustrates the vulnerability that African Americans, unsure whether their next encounter might lead to humiliation, could feel away from home. Such feedback paints a very different picture of travel for Americans of color. In this narrative, the nation was not a great expanse to freely roam across but a series of safe houses to jump between.

The postwar tourist boom was simply too big a social development to remain outside the era's political debates. While *Ebony* made travel discrimination part of a larger civil rights discourse, it was far more common for magazines to insert the vacation boom into laudatory narratives of American exceptionalism. By and large, magazine publishers saw their fortunes as yoked to the consumer industries they covered, not necessarily as hard news but as elements of contemporary culture. In a variation of auto executive and Secretary of Defense Charles Wilson's well-known, if misquoted, prescription, "What's good for General Motors is good for the country,"[84] magazine publishers believed that what was good for American business was also good for their enterprises, and they took it as a duty to publicize its virtues. Magazines were at times active in shaping this rhetoric, offering normative concepts like Henry Luce's "American Century" or *Holiday*'s "Mobile Man." More often, though, they explained how ideological concepts, such as the "People's Capitalism," related to readers' everyday lives. Whether readers accepted these explanations or not, they offer a window into the ways of understanding free time and mobility that commercial elites hoped would pass as common sense.

4 "This is How it Will Be When You Get There"
Destination Profiles and Middlebrow Geography

In March 1947, a lengthy profile of Mexico penned by author Anita Brenner appeared in *Holiday*. Brenner, an expatriate American journalist and anthropologist best known for her popular studies of mestizo craftwork and the Mexican Revolution, offered a nuanced picture of the nation, playing its stark contrasts off against one another. The Mexico that Brenner described was at once rich and poor, modern and traditional, European and Indian, and oppressive and liberating. Through this enigmatic land snaked a three-hundred-mile "tourist circuit" connecting Mexico City to the volcano Parícutin via a network of idyllic villages, where Americans saw "a Mexico served anxiously in the Gringo image." Brenner's editors at *Holiday* were delighted with the piece. The travel magazine was not the only publication to feature the article, though. A pirated, bowdlerized version ran in a number of Mexican newspapers as well, setting off a storm of controversy at the Mexican state tourism board. Bureau head Alejandro Buelna blasted the article as "utterly unfair" and inappropriate "for a foreigner living here and enjoying our hospitality." To make matters worse, *Holiday,* only a year old at that point, had already run a Mexico profile that Buelna found "derisive, crude and for the main, far from the truth." Brenner, aware of the outcry her piece set off in high circles, worried about her own well-being, telling *Holiday*'s editors that the whole affair rekindled "the impression that I am a dangerous character."[1]

Just one of many travel profiles that appeared in American magazines that month, "Mexico Fact and Fiction" may have been unusual in its quality of writing and insight, but it certainly wasn't unusual in form. Destination profiles filled postwar magazines, developing into a distinct promotional genre viewed as integral to the global tourist economy.[2] This chapter explores the processes and assumptions that guided the genre's production. By transforming multifaceted nations, regions, and cities into vacationlands, destination profiles acted as a type of geographic pedagogy. As individual articles, their intent was to shape popular conceptions of areas in ways that made them appear as desirable vacation spots. As a genre, though, their aim was to cultivate a particular way of seeing that rendered landscapes through the lens of middle-class touristic desire.[3] In doing so, destination profiles addressed readers as mobile people with both the itch and the affluence to roam, presenting them with catalogs of places out there to experience. Like other postwar cosmopolitan productions, travel profiles assumed a high-modern perspective that framed the world from afar as an endlessly complex, yet still ultimately orderable, collection of parts.[4] As sociologist Dean MacCannell has observed, this sense of fragmentation and synthesis lies at the heart of tourism. "Sightseeing is a kind of collective striving for a transcendence of the modern totality," he argues, "a way of attempting to overcome the discontinuity of modernity, of incorporating its fragments into unified experience."[5]

It was precisely this desire and geographic mind-set that destination profiles sought to nourish. Poking out of newsstands, resting on coffee tables, or laying open on waiting-room couches, popular magazines circulated these touristic representations of place through everyday life. Joined by everything from popular movies to vacation photos, they allowed the world of touristic fantasy to bleed into that of mundane reality.[6] The editors, writers, and photographers behind their production implicitly assumed that American vacationers, off on their annual jaunts, nursed a desire for geographic totality, racing across a global landscape to gather up as many fragments as possible. For boosters in Mexico and dozens of other locales, the easy mobility and popular cosmopolitanism voiced by midcentury magazines carried the promise of a booming tourist trade, as masses of American tourists poured in to collect whatever piece the region embodied. Thus it made sense for administrators like Buelna to keep close tabs on journalistic profiles, and he was by no means alone. During Ted Patrick's tenure editing *Holiday*, the governments of Italy, France, and the United States all awarded him honors for what they deemed helpful portrayals. Viewing these articles as unofficial supplements to their own promotional campaigns, industry boosters heaped praise on stories that pleased them and scorn on those that did not.[7]

"Lorelei of All Media"

As researchers at the Curtis Publishing Company surmised, travel narratives and photo-essays were a good way to attract a desirable audience and furnish a hospitable setting for tourism advertising. Crucially, publishers also recognized that these businesses still preferred magazines to television. While TV offered sound and motion to a national audience, magazines had the distinct advantage of reaching them in color. And more than any other variable, color was considered vital to selling travel. As J. Walter Thompson advised client Pan American Airways, a business especially dependent on overseas tourism, only color could "sell the romantic concept of travel to faraway places."[8] And color was vital not only to this kind of "lure" advertising but also to pitching sportswear, cameras, and dozens of other vacation goods. From a business perspective, then, travel was a growing ad market where magazines still enjoyed an important advantage.

Publishers responded by shaping their editorial mixes to attract as much of this booming ad sector as they could. Picture magazines, such as *Life*, *Look*, *Collier's*, and *Ebony*, made travel profiles a recurring feature, showcasing areas in tantalizing photo-essays. Over a two-month period in the summer of 1949, for instance, *Life* ran articles on Niagara Falls, the coastal regions of Western Europe, Virginia's Skyline Drive, and Yosemite National Park. Over time, many of these articles were developed into series with titles like "*Life* Visits," "Travel with *Look*," and "Armchair Traveler."[9] *Look* went on to package its profiles in a series of guidebooks in the late 1940s.[10] Even newsmagazines *Time* and *Newsweek* ran color photo spreads of popular destinations.[11] These articles were not simply geographic profiles, along the lines of an article that might appear in *National Geographic*, but specifically framed locales within the context of mass tourism. They were planned and executed from the American vacationer's point of view, and the guiding philosophy behind their production was that the upwardly mobile masses were eager to take part in rituals of enlightened tourist travel.[12] When *Life* photographer Eliot Elisofon proposed a photo-essay in 1957 on the islands of the eastern Mediterranean, for example, he explained that as American vacationers could more easily reach the area now, the story could be done from "both a tourist and historical perspective." The photographer wanted to do the same for "American motorists" looking to head down the Pan-American Highway the following year. Even remote areas like the "Rocky Sahara" were given similar treatment in *Life*, offering vacation tips such as hiring a Tuareg guide.[13] As the travel boom continued to grow over the late 1940s and 1950s, magazines expanded this type of coverage to create special issues aimed at vacationers. *Collier's* ran a semiannual guide, and *Look* issued a yearly "Vacation and Travel Special" in the early 1950s, complete with a twelve-month calendar of iconic tourist spots.[14]

At times, publishers were explicit about the link between the editorial climates they created and the travel advertising they hoped to attract. *Time*, *Newsweek*, and *American Magazine*, for instance, all ran "letters from the publisher" in the mid-1950s highlighting such a connection. Though addressed to the reader, these letters were clearly intended to catch the eye of advertisers. *Time*'s James A. Linen boasted that recent surveys at docks and airports found that nearly half of all departing and arriving vacationers were *Time* readers. Linen made sure to point out that the respondents used *Time* as a cue for "where to go and what to see abroad." John W. McPherrin, publisher of the relatively down-market *American Magazine*, was more direct, explaining in 1954: "It is to encourage our reader to realize their travel dreams that we publish so many travel adventures," before adding that "alert travel advertisers are giving many additional facts to our travel-minded readers."[15]

As destination profiles developed into a common sight, advertisers began to mimic their look and feel. Some sought out the same photographers and writers responsible for the eye-catching articles. Ad agency Doyle Dane Bernbach, which handled the account of swimwear giant Cole of California, contacted photographer Elisofon for this reason in 1959. "We are interested in maintaining an editorial look," art director Bert Steinhauser explained, "and after having seen your work on Tahiti in Life magazine . . . we feel that you would be an invaluable aid to us." And where magazines like *Holiday* enlisted well-known authors to write profiles, some advertisers did the same. Pan Am, for instance, tapped Ernest Hemingway in the mid-1950s to write about the Caribbean.[16] Sportswear companies and airlines had an intuitive connection to touristic profiles, but businesses with a more convoluted relationship found ways of appropriating the genre's conventions as well. Distiller Early Times showcased a circuit of hotspots for vacationing whiskey enthusiasts.[17] Heinz linked its condiments with American car culture. Advertisements like 1953's "I Wish I Were in Michigan" featured photos of the state's sights, restaurants, and diners, along with "Tips to Travelers." "In Dearborn, Michigan," one caption read, "the famous Ford Museum houses this venerable model T. Neighboring Dearborn Inn also attracts visitors from all 48 states. Here zestful Heinz Ketchup and Condiments add sparkle to the Menu."[18] Mimicking travel profiles was a way for advertisers to piggyback on the popularity of postwar vacation culture. But it was also a way for advertisers to stir up the carefree attitudes toward spending that Curtis called the "Holiday mood." To their eyes, the vivid imagery and gushing descriptions of place that were the genre's hallmark incited desires to shed restraint and dive into a world of consumer fantasy.

The notion that the magazine medium was uniquely suited to pique wanderlust and consumer desire was perhaps most clearly elaborated in a 1955 advertisement taken out by printer Fawcett-Dearing in *Printers' Ink*. Telling "the story of the magazine and travel," the printer called them the "lorelei of all media": "Only the magazine imposes no shackles on the writer and his wizardry with words, the artist and his eloquence with paints and photography. And as a creative salesman, it alone can print the intriguingly colorful advertising that pays off so handsomely for sellers. Sit back. Make yourself comfortable. Open it up, look and read. Leisurely. The world won't shout at you, flicker or fly by. Nor will it lose its lure in a sea of grey type faces, fighting the news of the day. For here in the magazine, you will first live your travels, place by place, page by page, as it quietly, compellingly whispers . . . go, go, go!"[19] Surrounded by crisp, color photographs of the Eiffel Tower, Washington Monument, Dutch windmills, and other iconic sights, the ad drew a direct connection between a magazine's fortunes and its ability to run striking travel content. "More and more people are going places today than ever before," Fawcett-Dearing explained. "More people are reading more magazines today than ever before. More travel advertisers are spending more money in magazines so far in 1955 than any other year in their history. Could there be any relationship?"[20] According to this calculus, it was magazine publishers' duty to stoke reader's wanderlust, placing before them an endless world of "lures" out there to see and experience. And as tourist travel grew, publishers could only expect the industry to lavish more and more spending upon them.

Just how destination articles took shape, transforming geographic *space* into narratives and imagery of *place,* was a complicated process grounded in a postwar "structure of feeling," or what Raymond Williams defined as the cultural currents and social structures that intuitively blend together at a particular moment. As Edward Said argued, these structures have a distinct geographic dimension in that they explain spatial contact—trade, colonization, war, tourism, or some other form—and provide frameworks for thinking about and representing the places brought together. Travel articles, no less than ethnographies, news, or intelligence reports, were products of how this "geographical sense" affixed certain narratives of identity to certain tracts of space and forms of mobility.[21] But at the same time, travel profiles were just as much the work of individual writers, editors, photographers, and illustrators who made creative decisions with specific objectives, aesthetic standards, and ideas about their audiences' sensibilities in mind.[22] By examining how travel articles were produced, we can better understand how popular geography was shaped by narratives of mobility as well as the dynamics of postwar cultural production.

"The Plus Factor"

No major magazine was more dependent on destination profiles than *Holiday.* While nearly all ran such articles, *Holiday* made them the bulk of each issue. And in doing so, it presented the geography of midcentury cosmopolitanism more explicitly than any other publication. Though *Holiday* was by no means the first travel magazine, it differed from the titles that preceded it in significant ways and struck observers as something new. As the marketing journal *Tide* remarked, "Many other magazines, like Asia and National Geographic, for example, have tackled some phase of the travel business, but none has devoted itself as fully to the subject as Holiday."[23] Travelogues were a regular feature of nineteenth-century magazines, and as early as the 1850s, enterprising printers created specialized titles, such as the short-lived *Magazine of Travel* (1857). Through the publication, which was founded at a time when tourism was exceedingly rare, Michigan printers Warren and W. Parsons Isham hoped to provide the state's farmers, shopkeepers, and craftsmen with "what would be almost equivalent to escorting them, at our own expense, thro' far distant countries."[24] As a tourist infrastructure of intercontinental railways, fast steamships, and automobiles grew over the late nineteenth and early twentieth centuries, a spate of new magazines, including *International* (1896–1901) and *The Globe Trotter* (1902–13), appealed to elite Americans. Other titles, such as *Around the World* (1893–95) and *Goldthwaites's Geographical Magazine* (1891–95), capitalized on the growing fascination with geography, natural history, and anthropology in middle-class culture. Publications like the *Bay View Magazine*, aimed at the many middle-class women who joined "fictive travel" clubs, or reading groups that took imaginative journeys by way of reading and discussion, tapped into the same currents.[25]

The most successful magazine to emerge out of this ferment, *National Geographic*, would become the most prominent outlet for popular geography throughout the twentieth century. Beginning in 1888 as the proceedings of the quasi-academic National Geographic Society, the magazine morphed into a popular periodical by early in the next century, running color photographs of places around the world. Although *National Geographic* grew to reach a large audience over the decades to follow, its view of travel remained couched in the late Victorian natural-history paradigm of its founders.[26] Other travel magazines of the early twentieth century struck a related but more explicitly expeditionary tone. From this perspective, travel was inextricably tied to imperial fantasies of discovery and conquest. Places outside the Western world provided sites for intrepid explorers to shed the emasculating strictures of modern life and test their mettle against the world's most trying climates and barbarous people.[27] In this way, magazines like *Nomad* (1927), *World Traveler*, and *Journeys Beautiful* (1924) tied themselves to groups like the Adventurers Club and presented their writers as authorities on expeditionary travel. Upon joining *Journeys Beautiful* in 1925, for instance, Henry Collins Walsh was touted as a friend of Robert Peary's and Theodore Roosevelt's, as well as a veteran of Arctic treks and desert battles with Moroccan tribesmen. *Nomad's* masthead featured a rifle-clutching figure astride a stallion as late as 1929. Like the *Magazine of Travel* before them, these publications billed themselves as a type of exploration by proxy. *Journeys Beautiful* promoted its "clearing house" of speakers, like Horace D. Ashton, "explorer of North Africa and the Troglodytes—cave men of the desert," available for lectures and dinner engagements. In another instance, the magazine touted a program through which, for a small fee, explorers would mail personal greetings to readers from around the world.[28] *World Traveler*, which allied itself with the aviators attempting the first transatlantic flights, took an updated approach that, even if it reflected the machine age, still left the unmistakable impression that travel equaled adventure. Even European tours were framed as opportunities for discovery, as one *Nomad* editor showed when he went missing in the catacombs beneath a German castle.[29]

Articles that eschewed an adventurous tone were backward glancing in their own right, evoking the luxury and distinction of the Grand Tour. *World Traveler* featured columns like "Notes for a Cosmopolite" and advertisements with titles along the lines of "Automobile Salon: The Aristocracy of Motordom." In one especially telling article, the author suggested a budget of at least $5,000 to $10,000 for a European vacation.[30] Connotations of virile adventure and elite cosmopolitanism would remain important to tourist imagery. But they would recede in importance during the mid-twentieth century as the intrepid explorer and society matron gave way to the globe-trotting middle manager, stenographer, and foreman. This image of tourism as a mass phenomenon rooted in egalitarian social trends was largely missing from the pages of travel magazines in the early twentieth century. Rather, they reflected the lingering influence of a late Victorian leisure class culture. Travel, within this Veblenesque context, was the domain of those Americans who enjoyed the rare capacity to forgo work, whether to set off on wilderness treks or genteel tours, and the luxury trades that catered to them.

Periodicals with the middle-class travel market in mind appeared in the 1920s and 1930s, but most were small publications on the fringes of the magazine trade. Many acted as organs for travel industry interests, and all were limited in scope. Travel expert Clara E. Laughlin, author of the popular "So You're Going to . . ." series, created a monthly newsletter for travel agents and enthusiasts in 1931 that self-consciously distanced itself from magazines about "remote places to which few travelers attain." Yet Laughlin was also aware that her collection of news and tips resembled something closer to a newsletter than a magazine.[31] Hoping to spur state development, the Arizona

Highway Department began issuing a pamphlet in 1925 publicizing its road-building efforts. *Arizona Highways* soon turned into a full-fledged magazine showcasing the state's scenic wonders and exoticized Native Americans. Similarly, the American Automobile Association (AAA), Greyhound, Hamburg American Line, and other industry groups all briefly published booster magazines.[32] Titles with origins in turn-of-the-century railroad promotion, including *Sunset* and *Travel* (which began as the *4-Track News*), grew in scope during the 1920s and 1930s, speaking to an increasingly modern, middle-class tourist sensibility.[33] Yet these magazines also suffered from constraints that kept their place in the publishing industry limited. *Sunset* was a regional title, serving the western United States, while *Travel* acted mainly as a promotional vehicle for its publisher's new books and an affiliated travel club's insurance plans.

Holiday represented something new in that it took the modern, middle-class tourist as its prototypical figure. Moreover, its origins in Curtis's marketing-research operations reflected a shifting structure of feeling in which popular enthusiasm about vacation travel was intertwined with the mass-marketing apparatuses that drove the nation's consumer economy. In true middlebrow form, *Holiday*'s editors pictured their audience as geographically curious Americans who had long enjoyed reading about the wider world but now felt the very real possibility of seeing it for themselves. As monthly columnist Clifton Fadiman explained, this possibility required a new type of travel writing: "The current literature of travel diverges sharply from that of the past. The reason is plain: the world has been discovered. Discovered not by adventurers, but by people. The travel writer can no longer start from the premise: Let me tell you about a place you will never see. On the contrary he must have in the back of his head: This is how it will be when you get there."[34]

Fadiman's involvement with the magazine was telling. Part of a small cadre of affable, accessible intellectuals who spoke to the broader public, he helped connect *Holiday* to the middlebrow media that thrived between the 1920s and 1950s.[35] Prior to his involvement with the magazine, Fadiman had been a book critic at the *New Yorker* and host of the popular radio program *Information Please!* Along with featuring well-known critics like Fadiman, *Holiday* adopted other hallmarks of middlebrow culture. "Good Reading," for instance, offered a tourism-oriented equivalent to the "Great Books" series, digesting classic pieces of travel writing complete with commentary by novelist and playwright Jerome Weidman. Like other middlebrow media, *Holiday* invited its audience into a corner of American culture that had historical connotations of privilege and distinction. This sense of shepherding an aspirant audience through new experiences permeated the magazine's editorial philosophy. "Good Reading" was clearly guided by a sense that *Holiday* gave its readers access to something they otherwise would not seek out for themselves. In one instance, Weidman wrote to an editor suggesting a story on George Borrow's *The Bible in Spain*, explaining that "he is precisely the sort of writer that we cooked up this Good Reading Series for. Nine tenths of your Holiday readers have heard about him but never read a word by him. A piece on Borrow would give them the plus factor we've discussed so often, the feeling that they've made contact with a writer they've been too busy or lazy to read on their own."[36]

The same attention to symbolic value marked *Holiday*'s travel writing as well. Its editors consciously steered clear of what they saw as hackneyed, "chamber of commerce" writing, for both aesthetic and instrumental reasons. Profiling the Curtis magazines for *Writer's Yearbook*, publishing-industry watcher Kirk Polking noted that "Holiday[,] . . . with a predilection for turning prominent novelists into travel writers, presents a door to the free-lancer that if not firmly closed, is open a bare crack."[37] While guided by desires to create an exemplary magazine, Ted Patrick and his editing team also recognized the cultural capital that came with an image of literary exclusiveness. Marquee names meant cachet, and *Holiday*'s contributors read like a who's who of mid-twentieth-century letters: William Faulkner, Ernest Hemingway, John Steinbeck, James Thurber, Arthur Miller, E. B. White, Budd Schulberg, S. J. Perelman, Eudora Welty, James Jones, Jack Kerouac, Truman Capote, William Golding, Arthur C. Clarke, and many others. Its lists of photographers (Robert Capa, Henri Cartier-Bresson, Ansel Adams, Arnold Newman, Slim Aarons, Elliott Erwitt, and Thomas Hollyman) and illustrators (Ludwig Bemelmans, Al Hirschfeld, Saul Steinberg, and Charles Addams) were just as impressive. In some instances, *Holiday* looked to build its cachet further by treating especially high-profile contributions as major cultural events. William Faulkner's 1954 article "Mississippi" was declared "the magazine story of the year" and introduced with an essay by critic Malcolm Cowley. Photo-essays by Cartier-Bresson were given less lavish treatment but showed similar efforts to highlight his prestige.[38]

Working with critically acclaimed writers came with a price, though. Although their lofty reputations lent distinction, *Holiday*'s editors worried at the same time that sophisticated material would confuse readers. With these fears in mind, they urged contributors to dial back their literary ambitions. As *Holiday*'s Harry Sions relayed to one literary agent in 1950, "The piece is hard reading—not so much for me perhaps . . . but I do feel that it would be rough going for the average reader."[39] Mexico's tourism head Alejandro Buelna objected to Brenner's article for much the same reason. Buelna's complaint with "Mexican Fact and Fiction" was not so much that it was damning but that it was overly complex. He charged that only readers who were "fully acquainted with the ideologies of both countries could discern what she was driving at. The average reader is not, neither here nor up there, and therein lay the dynamite of her article."[40] Careful to distance themselves, Sions and Buelna worried that sophisticated material stymied most people. Try as she or he might, the average reader could not be trusted to take away the correct meaning from a complex text. For *Holiday*, confused readers might sour on the magazine. For industry boosters, the prospects were worse: confused readers were the tourists who would never come. The solution, as they saw it, was straight accounts that left no room for confusion. So when Brenner hoped to meditate upon religious politics in rural Mexico in a later piece on Parícutin, editor Richard Field advised that "readers may be confused before they find out what the article is really about." He suggested something much more innocuous: "This is the story of a town that found itself sitting on the side of a volcano."[41] Over time, this heavy-handed editorializing came to irritate some of *Holiday*'s contributors. Jack Kerouac, a frequent contributor in the 1950s and early 1960s, summed up this sentiment well in a letter to his agent: "Tell HOLIDAY I'm honored to be invited to write travel stories for them all the time. . . . But please make it clear this time, huh, for them not to make their dopey changes on my prose, none whatever, unless mistakes of technical nature. . . . I mean why should they want my stories if they're going to be like someone else in the editorial dept. would like to write them?"[42]

The answer to Kerouac's question was that names like his carried "the plus factor" *Holiday* sought. According to this logic, the value of an article lay almost entirely in the byline. Most readers simply wanted the impression of having read an acclaimed writer; whether the piece was especially representative of a writer's broader corpus of work had little bearing on the cachet it carried. Watered-down Kerouac still allowed readers to draw a line between themselves and those who hadn't read him at all. Even though this picture of the reading experience may not have actually represented that of *Holiday* readers, it nevertheless formed the basis for the magazine's editorial philosophy. Moreover, it synced with notions of the other-directed person that by then had become common sense in advertising and market-research circles.

So what did *Holiday* readers want out of destination profiles, aside from the cachet of reading certain authors? According to the editors, readers wanted to confirm the presumptions they already had about an area. *Holiday* recognized that when readers cast their eyes on a travel profile, they peered through decades' worth of preconceived notions gathered at random from every corner of their lives. Impressions gleaned from school books, sermons, novels, newspapers, films, fairy tales, postcards, pop songs, conversations, and countless other sources slowly distilled in the mind's eye to form images of what a place was like. Only occasionally were these daydreams chastened by personal experience. *Holiday* aimed to use this collective knowledge to its advantage, building profiles around the mythologies of place that flowed through middlebrow culture.

Established writers were symbolically valuable in this regard, too, because many were closely associated with a particular area. Brenner, for instance, had already written three popular books about Mexico and thus was a logical choice for that country. Likewise, when *Holiday* wanted to run a series on the Pacific Northwest, it tapped one of the writers most closely tied to the area, Nancy Wilson Ross. Ross had garnered acclaim with a 1941 regional history, *Farthest Reach,* and had since then penned a number of novels set in the Northwest. Contacting Ross in 1956, editor Harry Sions suggested "a return to the scenes of Farthest Reach."[43] Editor Richard Field approached Carson McCullers with essentially the same pitch a few years earlier. "Your writing in 'Member of the Wedding' is so vivid, yet so sensitive and touching, and gives such an interpretive picture of the country and its people," Field wrote in 1953. "Would you have the time and the inclination to return to Georgia, to refresh your memories?"[44] In each case, *Holiday*'s hopes were that the author could revisit the themes, characters, and imagery that had earlier brought a place to life. This impulse was especially strong when an acclaimed writer's work had made the jump from popular literature to popular culture.

Richard Llewellyn's "Wales" (1951) illustrates the extent to which *Holiday* hoped to capitalize on other popular media. Llewellyn had risen to literary fame in 1939 with his Welsh mining saga, *How Green Was My Valley.* The bestselling work was well received by critics and audiences alike, and its popularity was boosted further by an equally acclaimed film version in 1941. Given Llewellyn's close connection to Wales, *Holiday* approached the author in the late 1940s to pen a profile of his homeland. The article appeared in 1951, but that was only after a series of revisions in which the editors prodded Llewellyn to present a very specific image of the country. Originally, the manuscript went into great detail on ancient lore and medieval history. But upon reading it, *Holiday*'s editors advised Llewellyn to change his focus entirely. "You should stay much closer to today and to the people of today," Field wrote; "it would be extremely interesting to American readers if you would tell more about the miners of today, their working conditions and way of life . . . for Wales means coal and coal miners and their hardships to most American readers."[45] While the final version retained allusions to "murmurous forests" and druids in "azure robes," it conformed more closely to the hardscrabble image *Holiday* wanted. Llewellyn spent much of the article chronicling the isolated, gritty way of life eked out by Welsh miners and villagers under England's daunting shadow.[46]

Even more than Llewellyn's account, *Holiday*'s layout, photography, and captioning stressed the coal-country image of Wales. The article opened with a two-page shot of a pastoral village flanked by a pair of emerald hills. On the next page, a subhead announced that "the author of 'How Green Was My Valley' takes you to his native Wales." Readers could find another two-page photograph of a valley further into the article, this one home to an industrial town, slag heap, and hulking complex of mine equipment. Again cajoling readers to view the landscape through the prism of Llewellyn's famous novel, the caption explained that "Gelli Colliery in Ystrad Rhondda might have come directly from pages of *How Green Was My Valley*." To the left appeared an archetypal soot-covered miner—the tragic figure fated to descend into the dark shafts each morning.[47]

As the anthropologist Edward Bruner has observed, foreign lands become known in a general way through "master stories" and iconic images that encapsulate some perceived essence of place. Wales's "master story" with American audiences centered on coal mining, and Llewellyn was probably more responsible for writing it than anyone else. Yet despite his authority, *Holiday* was reluctant to allow him to veer from the image of Wales he had etched a decade earlier. Instead, the magazine's chief concern was to produce an article that closed the circuit of popular geography it imputed to readers. By crafting an image of Wales in the likeness of popular knowledge, *Holiday* created a scenario in which familiar figures could circulate from the reader's imagination through a recognizable landscape on the magazine page and then back into the mind's eye.[48] In a similar instance, editor Harry Sions contacted *From Here to Eternity* (1951) author James Jones in 1956 about a profile of the U.S. Army. The editor pitched the story as a homecoming in which Jones revisited the settings and ways of life he had earlier immortalized. Like Llewellyn's *How Green Was My Valley*, Jones's book had been a critical and popular success that was made into a landmark film. Jones was undoubtedly a popular authority on army life; but he was not alone in this regard. Rather, what made Jones "a natural choice," as Sions called him, was that he alone could lend the name that reanimated the bases, soldiers, and women that Americans had watched on-screen a few years before.[49]

By working with famed authors, especially those closely associated with an area, *Holiday*'s editors could capitalize on earlier depictions of place that left a mark on the geographic imagination. And in the process, they could further bolster the magazine's cachet by offering *the* definitive account. After all, who other than Faulkner could truly describe Mississippi? As *Holiday* imagined it, readers placed great stock in this aura of authority, confident it had given them special insight into some corner of the world. But just as the editors doubted readers' comprehension skills, they also questioned the depths of their geographic curiosity. Ultimately, profiles needed to echo the narratives that readers had encountered before in memorable media texts.

"Making Real Places and People"

The use of archetypal figures and mythologies served a function similar to popular touchstones, bringing places to life in ways that synced with the public imagination. Novelists' experience in conjuring whole fictional worlds made them particularly well suited for this task. "As Holiday writers," editor Ted Patrick explained, "they channeled these talents into making real places and people come into vivid perspective."[50] While the magazine's articles were putatively works of journalism, there were real limits to their verisimilitude. For one, editors worked with writers to craft figures, such as the "real New York cabbie," who personified some aspect of a place. At times, *Holiday* gave writers leeway to create fictional characters wholesale. In a profile of Buenos Aires, one editor instructed Llewellyn to simply transform a goddess figure he used as a literary device into a real woman.[51]

In other instances, contributors developed their travelogues more as short stories than journalistic reports. The travel and nature writer John Graves's 1959 account of a solitary canoe trip down Texas's Brazos River illustrates this well. The article later formed the backbone of the proto-environmentalist travelogue *Goodbye to a River* (1960).[52] Before making the journey, Graves contacted his agent to tell him what he had in mind for the piece. His plans ranged from very general ideas about how to convey the river's mood, scenery, and wildlife to predicting specific events and encounters along the way. Graves noted that he wanted to "get down what it looks like, how it sounds, the birds and animals I see, how duck-breasts taste broiled over mesquite coals, what a leathery rancher says to me from the bank where he's trying to untangle an Angora goat from the wire, and the Comanches and the stolen horses and the two little redheaded boys scalped and murdered always behind it all. What I mean is that I'd like to set my feelings about that river down now, before they drown it, and the framework for setting them down will be the trip." Graves's letter read like a preview of the article he eventually penned.[53] The piece also seemed to be heavily shaped by editorial requests. One editor at *Sports Illustrated*, where Graves had also shopped his manuscript, asked for more of a sportsman flair. "Graves could reflect on his earlier trips," the editor suggested to the author's agent, "when a catfish as big as a sperm whale came out of the depths and swallowed the whole canoe—that sort of thing." Just this sort of fish tale appeared in the final article.⁵⁴ *Holiday*'s editors, for their part, wanted to see a greater emphasis on the "pleasure-of-being-along [sic] philosophy," which showed up in transcendentalist passages on "solitude" and "the pulse of being."⁵⁵

Given the correspondence between Graves and his editors, it is difficult to surmise which parts of the journey were actual events, which were memories of previous journeys, and which were products of his imagination. The writer had drifted down the Brazos enough to foresee many of the sights and sounds he was likely to encounter. But it is also clear that the journey's events were malleable—subject to Graves's and his editors' dictates. Graves himself admitted that the trip was a vehicle for saying the things he felt needed to be said about modern man's cavalier treatment of wilderness. In a preface to the book version of *Goodbye to a River*, he freely admitted some "fictionalizing" around a general body of real events.⁵⁶ But the actual, embellished, and fabricated aspects of the *Holiday* article were all presented as a factual account. This suggests an openness to blurring the line between fact and fiction. Writer, and for a short time *Holiday* editor, John D. Weaver noted that the magazine's articles were a unique genre. According to Weaver, they required "a summation of every field I've worked in: the imaginative quality of fiction writing, some straight reporting, and the scholarly checking of facts as a researcher."⁵⁷ While Weaver did not outline the full editorial parameters, the wholesale creation of characters and events would seem to compromise the value of straight reporting and fact checking. Ultimately, though, stories like Graves's tell us less about *Holiday*'s journalism than how thematic considerations drove depictions of place. Verisimilitude was less important than animating places though figurative characters and action.

By rendering geographic areas into mythic landscapes, profiles became a way of discussing cultural tensions. This was especially so for areas, like the western wilderness, that had long been romanticized in American culture. Graves, for instance, portrayed the Brazos as one of the last bastions of a bygone American primitivism. Scene of unspeakable acts of violence just a few generations before, the river valley was still haunted by the ghosts of Comanche warriors and white settlers. Macabre imagery was key to romanticizing the parched, scrubby land that ran along the riverbank. An early draft detailed a grisly series of scalpings and murders.⁵⁸ Many of the goriest passages were later excised or toned down, but *Holiday* retained one horrific account of a rape and murder that *Sports Illustrated* editors had earlier said was "definitely too violent for us." *Holiday*'s editors must have been pleased with Graves's gritty depiction of the region because they went on to solicit profiles of the Rio Grande, Carlsbad Caverns, Colorado, and Wyoming over the next two years.[59] Similarly, western author A. B. Guthrie Jr., in an article that *Holiday* praised as a model profile, framed Montana as a place where confronting corporeal danger was a way of life: "The Montanan's bloody head unbowed sees something funny in the blood. He makes a joke out of it." In Guthrie's Montana, brute force, personified by the marauding lynch mob, was the law of the land. Yet as fatal as men could be, nature posed a graver threat. Illustrating "the element of peril" that had always characterized life in Montana, Guthrie devoted an extended passage to graphic description of a recent bear attack. Pondering what exactly bound residents to this difficult land, the author settled upon the subtle reassurances that savagery always lay dormant in even the most tranquil settings. "It is the cool summer nights with the coyotes crying," he concluded.[60]

While the postwar years saw a resurgence of popular interest in the frontier, *Holiday*'s profiles ran counter to the sanitized image offered in most film and television westerns. With their sense of moral uncertainty and random, unflinching violence, these accounts presaged the move to what would become known as a revisionist perspective of the West. Critic Dayton Kohler classified Guthrie in this camp, explaining that his work spoke to "the emotional erosion which frontier life imposed . . . the cost of hardship and the casual cruelty of things." Guthrie and Graves seized on this "casual cruelty," implicitly contrasting it with the coddled world of modern suburbia.[61] An image of the West as proving ground for white American valor had been central to its popular mystique and touristic appeal since the mid-nineteenth century. And for nearly as long, the region had been promoted as a cure for the softening effects of middle-class complacency. To the eyes of critics, this sense of satisfaction had reached alarming heights in postwar America as comfort, security, and material acquisitiveness were elevated to a sort of civil religion. Behind chrome-laden sedans and sportswear-stuffed suitcases, critics saw a shackling of the human spirit. For them, modern living exacted an especially severe toll on American manhood as men insulated themselves from the hardships that bred virility.[62] There were still places out there that offered redemption, Guthrie and Graves wrote, but they were steadily disappearing. In their hands, travel profiles became a canvas for depicting preserves where a primal type of American masculinity still thrived amid a sea of emasculating comforts. And by eulogizing violence's diminished presence in everyday life, western profiles offered a means of exploring the darker sides of human nature.

Holiday's articles thus became screens on which to project the tensions straining the American psyche. Acting as modern mythologies, they offered a way to reconcile incompatible values—virility and refinement, risk and security, work and leisure, domesticity and wanderlust, and so on. Not uncommonly, authors adopted a pseudopsychological argot, conceptualizing areas as personifications of deep psychic impulses. Graves, for instance, conceived of a profile of the Rio Grande borderlands in heavily Freudian terms. "It is a romantic and rough and tawdry and bawdy region," he wrote, "almost Arab in its contrasts of austerity and self-indulgence." Building on this theme, Graves continued: "The towns of the Mexican side have long been a kind of expression of the American id, where thousands of square miles of Calvinistic inhibition can blow off steam at brothels and saloons and bad bullfights and dirty shows and, occasionally, for a night in jail."[63] Other *Holiday* writers built their profiles around socio-psychological themes as well. Nancy Wilson Ross diagnosed Portland, Oregon, as "a 'schizophrenic' city."[64] Given the pervasive role psychology played in postwar discourse, it is not surprising that *Holiday*'s writers dipped into it to craft geographic meaning. Popular books as varied as Mickey Spillane's bloodbaths and Benjamin Spock's *Baby and Child Care* (1946) channeled Freudian notions of repression and development. Similarly, works like *The Manchurian Candidate* (1962) and Vance Packard's *Hidden Persuaders* pointed to the prospects of mind control.[65] For academics speaking to a broad audience, social psychology offered a sort of intellectual lingua franca. David Reisman, C. Wright Mills, Arthur Schlesinger Jr., Erich Fromm, Richard Hofstadter, and others all described social change in terms of personality characteristics.[66] *Holiday* tapped into the same psychological lode. As Graves and Ross suggested, places could be understood as geographic outgrowths of psychic tensions. Repression on a wide-scale basis was bound to find outlet in rough-and-tumble towns like Juarez City. And in the same way, embracing a pair of conflicting personas was bound to bring about a sense of civic cognitive dissonance.

Capturing "Tigerishness"

As these authors' experiences demonstrate, *Holiday* contributors viewed travel writing as a way of making broader social statements. All were successful authors who understandably wanted to go beyond description and mood setting. As Graves put it in a 1960 letter, he wanted to avoid "guidebookishness." He hoped to keep what struck him as an otherwise mundane assignment on the Carlsbad Caverns fresh by "tying the Caverns part of the piece into a framework of understated, thematic material (wildlife, commercialism, regional history, and so on)." Much to Graves's consternation, *Holiday*'s editors stripped out most of this material in their edits.[67] As others found, the magazine's willingness to explore intellectual themes was limited. If they fit with the image of place *Holiday* had in mind, these kinds of ruminations were permitted to a degree. But if they ran counter to or complicated the picture in some way, the magazine had less tolerance. This ability to police the creative process was a source of pride for the magazine. "Unlike most other magazines," a 1959 Curtis educational guide noted, "Holiday is completely planned by the editors."[68] While these plans were very different from those yielded by the mechanistic reader research behind *Holiday*'s first issues, they were still built on a very specific understanding of readers' expectations. The difference was that these plans were hatched from a gut understanding of the middlebrow mind, rather than actuarial tables or "predictograph" machines. Extensive planning meant that editors could identify angles they wanted to see explored at the outset, and they could then guide contributors toward them. And at the end of the process, their final say over how profiles were laid out, packaged with artwork, and captioned gave the editors a powerful tool for reasserting creative control.[69] "It's not that we are disinterested in the text," editor Louis R. Glessmann explained about *Holiday*'s philosophy toward imagery, "but rather that we feel the art must carry its own weight. Quite often we frankly don't care what the author is trying to say—we assume he uses the words he requires to get his point over."[70]

The magazine's handful of themed issues every year provided the best opportunity to implement carefully thought-out editorial plans. By the mid-1950s, *Holiday* annually devoted its January issue to European travel and its July number to seeing the United States. On top of that, the editors usually devoted at least one issue per year to a major tourist destination. Themed issues were major undertakings that allowed the editors to organize their depictions of place around some larger concept. The April 1953 issue, for example, was framed as one last "portrait" of the Paris of old before the "*grande dame* of the world's cities" was forever changed by mass tourism. Similarly, the editors devoted the October 1949 issue to Gotham "from the point of view of the indigenous New Yorker." Featuring E. B. White's ode to the city, "Here Is New York," the issue was planned as "a portrait from within."[71]

When *Holiday* revisited New York City ten years later, it took the opposite angle. A case study Curtis produced for college journalism students in 1959 details how the issue was crafted. In doing so, it offers a window into the production of middlebrow geography, showing how *Holiday* planned the issue to emphasize a certain conception of New York predicated on tourism's fragmentary perspective. As Sions explained, "Our 1959 issue was built around the concept of the world's New York, the outsider's New York. . . . It was a discovery of the many small worlds that make up New York, a picture of the city as an inspiration and a guide to the perceptive visitor."[72] The overriding function of the issue was thus to impose a framework on the endless array of sensations that attracted, but also bewildered, visitors to the city. An opening editorial explained: "What stuns at first in New York is the overwhelming number of these small worlds which overlap and intertwine in one city, so that for the newcomer who does not recognize the threads, does not see the pattern each world forms for itself, the city is simply a megalopolis, confusion compounded, chaos."[73] In line with what MacCannell characterized as tourism's longing for totality, or the sense of steadily gathering up shards to one day achieve a holistic understanding, *Holiday*'s editors saw the magazine as a way of providing this kind of Olympian perspective. Over the next year and a half, *Holiday*'s editors went through a series of ideas on which "small worlds" to feature, debating the merits of theater, media, nightlife, sports, parks, music, literature, art, architecture, and high society. For each, they targeted a handful of writers closely associated with the field. Arthur Miller and Truman Capote, for example, were suggested for the theater and nightlife pieces.[74]

Though the interplay between images and words was always central to *Holiday*'s profiles, photographs were especially integral to the New York issue because they provided a way to attach a tangible identity to each microworld. "Each has its own special distinctive flavor," a planning memo explained, "its own set, its individual background, its own 'capital,' as it were. . . . Our aim, then, would be to show in text and pictures these different small worlds against their setting, or backgrounds, with representative people who typify them."[75] In presupposing that each fragment of the city could be captured and made knowable by the camera, the editors embraced the fundamental assumptions of what critic Susan Sontag called "photographic seeing." Describing the medium in its high-modern heyday, Sontag argued that photography's "main effect is to convert the world into a department store or museum-without-walls in which every subject is depreciated into an article of consumption. . . . Through the camera people become customers or tourists of reality."[76] While Sontag's comments were critical, *Holiday*'s editors and photographers saw cataloging the world as both a plausible and desirable endeavor. The magazine's plan for executing this concept was to photograph iconic New Yorkers against their natural environment. Like other forms of touristic iconography, the images acted metonymically to express some larger essence of place. Architect Philip C. Johnson was pictured in front of the new Seagram building, standing in for the chic world of international design and architecture. Similarly, beatnik New York was personified by African American poet Ted Joans, photographed by Burt Glinn at a lively Greenwich Village coffeehouse. Home to a mixed-race crowd and festooned with avant-garde décor, the scene was meant to capture the Beat's unconventional way of life.[77]

According to art director Frank Zachary, it was exactly this kind of "subjective" quality *Holiday* aimed for in photographs. As he explained, photography "creates illusion rather than transcribes mere fact. In the words of a famous art dictum, it is not the tiger we wish to portray; it is his tigerishness." In some instances the magazine went to great lengths in pursuit of this "tigerishness." Photographing actress Helen Hayes against the shimmering, ethereal lights of Broadway meant erecting a scaffold over Times Square, along with securing a city permit and a one-million-dollar insurance policy.[78] The photos that surrounded the portraits further teased out the distinctive quality of each Gotham microworld. *Holiday* represented beatnik "inscrutability," for instance, with a photograph of actress Mimi Margaux. The actress's flowing black hair framed her brooding face against the Lower East Side skyline. Another photo depicted beatnik melancholy in the form of a solitary folk singer, dressed in black and strumming his guitar in the Washington Square darkness.[79] Altogether, the issue featured more than a dozen portraits, each intended to show the reader a different microworld and all that it encapsulated. To read the magazine, then, was to supposedly simulate the process of gathering up fragments: as the reader turned each page, she or he pieced together a more and more complete understanding of the city.

The photographic centerpiece of the issue, an Arnold Newman portrait of public works czar Robert Moses, was meant to communicate exactly this sense of order from chaos. According to the case study, the image was a "a theme picture representing the entire city, its progress, its civic life, its dynamism."[80] If order was *Holiday*'s desired master narrative for the Big Apple, Moses was an appropriate choice. The planner and public works director had since the 1920s steadily accumulated one mantle of power after another, overseeing the construction of every major municipal project of the era. As Moses described it, his parks, expressways, bridges, and tunnels were intended to "weave together the loose strands and frayed edges of the New York metropolitan arterial tapestry." This infrastructure opened the way for the Greater New York area that sprawled across the five boroughs, up to New Haven, outward through Long Island, and over into northern New Jersey.[81] To capture Moses as a metaphor for the city, Newman again erected a girder for the shoot. This one he suspended over the East River with Midtown Manhattan and a brilliant blue sky as the backdrop. The builder, wearing a dark wool suit, clutching blueprints, and standing erect on the beam with arms akimbo, peered confidently into the camera. "Robert Moses on a symbolic girder," the caption read, "blueprints in hand, across the East River from the awesome cosmopolis whose shape he is charged with controlling."[82]

For *Holiday*'s editors, Moses represented what they understood to be New York City's ultimate "tigerishness"—its constant state of flux. The master builder was indeed a personification of New York's dynamism. His endeavors had unleashed a thirty-year flurry of what critic Marshall Berman has called "creative destruction," or the perpetual building up and tearing down at the heart of capitalism. Moses's projects slashed through the city's neighborhoods, creating a network of roads, bridges, and tunnels that nourished an automobile-based suburban culture. "Moses' historical mission, from the standpoint of this vision," Berman writes, "is to have created a new superurban reality that makes the city's obsolescence clear."[83] While obsolescence might be too strong a word, the meaning of the city did change dramatically as suburban living became the norm after World War II. Placing Moses outside the city for the shot, in this sense, was a masterstroke because it replicated a driver's view and showcased New York as something the eye could consume in whole. The city, then, was something to contemplate from afar rather than be a part of and experience. It was an image that could be packaged and marketed to the tourist gaze, or the traveler's appetite for spectacular new environments.[84]

Holiday's use of photos to suggest parts of a whole could be seen in other issues as well. The magazine's 1953 Paris issue, for instance, featured a collection of Henri Cartier-Bresson photographs titled "Paris! City of Types." Including images of young lovers, haggard old pensioners, and the ubiquitous American tourist, picture editor Louis F. V. Mercier called the essay "a documentation of the spirit of Paris."[85] In the European travel issue the following year, the magazine featured yet another Cartier-Bresson photo-essay. "The Face of Europe" took the whole continent as its subject, presenting Italian street musicians and British aristocrats as distillations of national spirit. In an introduction to the piece, *Holiday*'s editors adapted Cartier-Bresson's photographic maxim of the "decisive moment" to tourism, explaining that "the real traveler, like the great artist, learns to make his instants count, to see with a trained eye the flick of life, the exact moment of significance." Just as the camera could capture the essence of an event with the snap of a shutter, the tourist's eye could capture an essence of place when it fell upon an iconic sight or archetypal figure. Those fragmented moments culminated, according to this philosophy, in a holistic understanding of place. "From the little things one sees," Cartier-Bresson wrote, "a sort of synthesis builds itself, possibly superficial but with truth and fragrance."[86]

Synthesis, or the sense that everything could be pieced together, speaks to the pedagogical intent behind destination profiles. Aimed at the legions of

American readers who marketers hoped had at last risen from their armchairs and climbed into automobiles and airplanes, the articles offered instruction on how to see the world from a tourist's point of view. In one regard, this meant publicizing an area's sights, history, and charms. But in another, it meant encouraging readers to look for an ultimate geographic essence. As magazine profiles showed them, places were alive with distinctive spirits that tourists could experience for themselves once they made the trip. Moreover, destination profiles suggested a whole geographic disposition and vantage point on the world. Situating readers as part of an urbane, supermobile, and quintessentially modern culture, the profiles spoke to a cosmopolitan way of being that carried great resonance in midcentury America. The genre implied that, for readers, the world was their oyster, offering all the finer things that life had to offer, whether it be great writers or fascinating places. This highmodern sensibility was especially visible in "slick" picture magazines, like *Holiday*, *Life*, and *Look*. Their clean, modernist photo-essays, like the glass and steel skyscrapers that began to dominate city skylines, offered an aesthetic counterpart to the structural-functionalist thought that animated midcentury dreams of a smooth-running American Century. By showcasing disparate areas and explaining how they could be understood in totality, destination profiles represented a world that ran like a well-engineered system. They embodied a modernist "heroism of vision," as Sontag called it, through which everywhere could be seen, appreciated, and properly fit within a larger framework.[87]

This flattering image of the modern world was predicated on an equally complimentary picture of the reader as connoisseur. Yet as magazine editors sought to cultivate this view of the self, they questioned the depths of their readers' curiosity. Seeing audience members' geographic imaginations as essentially circumscribed by what they already knew, *Holiday* skewed profiles toward the recognizable figures and themes that flowed through popular culture. Although the magazine's profiles avoided the "chamber of commerce writing" that boosters like Buelna would have preferred, their literary merit served commercially instrumental purposes. By offering acclaimed contributors, the magazine looked to corral to what it saw as an aspirant, fun-oriented, and free-spending readership. Showing a more canny understanding of the dynamics behind selling tourism than most boosters, *Holiday*'s editors recognized that marketers ultimately needed to reach the subset of consumers who saw cosmopolitan travel as integral to their core identity. Before long, destination advertisers influenced by new ideas about consumer desire would also learn that flattery could work wonders.

Federal projects during the Depression promoted tourist travel to regions throughout the country. The New Deal's most direct intervention in the growing tourist economy saw the creation of the United States Travel Bureau in 1937. New York City Art Projects, Works Progress Administration, 1940.

The Family with *Everywhere* to go

AMONG grandmother's first reactions to the automobile was this one: "What would we *do* with it? We've no place to *go!*"

But the automobile unlocked a thousand doors to the world outside for millions of people in all walks of life.

Now comes the airplane and repeats the process, increasing many times over the number of "places to go." What's more, its tremendous speed *creates* the time for travel, whether for business or pleasure. Its indifference to the winding paths of earthbound traffic, its ability to fly direct to its objective—brings within the reach of everyone the farthest places of the continent and of the earth.

Today, the family has everywhere to go! Air transportation hands over the keys . . . a couple of hours to the city, which the family never had time to visit before, a brief afternoon to reach the playgrounds of mountain or sea, overnight to the enthralling drama of another hemisphere . . . and a score of new markets brought almost to father's office door.

Busy at war today, the Airlines of the United States expect to be equally busy in peace . . . serving a nation whose market places and whose playgrounds are now, literally, everywhere!

When you travel by Air *make reservations early; please cancel early if plans change.* When you use Air Express *speed delivery by dispatching shipments as soon as they're ready.* Air Transport Assn., 1515 Massachusetts Ave., N.W., Washington 5, D.C.

This advertisement is sponsored by the nation's airlines and leading manufacturers in the aviation industry

THE AIRLINES OF THE UNITED STATES
LEADING THE WORLD IN AIR TRANSPORT

During the later part of World War II, advertisers described the war as a fight for a leisured, consumer-oriented way of life. Travel marketers, in particular, framed the coming peace as the advent of a supermobile society. Duke University Digital Collections, Ad Access.

For many Americans, vacation travel, and the sense of mobility that came with it, came to be seen within the framework of consumer entitlement after the hardships of the Depression and war. Bill Mauldin, *Back Home* (New York: William Sloane Associates, 1947), 151. Copyright by Bill Mauldin (1947). Courtesy of Bill Mauldin Estate LLC.

The slick, colorful, and jumbo-sized *Holiday* grew into the premier outlet for travel writing and photography in postwar America. E. B. White's *Here Is New York* (1949) and John Steinbeck's *Travels with Charley* (1962) were among the pieces that first appeared in its pages. *Holiday,* May 1948 and August 1953.

Magazine coverage of the postwar vacation boom used the language of citizenship to describe tourist travel as among the unique folkways of a democratic, classless society. *Holiday,* April 1951, 30. Courtesy of Roy Doty.

B·O·A·C makes your Two Weeks Vacation a Full 14 DAY European Holiday!

SUN	MON	TUE	WED	THU	FRI	SAT
		1	2	3	4	5
6	7 AND HERE'S HOW...					LEAVE N.Y.

ARRIVE LONDON 7 A.M.

Stay awhile in Britain... then visit Paris... or Rome... or Zurich... or Vienna... or Copenhagen... or Stockholm ...or any of eighteen other Key Cities

LEAVE LONDON 8 P.M.

ARRIVE N.Y.   29   30   31

STRATOCRUISER SPEEDBIRDS TO LONDON CONNECT WITH 325 FLIGHTS WEEKLY TO ALL EUROPE!

Sounds like magic—doesn't it—to enjoy 14 full days in Europe on your two weeks' vacation?* But you can do it, *this summer or autumn*, thanks to BOAC's daily Stratocruiser Speedbirds to London and most frequent onward service to 18 countries via BOAC or BEA.

Think what this means! Now Europe, with all its history, art, scenery, and family ties, comfortably comes within the scope of your normal two weeks' vacation —this summer! Your ocean crossing is by de luxe, twin-deck Stratocruiser, the finest airliner flying.

Plan now for that dreamed-of European trip. Ask your travel agent to help you choose your Speedbird itinerary. Whether you wish to concentrate on one city or country, or visit several—you'll be amazed how much you can see and do—on your Speedbird holiday!

* *Of course, your customary two weeks' vacation is actually 16 days, including that extra week-end!*

WRITE FOR THIS ALL-INCLUSIVE TOUR BOOKLET

Still time *this* summer to join one of these 16-day-and-up *escorted* tours via BOAC. Twelve thrilling itineraries including Britain, Low Countries, Germany, France, or Rome and other shrines for Holy Year. Write BOAC for "12 Tours Booklet."

See your travel agent now, or contact BOAC

BRITISH OVERSEAS AIRWAYS CORPORATION

420 Madison Avenue, New York 17, N.Y. Telephone: PLaza 5-5960. Offices in Washington, D. C., Miami, Chicago, Los Angeles, San Francisco, Montreal and Toronto.

In popular vernacular, "two weeks" became synonymous with vacation travel, describing a block of time during which Americans could venture outside the shadow of work. Framed as an annual event, the term suggested a shared folkway of consumption. *Time*, June 12, 1950, 44.

Revelers lift pharmaceutical manufacturer Claiborne Robins in celebration during a company holiday to Havana. Robins paid for 132 of his employees to make the trip. Press accounts of such employer-sponsored vacations, which appeared throughout the 1950s, emphasized American business's role as patron of the leisured "good life." *Life,* December 16, 1957, 125. Photograph by Paul Schutzer, Getty Images.

Poet Ted Joans, photographed at a Greenwich Village coffeehouse, was intended to represent beatnik New York in a 1959 *Holiday* theme issue that depicted the city as a collection of "micro-worlds." Photograph by Burt Glinn, Magnum Photos. *Holiday,* October 1959, 83.

West Germany's postwar travel advertising omitted images of the adult generation after market research revealed that Americans were most likely to associate them with Nazism and the Second World War. The elderly and children stood in for stood in for traditional German culture and the nation's future. *Holiday*, January 1955, 1.

Pablo Casals, whose cello appeared in advertisements promoting tourist travel to Puerto Rico in the late 1950s, provided marketers with an opportunity to associate the island, which had long connoted poverty and blight to many mainland Americans, with a refined, cosmopolitan culture. Photograph by Elliot Erwitt, Magnum Photos.

The British expatriate adman David Ogilvy, responsible for midcentury icons such as Schweppes' Commander Whitehead and the Hathaway Shirt Company's eye-patched aristocrat, was masterful at plucking archetypal figures and settings from the middlebrow imagination. *Life*, May 14, 1956, 78.

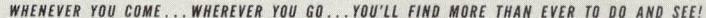

Prior to hiring Ogilvy, Benson & Mather in 1951, the British Travel Association's advertising employed the same cluttered aesthetic and catchall approach that characterized most destination advertising at the time. *Holiday,* March 1951, cover II. Courtesy VisitBritain.

Henry VII, Elizabeth I and Mary Queen of Scots are buried in this chapel.

Tread softly past the long, long sleep of kings

THIS is Henry VII's chapel in Westminster Abbey. These windows have filtered the sun of five centuries. They have also seen the crowning of twenty-two kings.

Three monarchs rest here now, Henry, Mary and Elizabeth. Such are their simple names in sleep. No titles. No trumpets. The banners hang battle-heavy and becalmed. But still the royal crown remains—*honi soit qui mal y pense*.

When you go to Britain, make yourself this promise. Spare time to visit at least *one* of the thirty great cathedrals.

Their great names thunder! Durham and Armagh. Or they chime! Lincoln and Canterbury. And sometimes they *whisper*. Winchester, Norwich, Wells and Salisbury. Take a map and a good guide book. Then make your choice.

Each cathedral transcends the noblest single work of art. It is a pinnacle of faith and an act of centuries. It is an offering of human hands as close to Abraham as it is to Bach. Listen to the soaring choirs at evensong. And, if possible, go at Christmas.

You will rejoice that you did.

For free illustrated literature, see your travel agent or write Box 123, British Travel Association.

Looking to activate reader's deep-seated travel fantasies, Ogilvy, Benson & Mather pioneered a photographic-intensive aesthetic for the British Travel Association that soon became the default look for magazine advertising across the tourism industry. *Holiday,* November 1958, 116. Courtesy VisitBritain.

In its campaign for the French Government Tourism Office in the early 1960s, Doyle Dane Bernbach, another agency associated with advertising's creative revolution, also considered fantasy-laden photographs integral to evoking the therapeutic, experiential appeals of travel. New Yorker, February 4, 1961, 9. Photograph by Elliot Erwitt, Magnum Photos.

Lovely. Everyone knows.

Lovely. Heaven only knows.

on the peak of one of the wooded hills of Southern Rajastan and you can look down on Udaipur, "City of the Dreams". Below you, 16th century palaces seem to float on the dark blue waters of an too-perfect lake. Over one of the bridges, perhaps, trudges a string of camels, carrying wood and grain. you like to stay in the sumptuous palace of a Maharana? You can, for as little as 'ay (including 3 delicious meals—and high tea!) If you'd like to know more about her modern hotels and travel facilities, see your Travel Agent. Or write to the vernment of India Tourist Office.
w York, 19 East 49th Street. Chicago, Palmer House. San Francisco, 685 Market Street. Toronto, 177 King Street, West.

India

By the mid-1960s, India and other "off-the-beaten-path" destinations recognized that remoteness could serve as a virtue in ads targeted at the subset of vacationers who searched for a perceived authenticity of place outside the mass tourism circuit. *Harper's,* January 1965, cover II.

When the federal government recognized the travel gap's contribution to a growing trade deficit, it created the United States Travel Service in 1961 to oversee international marketing efforts. Ogilvy, Benson & Mather handled advertising throughout much of Europe, selling a mythic American landscape and seeking to defray concerns that U.S. travel was unaffordable. Reproduced in David Ogilvy, *Confessions of an Advertising Man* (New York: Ballantine, 1963), plate facing page 89.

5 CASTING LURES
Tourism Advertising and the Experiential Ethos

Poking fun at the barrage of ads pitching cities, states, and nations in postwar magazines, *Advertising Age* featured a cartoon in 1947 showing an agitated railway stationmaster snapping at a customer. "Look, mister, it may be advertised as America's ideal vacation spot in all the magazines," he barked, "but you've got to remember the name of the place before I can sell you a ticket."[1] The cartoon alluded to a nation on the go, packed with novice tourists learning the ins and outs of vacation travel. But at the same time, it lampooned the incredible uniformity exhibited across tourism advertising as a genre. The cartoon playfully pointed out that everywhere claimed to be "America's ideal vacation spot."

Glancing at the cartoon, admen in the know could chuckle at the genre's anachronistic aesthetic. Owing as much to nineteenth-century boosterism as modern advertising, community advertising, or the notices placed by tourist boards and semiofficial booster groups, usually presented readers with a hodgepodge of generic lures that could just as easily be claimed by countless other places. "Smiling fisherman with gigantic catches, scenic panoramas, gay crowds, lovely beaches, lofty peaks, historical places" along with "luscious gals in swim suits" constituted the genre's typical mise-en-scène, observed a pair of marketing professors in 1938. But industry insiders could also appreciate the unique problems that selling travel posed to advertisers. Nearly every region had awoken to the economic powers of tourism by the late 1930s, and most offered some variation of the same basic set of attractions. As one 1939 *Printers' Ink* article summed up this quandary: "What can a community say? Aren't all travel copy angles more or less alike? Where is the chance for variety? . . . How can we give our community an individuality that will make tourists prefers us to other communities?"[2]

The stationmaster cartoon exaggerated the extent to which all community ads offered a chorus of identical calls. Throughout the 1930s and early 1940s, a number of aggressive boosters and tourist boards had embraced systematic advertising methods. As seen earlier, ads crafted for California and other spots went well beyond pitching the sandiest beaches, instead tapping into Depression anxieties and wartime hopes. And while the authors of the 1939 report in *Printers' Ink* acknowledged that originality posed a real problem, they identified a range of novel angles that savvy advertisers had used to their advantage. In the early 1930s, Bermuda targeted allergy sufferers, boasting "no hay fever in this glorious blue golden island." At other times, advertising explicitly cast the island as a step outside machine-age clamor and into a peaceful, bygone past. "Yes, we have no factories, street cars, motorcycles, or automobiling," the tourist board trumpeted. The All-Year Club targeted the same frazzled crowd, imploring "men worried about breakdowns" to "Bake Out Your Troubles in S.C."[3] But even with these notable exceptions, much tourism advertising looked atavistic and unsophisticated in the mid-1940s. For every group like the All-Year Club that embraced the scientific ethos of modern advertising, there were many others for which it was completely foreign. And the latter overshadowed the former enough to where *Advertising Age* could make the genre's self-defeating uniformity a laughing matter.

Yet tourism advertising would look very different a decade later. This chapter tracks its transformation, examining how midcentury advertisers forged new ways of casting areas as vacationlands through narrative and imagery. No less than editorial profiles, tourism ads were produced as a form of geographic pedagogy, created to persuade readers to think about faraway landscapes in highly particular ways. As travel boomed, public and private boosters aggressively marketed their regions in the hope of establishing themselves as preeminent vacationlands. Many turned to Madison Avenue, where leading agencies systematically approached the problem of luring would-be tourists to an area. Early efforts ranged from boosting off-season traffic to vetting out and refuting the negative stereotypes that kept tourists away. Influenced by new strands of social thought and consumer psychology, the most sophisticated ad agencies of the era recognized that the desires animating leisure travel were highly experiential in nature. Pitching areas as sites of personal transformation and transcendence, these marketers combined enduring narratives of place with patently therapeutic conceptions of consumer fantasy. In doing so, they recognized that it was much more persuasive to sell tourist travel as a ritual of social distinction than an egalitarian folkway.

Directing Traffic

Community advertising's earliest roots lie in the simple notices taken out by resorts in mid-nineteenth-century newspapers. Looking to attract well-heeled summer visitors, hoteliers promoted the healthful benefits of local scenery and attractions.[4] By the turn of the century, railroads, travel agencies, boosters, and exposition organizers began mounting extensive publicity campaigns that enlisted everything from magazine advertising to promotional literature to press junkets. The most forward looking drew on themes in contemporary culture to project consumer desires onto the landscape. Some hoped to capitalize on feelings of middle-class malaise. The Boston and Maine Railroad, for instance, tempted urban businessmen fearful of emasculation with promises of "waters that are alive with the 'Fighting Kind.'" Others drew on romanticized notions of western scenery. Mindful of the pull Europe cast on American tourists, western boosters issued patriotic calls to "See America First."[5] No group was more active than the western railroads in promoting vacation travel. With each boasting a scenic wonderland along its route, including the Grand Canyon and Yellowstone Valley, the railroads built luxurious hotels and tagged local Native American tribes, landscapes, and wildlife as attractions. Taking a page from national advertisers, they promoted these spectacular areas—many of which were designated national parks—as branded destinations complete with recognizable trademarks and logos. The Great Northern went the furthest, appropriating the "See America First" slogan from a Salt Lake City booster and turning it into a catchphrase for the railway's Glacier Park. The National Park Service, under the guidance of former journalism and marketing executive Stephen Mather, fully understood the value of this publicity, actively encouraging the western railroads, hotels, and even dude ranches to feature the parks in national ad campaigns.[6]

"Lure" advertising would remain central to transportation marketing over the decades to follow. Railways, ocean liners, and airlines all served particular geographic regions, and each recognized that promoting the areas they serviced was tantamount to advertising themselves.[7] The advertising industry's choice of metaphor, lure, offers insight into how marketers thought about selling tourism and, more generally, how they thought about consumers. Destination advertisers saw the challenge before them as fundamentally akin to that faced by hunters: how to attract one's prey; and for both, the obvious solution seemed to be dangling the right inducements. This logic was at the heart of selling travel, fully pervading the language marketers used to describe the process. So for instance, when the printer Fawcett-Dearing described magazines as the "lorelei of all media," it spoke in an idiom of enticement and impulse. Lorelei was a golden-haired siren who, in a well-known legend of German mythology, drew sailors to their deaths along a perilous bend of the Rhine. Entranced by her call and striking beauty, men were powerless to resist her lures.[8] For destination advertisers, the objective was much the same. Selling travel was a matter of coaxing consumers to follow their instincts.

By the early 1920s, a spate of new boosters on both sides of the Atlantic began to aggressively market tourism services. European governments seemed to discover in unison the economic value of vacation travel and opened official bureaus to grow their domestic trades.[9] Generally cooperative ventures involving railroads, steamship lines, hotels, entertainment vendors, and national governments, these bureaus capitalized on the glamour and prestige long associated with European travel. In terms of marketing, they favored a deluge of promotional material, such as glossy posters and brochures, over paid advertising. The German effort, coordinated by that nation's railroads, sent out thirty million booklets between 1924 and 1934, which, as one observer pointed out, was enough to stretch from New York City to Berlin. The sheer volume of publicity made paid advertising hardly necessary, as it fed the romance surrounding transatlantic travel, which in turn fed complimentary press coverage. As one observer noted, newspapers were filled with European travel ads, but they appeared in the rotogravure section's photos of foreign cities and ocean liners, rather than in advertising columns. Together, these coordinated efforts constituted what *Advertising and Selling* in 1929 called "a vast system" for "the extraction . . . of a billion dollars a year from the pocketbooks of the public."[10]

In North America, much of this work was handled by semiofficial boosters such as Southern California's All-Year Club and the New England Council. Learning from the railroads and steamships, these groups looked to sear themselves into consumer consciousness through national advertising campaigns. They saw the selling of vacationlands as akin to mass-marketing any other product and eagerly embraced what was congealing into modern advertising's coordinated blend of market research, image crafting, and selective media buying. As the All-Year Club's Don Thomas explained, selling Southern California was like merchandising any other "commodity." It required disciplined analysis rather than "guesswork." Back east, groups like the New England Council looked to Los Angeles as a model and touted their own systems of "research, planning, and publicity."[11] The All-Year Club's name itself belied this more nuanced approach to luring tourists. The group was founded by a group of Los Angeles businessmen in 1921 to grow the area's tourist trade and in particular attract visitors during the lean summer months. Identifying its biggest problem as the perception that Southern California summers were broiling hot, the club dedicated itself to disabusing easterners and midwesterners of this notion. The first "four years we harped on Summer climate," Thomas explained. "The next four we kept up the heavenliness of our Summers, but stressed the sheer comfort of our Winters." By 1932, summer visitors exceeded and outspent winter guests. Southern California was not alone in battling "climate prejudice." Jamaican boosters, also interested in growing their summer trade, recognized that American tourists assumed the island was hot and sticky. In response to such concerns, advertisements included temperature charts, copy, and imagery meant to show that Jamaican summers were actually quite mild.[12]

Such efforts reflected rationalistic business hopes that, if wielded correctly, advertising promised systematic control over industry conditions. In the context of tourism, this meant that ads could not only lure more visitors but also direct their spatial and temporal flow—telling them exactly where to go and when. This traffic control function was almost a pure distillation of the behaviorist psychology and functionalist thinking trendy in advertising circles during the second quarter of the twentieth century. Rooted in animal research, including the proverbial rat-in-a-maze experiment, and predicated on stimulus-response models, behaviorism called for enticements that could trigger certain desired behaviors. Attracting tourists was a matter of strategically presenting the right lure. The New Jersey Council, for instance, identified "seasonal sports and uncrowded, low-cost vacations" as the best stimuli for attracting more tourists in the late spring and summer.[13]

Traffic control would remain an important part of destination advertising over the decades to come. Amid the postwar travel surge, other winter havens, such as Florida, stepped up efforts to promote their summer trades. Likewise, if an area hoped to disperse the tourist crowds by drawing visitors out of major cities and resort areas, advertising could emphasize more remote districts. Hawaii, where hotel overcrowding in Oahu had become so severe that there was no longer anywhere to house trial jurors by the late 1940s, looked to spread guests across the island chain.[14] Traffic control efforts owed a heavy debt to functionalist preoccupations with efficiency and peak performance, viewing tourist infrastructure through the fulcrum of management science. Thomas and others drew on that field's terminology, calling their local resources and attractions the "vacation plant." Looked at in this manner, a Miami Beach hotel that sat empty May through October was no different than a foundry that went unused for half the year. Both represented dormant capital. Similarly, the sunshine that fell on empty beaches in Maui while a backlog of tourists waited for rooms in Waikiki represented wasted resources. To industry eyes, advertising copy that synchronized tourists' behavior with local objectives brought the area's infrastructure closer and closer to full capacity. "When you have a plant that markets a half-billion dollars' worth of goods yearly," Thomas asserted, "you keep it operating efficiently."[15]

While community advertising had grown active by the late Depression years, the postwar travel boom set off a flood. As *Advertising Age* wryly put it in 1946, "Every state will be going over its terrain, its institutions, its history and its people with a high-powered microscope, trying to discover or embellish attractions which can help it dip more heavily into the tourist lode."[16] Very few boosters showed the sophistication of seasoned advertisers like the All-Year Club, though. Many simply pitched the old standbys: "Most beautiful mountains, best beaches, etc.," as Thomas described them. Others took a catch-all approach, squeezing in as many lures as possible to show that an area offered something for everyone. One notice from New Mexico's tourist board managed to fit a Spanish belle, crested butte, colonial church, dancing Native American, pueblo village, modern resort, golf course, downtown Albuquerque, and a ghostly procession of conquistadores and wagon trains into a single illustration. Foreign bureaus went to similar extremes. The French National Tourist Office boasted of "Her [France's] infinite variety" and featured a map overlaid by photos of a port, castle, peasant women, Riviera beach, alpine skier, and the Eiffel Tower in one 1948 ad. For good measure, it also included an endorsement from singer Lily Pons.[17]

The glut of ads coupled with tourism's growing importance to local economies pushed some communities to take a savvier approach. Those that had already adopted systematic methods became even more scientific, recognizing that they were in stiff competition with each other and other expensive purchases. For the All-Year Club, the emergence of mass tourism meant that advertisements needed to target consumers with even more detailed information. Taking an approach akin to advertising wizard Rosser Reeves's "unique selling proposition" (USP), the booster emphasized a handful of specific attributes that could set the region apart from competitors. While the group's account was handled by Foote, Cone, & Belding, it showed all the hallmarks of the USP approach that Reeves had made famous at Ted Bates & Company, hammering away at a specific selling point over and over again. "Getting the message into the heads of the most people at the lowest possible cost," Reeves observed of this method, "it's almost a problem of engineering."[18]

Despite the dominant role leisure had assumed in American culture by midcentury, a marked suspicion toward play and idle activity lingered among many Americans, who, as anthropologist Margaret Mead wrote in 1957, were still sensitive about upsetting the traditional "rhythm of work, virtue, and leisure."[19] The reams of academic and popular commentary treating leisure as a problem of modern society evinced the trouble that many Americans felt reconciling the new fun morality with traditional narratives of productivity, industriousness, and thrift. Thanks to these persistent moral concerns, tourism marketers saw their product as a purchase that, more so than other expensive items, consumers found difficult to justify. "These money spending tourists do not come here automatically," one All-Year Club official explained in 1956; "they have to be sold on the idea. They have to be sold in competition with other selling campaigns—'Buy a new car'; 'Go to Europe'; 'Come to

Florida,' etc."[20] "Reason why" advertising aimed to provide the rationale. It zeroed in on the key benefits that a vacation could offer and emphasized them again and again. Armed with sound reasoning, marketers hoped, consumers could get past their unease with such an extravagant purchase.

For the All-Year Club, adventure and variety were their unique appeals, offering the most convincing reasons for an expensive and time-consuming trip to Southern California. The group homed in on "adventure" after studies revealed that the average visitor had to travel twenty-four hundred miles to reach Los Angeles. Copy highlighted this sense of journey, exclaiming: "No other U.S. trip is such a big experience. It's *the* great American travel adventure." The idea that a trip to California should be understood in terms of adventure and national identity played into narratives of American wanderlust. "You cross the U.S. . . . See the West," one 1954 advertisement explained. Below, a boy in a coonskin cap could be seen playfully surveying the landscape around him. Copy pointed out that a Southern California vacation allowed most Americans, still largely huddled in the Northeast and Great Lakes regions, to cross the Great Plains, pass over the Rockies, traverse the desert, and finally reach the Shangri-La that was Southern California. Couched in these terms, the vacation was transformed from leisure activity into traditional folkway: the cross-country trek was one of things that made Americans who they were. Explorers, prospectors, and pioneers had passed through the same territory to create the nation; and as the boy's coonskin cap signaled, the notion that seizing the continent was a defining act of American nationhood was reiterated week in and week out in the frontier dramas that played out on TV and movie screens throughout the 1950s. A vacation out west, in this context, allowed modern Americans to entertain fantasies that they were making their own westward trek, ritually affirming patriotic bonds across time in the process.[21]

The All-Year Club's second unique proposition, variety, was selected to convince consumers that the considerable expense of a Southern California vacation would be well worth the money. To get this message across, ads emphasized the sheer number of things to do around the region. The "See the West" ad discussed above, for instance, featured eighteen color photographs showcasing specific sights around the region. "Flowers forever blooming here!" a typical caption gushed. "World's largest rose garden—15,000 bushes—in Exposition Park, Los Angeles." What differentiated this approach from other catchall appeals was the explicit use of advertising theory underlying its construction. Convinced that consumers saw a Southern California vacation as a major time commitment that would last for roughly two weeks, the club set out to show that the region's remarkable variety of landscapes and attractions made it a good return on investment. The ad's layout suggested this temporal quality, resembling a calendar or schedule of distinct daily activities, each accounting for a unit of vacation time. Details about tourist sights were key in this regard because they pointed to concrete activities that could fill an itinerary. "Facts in community promotion are like special aisle displays of merchandise in a market," Thomas explained. "The closer merchandise is brought to the shopper, the more attention it attracts and the more is sold."[22] In the same manner, the club recognized that Southern California offered a more diverse set of climates, topography, and activities in a short drive's distance than any other part of the country. Advertising images were carefully chosen to communicate this compact diversity. One photo showed a car with skis strapped to the roof passing a convertible packed with sunbathers. Orange groves bloomed in the foreground against a backdrop of snowcapped mountains. Over the rest of the 1950s and early 1960s, the club's advertising followed along the same lines, asking consumers "Where Else Can You See So Much So Easily?" and imploring them to "choose a new kind of vacation fun everyday in Southern California."[23]

The heavy emphasis on concrete benefits in the All-Year Club's advertising brings to light the extent to which many Americans still viewed vacationing in terms of cost-benefit analysis. According to this rationale, the best vacation was the one that delivered the most bang for the buck. In a 1955 article for *Holiday*, the critic Bernard DeVoto blasted this aspect of the American character, suggesting that the "resolution, doggedness, and grit" that enabled Americans to take vacations en masse precluded them from enjoying their trips. "Having succeeded in getting a headlock on pleasure," DeVoto surmised, "they have gone on to choke it to death." Having adopted the relentlessly functional ethos of modern business, the typical American's work instincts "professionalize his pleasure, put it on a sound business basis, make an investment of it. It has got to show a profit. . . . Are we investing for safety of principal, for income, or longterm appreciation? Program this trip accordingly—budget it, it's costing plenty isn't it?"[24] Critics like DeVoto recognized that this functionalist mentality missed the deep psychological satisfactions and sense of play that were central to pleasure travel. These elements were not lost on the era's more creative tourism advertisers, though, who well understood the selling powers presented by the not-always-rational life of the mind.

Substituting a Lovely Image

For advertisers eager to probe the nuances of touristic desire, motivational research (MR) offered an alternative approach that also carried the cachet of science. By uncovering the subconscious desires and prejudices that made a community more or less attractive, advertisers could craft copy and imagery that attacked those motivators head-on. McCann-Erickson, for instance, used motivational studies to probe consumer thinking on behalf of the New Mexico State Tourist Bureau in the mid-1950s. The agency found that participants expected the state to be scorching hot and home to second-rate facilities. Armed with these findings, McCann-Erickson built a campaign around the dual themes "*high, cool, New Mexico!*" and "*comfortable as home!*" An ad featuring Carlsbad Caverns made sure to note that the caves had "*three elevators for your convenience.*" Others depicted super highways to show that Route 66 was not the state's only modern road.[25] Over the next two years, bureau advertising struck a careful balance. On the one hand, it conveyed notions of Native American and Hispanic exoticness so central to establishing New Mexico's touristic identity in previous decades. A Zuni dancer, for example, served as a sort of logo for the campaign in 1957. Wrapped in a woven blanket and wearing a bright blue ceremonial mask fitted with a beak, horns, and feathers, the otherworldly figure dominated advertisements, connoting the state's enchanted landscapes. But at the same time, the ads sought to counter assumptions that indigenous spectacle also meant technological backwardness. With this consideration in mind, copy alluded to "the great work being carried on here by our nuclear scientists" and assured readers that "fine highways speed you along."[26]

Campaigns like New Mexico's offer a window into how areas dealt with negative perceptions that could keep tourists away. While groups like the All-Year Club had been combating stereotypes since the 1920s, postwar efforts tackled image issues related to culture and geographic identity that were far more sensitive than perceptions of bad weather. Drawing on market research and theories of persuasion, midcentury campaigns sought to tap into touristic desires for otherness without activating prejudices. In the case of New Mexico, this meant that white middle-class tourists could venture into the Land of Enchantment without leaving industrial modernity's zone of comfort.

Community advertisers, in this regard, hoped to manage what they saw as a cognitive dissonance that rendered vacations at once attractive and distressing to many consumers. At a general level, many ads targeted lingering moral reservations. As historian Michael Berkowitz has argued, they emphasized a vacation's practicality within staid, middle-class terms.[27] After suggesting a Florida package trip as a good wedding gift, for instance, one 1948 ad reassured readers that "you don't need an 'occasion' to give *yourself* a winter vacation in Florida. You know it will be good for you. . . . Restful days in the warm, healthful sunshine."[28] Others found alternative psychic chords to pluck. Echoing celebrations of the sentimental family that resounded throughout

American culture at the time, Californians, Inc. stressed how vacations could strengthen domestic bonds. One 1946 offering depicted a young family sightseeing at Fisherman's Wharf. The ad included a coupon redeemable for a booklet called "The Chapter in Your Life Entitled San Francisco." Without mentioning the war, the group clearly framed vacationing in terms of reunion. No longer an extravagance, the trip provided a means of segueing between wartime absence and postwar togetherness.[29]

Dealing with reservations and prejudices in advertising often meant obscuring problematic issues rather than trying to explain them away. Germany, perhaps more than any other place, provides a window into this dynamic of travel marketing. In the 1920s and 1930s, Germany was second only to France in popularity among American tourists. After the Second World War, the nation faced obvious challenges to regaining that spot. The war's colossal destruction, occupation logistics, and early Cold War tensions prevented Germany from reestablishing its tourist trade as quickly as its neighbors had. Despite these obstacles, the German Tourist Association was ready to open a Manhattan office and launch its first postwar U.S. ad campaign by 1950. Centered around the theme "See You Again in Germany," the ads featured waving Deutschlanders in traditional dress. Alluding to the country's prewar popularity, they implied that an old favorite was open again for business. Before long, American tourists were back in droves. While only 38,000 Americans vacationed in West Germany in 1950, 200,000 flocked there in 1952 and 400,000 streamed in by 1958.[30]

Logistics, however, may have been the least of Germany's worries. As *Advertising Age* observed in 1952, "Public relations had its problems. Not a few newspapermen could remember Germans in ME-109s, Tiger tanks or E-boats." Unmentioned was that Germans had not just been recent foes but perpetrators of genocide on an unimaginable scale. While the Germany of popular imagination—quaint villages, Alpine castles, and Bavarian beer gardens—may have retained its appeal to American tourists, behind this idyllic screen lay a landscape of systematically orchestrated slaughter. Evidence of the war abounded into the 1950s, and Nazism's artifacts dotted the landscape. As the *Saturday Review*'s Horace Sutton reported in his 1951 article "Return to the Reich," the party's Munich headquarters survived as an information bureau renamed America House. Similarly, the site of the protean beer-hall putsch was now "an American snack bar complete with Coca-Cola sign."[31] These types of reminders raised unpleasant questions about the value of cultural tourism because they challenged Eurocentric narratives of civilization and progress. Germany's recent past suggested that American links to an idealized European culture may not have been worth venerating if it could mutate into such calculated brutality. Further, the country raised unpleasant questions about a white American identity that at its core was racially constructed around filial connections to European people.

Stephen Goerl Associates, the German Tourist Information Office's advertising agency in the 1950s, was aware of the image problems Nazism posed and designed the group's campaign to circumvent them. Visit Germany ads, Goerl explained, were made to emphasize "the old and the new." One advertisement, which Goerl selected as his agency's top ad for 1954, featured an illustration of a kindly old burgher handing an apple to a schoolgirl. A quaint medieval village served as the backdrop. The tagline promised: "The old and new will delight you in Germany." Copy elaborated on this theme, adding that "the patina of age and vigor of youth blend into a pattern of vivid contrasts." Missing from these images of children and the elderly were German adults. Goerl explained, "We have purposely omitted the generation in between with the thought in mind that a great many Americans are still thinking of Germany as a recent enemy, and a man of about 30 or 40 years of age might be regarded as the representative of the war period. In making tests, we have found that readers are less likely to associate the war with the older or the new generation."[32] To create an attractive image of Germany, then, Goerl erased the adult generation, writing Nazism out of nation's touristic master story. In doing so, the agency and booster hoped to strike a decade of barbarism from American memory and recast Germany as a land of storybook villages. Given the speed of West Germany's ascent back into the top tier of foreign vacation spots, many Americans had little difficulty embracing the sanitized image of "the old and the new."[33]

Puerto Rico was another place that sought to screen out Americans' negative perceptions. In the U.S. territory's case, tourism boosters hoped to forge an altogether new image. For decades, business leaders in Puerto Rico had longed for a mass vacation trade but were stymied by mainland perceptions that the island was hopelessly slum ridden. In the 1930s, the territory carried out beautification projects, built infrastructure, opened a visitor's bureau in New York City, and hired a public relations firm. But as historian Dennis Merrill has noted, "The effort portrayed Puerto Rico in condescending terms: a poverty stricken land whose simple people awaited the opportunity to serve their northern benefactors." This disparaging picture stuck with the island over the next two decades. By the 1950s, Puerto Rico's image on the mainland began to change. A postwar alliance between modernization champions in territorial government and mainland industry, called Operation Bootstraps, led to a string of new luxury hotels, most famously the Caribe Hilton in 1949. Along with the construction projects, the Commonwealth of Puerto Rico Visitors Bureau launched a series of ad campaigns.[34] As in New Mexico, the bureau played up the island's exotic atmosphere while at the same time stressing its modernity. Advertising copy referred to the island as "Puerto Rico, U.S.A.," and photo montages balanced depictions of the island's Spanish colonial heritage with those of ultramodern, deluxe resorts.[35]

It was not until the second half of the decade, though, that Puerto Rico's transformation from "vast slum" to luxurious getaway would become complete. At that time, advertising man David Ogilvy assumed publicity duties and lacquered the island's public image with a sheen of high-class sophistication. Upon taking over the account, Ogilvy, Benson & Mather (OBM) commissioned studies to gauge American impressions of the island and its Caribbean neighbors. Their findings were that, despite recent gains, Puerto Rico was still perceived to be the poorest and dirtiest part of the region. According to the report, these stereotypes were firmly rooted in mainland racism. Puerto Rican migrants had moved to big mainland cities, especially New York, in large numbers over the previous few decades. For many midcentury white Americans, these newcomers became synonymous with big-city blight, crime, and disorder. Films like *West Side Story,* though largely sympathetic to its characters, still spoke to the close association in American culture between Puerto Ricans and urban decay. OBM recognized that most white Americans knew little about the island itself. "In this state of ignorance," Ogilvy observed, "most Americans ascribe to Puerto Rico itself the prejudiced ideas they apply to the Puerto Rican minorities on the Mainland."[36] Simply countering white American prejudices with images of sandy coves and the Caribe Hilton was not enough because it failed to give the island a new identity. What it needed instead was a total image overhaul. "We must substitute a *lovely* image of Puerto Rico for the squalid image that now exists in the minds of most mainlanders," Ogilvy wrote Operation Bootstraps head Ted Moscoso.[37]

The result was an intensive campaign meant to recast the island as a place that oozed upper-middlebrow refinement and sophistication. "Puerto Rico in renaissance," as the campaign dubbed it, was a land of colonial gentility and world-class symphonies. It was an island that bore "the Royal Arms of Spain . . . new hotels . . . four-lane highways . . . landscaped apartments . . . men of industry who also love poetry . . . [and] men of vision who can also respect the past."[38] In the campaign's most celebrated advertisement, Pablo Casal's cello could be seen resting against a wicker chair in an empty room lined with Spanish tile. Light flooded in through a stained-glass window atop a long, slender doorway. "The big black fiddle is a stopper," one public relations executive remarked of the Elliott Erwitt photograph in 1962. Its picture of classic refinement posed such a stark juxtaposition with ugly stereotypes, he argued, that mainlanders would have a much harder time deriding the island as a "litter of cribs and crazy shacks on stilts."[39]

Mouth-Watering Images

In Ogilvy, Puerto Rico employed one of the most innovative advertising men of the postwar years. Along with Leo Burnett and Bill Bernbach, Ogilvy was viewed within industry circles as a maverick newcomer responsible for ushering in a more creative and up-to-date brand of advertising. Brought up in a middling but socially connected and well-educated family in early twentieth-century England, Ogilvy at a young age developed a fascination with American culture. After a year at Oxford, he left to travel Europe and the United States, pursuing a string of wildly disparate jobs: sous-chef in Paris, social worker and oven salesman in Scotland, advertising account manager in London, farmer in Pennsylvania Amish country, British intelligence man during World War II, and pollster in George Gallup's public opinion lab. When Ogilvy helped to found Hewitt, Ogilvy, Benson & Mather in 1948, his start on Madison Avenue was inconspicuous. Thanks to his time at Gallup, he was initially recognized as more of a market-research expert than copy wizard. But after the dashing, eye-patched aristocrat he created for Hathaway shirts became a hit in 1951, he was soon hailed as a creative genius. Over the decade to follow, industry watchers fawned over Ogilvy's graceful prose, and his unusual characters garnered him attention in the popular press.[40] It also helped that Ogilvy was a shrewd self-promoter, cultivating the persona of a fey bon vivant, enshrined in his best-selling *Confessions of an Advertising Man* (1963).

Merging the art and science schools of advertising, Ogilvy adhered to a "formula" of "disciplined thoroughness and creative brilliance."[41] While the agency's ads often used creative, fantasy-tinged themes and imagery, they were almost formulaic otherwise. Each advertisement offered the same three elements—a striking photograph; a short, graceful headline; and a small blurb of fact-filled copy—arranged from top to bottom. Ogilvy's insight into the popular imagination allowed him to pluck out archetypes, like the Hathaway Man, and place them on the magazine page. During an era that stressed conformity, this intuitive understanding allowed him to see that quirky, even odd, imagery could resonate with deeply entrenched desires among millions of Americans. Played by George Wrangle, a White Russian expatriate, who had also worked a panoply of jobs ranging from foreign correspondent to fur salesman, the Hathaway Man's elegant dress and eye patch suggested a suave, masculine ideal and sense of cosmopolitan intrigue. "An eye-patch on a man had always struck me as having overtones of heroism and mystery," Ogivly explained. "When such a man came into a restaurant, people would always tend to whisper, 'Who's that?'"[42] Commander Whitehead, the bearded sea captain that OBM made the face of a long-running Schweppes campaign (played by the company's actual president of North American operations), tapped into the same masculine fantasies.[43] Explaining his success, Ogilvy frankly remarked that "the ideas came to me when the telephone line to my unconscious was functioning—when I was at stool, or tipsy, or asleep."[44]

Over the 1950s and 1960s, OBM built a niche specialty in tourism advertising—first with the British Travel Association (BTA), then with the Commonwealth of Puerto Rico, the United States Travel Service, French National Tourist Office, American Express, KLM Royal Dutch Airlines, Cunard Lines, and P&O-Orient Lines. The collection of accounts spurred Ogilvy to later joke that he was "supposed to be the Grand Panjandrum of travel advertising."[45] But even discounting Ogilvy's penchant for self-aggrandizing, his agency did revolutionize the look of tourism advertising. It cast aside the cluttered aesthetic and hackneyed writing of old and replaced them with a sleek, photocentric layout that became the default look for tourism ads by 1960. Looking back at the BTA campaign's impact from the vantage point of 1970, industry watcher Robert Glatzer remarked that it "influenced—for years it overwhelmed—all other tourist campaigns." Indeed, Ogilvy's impact on the industry led the *Saturday Review* in 1967 to name him, along with industry titans Conrad Hilton, Juan Trippe, Walt Disney, and five others, to the pantheon of "Men Who Made the World Move."[46]

Rejecting the behaviorist, stimulus-response lures of groups like the All-Year Club, Ogilvy's BTA advertising was much more attuned to the fantasies and desires that animated Americans' geographic imaginations. As he explained shortly after taking over the account in 1951, "It is unrealistic to believe that any advertisement can do a complete selling job—that it can sell anyone four weeks expedition costing $1200." But it could "plant in the virgin mind a mental picture of what Britain looks like and feels like, and this picture can be damned enticing." Ogilvy recognized that tourists were not simply going somewhere but were making something closer to a pilgrimage.[47] In choosing a vacation site, they set out to physically inhabit the places that had been backdrops for earlier daydreams and fantasies. Luring tourists was a matter of cultivating imaginative desires to the point where consumers felt compelled to act on them. Selling tourism was thus about selling experiences. While Ogilvy had the savviest understanding of tourism on Madison Avenue, he was not the first to recognize tourist travel's experiential qualities. Fairfax

Cone, who handled the copywriting duties for Californians, Inc. in the late 1930s and 1940s, saw their value, as well, penning ads meant to "take their readers by the hand . . . and conduct them through the experience of a San Francisco vacation," as opposed to simply listing the "city's attractions and distinctions."[48] Ogilvy's advertising for the BTA built on this fundamental insight, overlaying it with a rich understanding of how fantasy, desire, and self-affirmation interplayed in the tourist imagination. Indeed, the agency's "Come to Britain" campaign would usher in a new standard for destination advertising that took the idealized encounter and transformative moment as its base. In this way, Ogilvy and the BTA offer a window into how the most sophisticated marketers of the era were thinking about popular geography and touristic desire in ways that would be foundational for a consumer culture shifting toward the buying and selling of service experiences.

While most industrialized nations took tourism as a serious economic matter by the postwar era, Great Britain was especially determined to grow its industry. Even before the end of fighting, the country had identified foreign tourism as a means of rebuilding the British economy. The BTA targeted American vacationers throughout the late 1940s and 1950s as an important source of reconstruction dollars. Although faced with severe logistical hurdles, tourism had already become Britain's number one trade export with the United States by 1948.[49] Before Ogilvy took charge of the account in the spring of 1951, BTA ads adhered to the jumbled, catchall aesthetic favored by most boosters of the day. Ads used the tagline "Come to Britain" and featured illustrations of iconic sights, activities, and people.

OBM soon discarded this look and replaced it with a "cordially English" institutional campaign meant to "play up England's permanent and characteristic virtues." In terms of design, the BTA campaign adopted the Hathaway layout as a means of emphasizing photography and showcasing archetypal imagery.[50] In one of its most celebrated advertisements, a headline implored readers to "Tread softly past the long, long sleep of kings." A full-color photograph showed the tombs of Henry VII, Elizabeth I, and Mary, Queen of Scots, in their Westminster Abbey chapel. Flooded with sunlight, the room glowed with golden hues. "These windows have filtered the sun of five centuries," explained copywriter Clifford Field's hushed prose. Brightly colored pennants cut diagonally through the frame while ornate, stately tombs rested in the bottom right-hand corner. "Three monarchs rest here now. Henry, Elizabeth and Mary. Such are their names in sleep. No titles. No trumpets. The banners hang battle-heavy and becalmed. But still the royal crown remains." The scene, shot from a slight angle and partially framed by a proscenium archway, replicated the oblique vantage point of a visitor who has just caught a glimpse of the chapel. As he or she peers inside, the room seems to radiate brilliant light, suggesting the crown's eternal vibrancy. "Tread softly," the headline whispered, demanding reverence for monarchs who were at once centuries deceased and yet still alive within the abbey's sacred space.[51] Other advertisements aimed for the same atmospheric feel. "It's a short lane that has no Hollyhock," one 1955 ad explained. The photograph's first-person perspective offered readers a peak down a village lane where ramshackle cottages and flowery gardens lined the way.[52]

The emphasis on iconic British imagery stemmed from Ogilvy's philosophy on the nature of tourism. "The foreign tourist," he wrote, "is out to collect clichés." In this way, Americans' popular knowledge of Great Britain was the campaign's greatest resource. Copywriters were advised to "use one 'stereotype' to flag your audience—Tower Bridge, Union Jack, Guardsman, etc."[53] "Stereotypes" were so integral to BTA advertising that the agency dubbed them "Fundamental Pictures." "We cannot have too many photographs of the things that make Britain an eternal magnet for tourists," a 1957 planning document explained. "Stately homes, cathedrals, castles, rich interiors, inns, thatched cottages—will all make marvelous advertisements."[54] Iconic sights invested the image with what critic Roland Barthes called "certain tourist stereotypes," or "the condensed essence" of a particular geographic identity.[55] Estates, villages, cathedrals, and pubs were thus a kind of coded language Americans could understand as allusions to a unique Britishicity.

Tourists would ultimately come to Great Britain, OBM surmised, so that they could experience this distinct, and patently non-American, British essence for themselves. "Tourists do not travel thousands of miles to see things which they can see next door," Ogilvy wrote in 1963. Eager to amplify differences, campaign imagery stayed away from architectural styles any newer than the seventeenth century. Americans could see Georgian and Victorian cityscapes without traveling across the Atlantic; they could only see medieval, Gothic, and Tudor environments, however, by going abroad.[56] The result was a heavy focus on castles, thatched roofs, and quirky "Olde-Curiosity-Shoppe aspects" of British culture. The colorful uniforms donned by royal pikemen, barge masters, and choir boys, along with the idiosyncratic nature of British currency, suggested that Britain offered a charmingly anachronistic counterpoint to the hard rationality of American modernity.[57] Such distinctions were reinforced elsewhere in popular culture. Stanley Donen's *The Grass Is Greener* (1960), for instance, acted them out via a love triangle set against the backdrop of a stately English mansion turned American tourist stop. Living amid an estate stocked with the relics of seventeenth- and eighteenth-century gentry life, Cary Grant and Deborah Kerr spend their days maintaining the manor and running a small mushroom farm. After a suave American oilman, played by Robert Mitchum, tours the estate, he relentlessly sets out to woo the elegant Kerr away from Grant's befuddled, but refined, country gentleman. Poised to join Mitchum for a life of international jet-setting, Kerr at the last minute opts to return to Grant and his antiquated world of tweed coats and country gardens.[58]

For the BTA's image crafters, tapping into popular geography also meant alluding to famous books, films, and other popular texts. As Ogilvy explained to a bureau representative in 1954, a consumer's decision to vacation somewhere "is the result of many influences—books read in childhood, films seen at the cinema, a desire to keep up with the neighbors, advertisements read in magazines."[59] Each offered a stock of symbols, themes, and narratives that could be appropriated into the campaign. Pointing to the popularity of director Alfred Hitchcock's train thrillers, for instance, Ogilvy suggested railway-themed ads. J. M. Barrie's *Peter Pan*, just made into a Disney film in the 1950s, and A. A. Milne's *Winnie-the-Pooh* were other fond British touchstones that could be worked into the campaign. One ad, OBM suggested, could feature a child modeled after "Christopher Robin (but without the long hair!)."[60]

By the late 1950s, more Americans than ever were traveling to Britain. Whereas roughly 335,000 American tourists visited the country in 1947, more than 1,175,000 came ten years later. The following year, they left an estimated $150 million behind them.[61] Britons, curious as to how their nation was being packaged and sold across the Atlantic, followed the campaign at home, and many grew dismayed. The *Sunday Times, Manchester Guardian,* and others leveled scathing attacks throughout the 1950s and early 1960s, charging that the campaign's deliberately antiquated "cottage and smocks" image slighted modern Britain and worked against efforts to bolster the nation's industrial base.[62] Ogilvy defended himself in *Confessions of an Advertising Man:* "I am rebuked for creating the impression that England is a bucolic little kingdom living on the glories of an ancient past. Why don't I show England 'as she really is,' the vital, industrialized, welfare-state which has given the world penicillin, jet engines, Henry Moore and atomic power stations?" Answering this question, Ogilvy thundered: "No American is going to cross the briny Atlantic to look at a power station. He would rather see Westminster Abbey; so would I." Others agreed. The *Economist*, itself no fan of "those gaffers in the New Yorker," applauded its effectiveness.[63]

Objections raised against the BTA's imagery and themes illustrate just how politically fraught tourism advertising could be. While OBM was never forced to run images of cooling towers and council blocks, the agency did bow to domestic pressures, looking for ways to "inject an atmosphere of economic vitality, social progress, and cultural renaissance" into the campaign.[64] At other times, the agency nixed promising copy ideas that might upset domestic observers. BTA officials, for instance, quickly dashed Ogilvy's plans to feature a Victorian locomotive—a photo that would certainly roil critics who worried about perpetrating an image of British technology as backward.[65] Agency and client feuded over not only the content of advertisements but their format as well. Despite the campaign's commercial and critical success, the association resisted the spare "Hathaway" format for years, preferring layouts that used multiple photographs.[66]

The friction surrounding photography stemmed from two fundamentally different understandings of the medium in a way that highlights Ogilvy's nuanced understanding of both the photographic image and the touristic mind-set. The BTA looked at photos as a means of showcasing a long roster of attractions. Images simply indexed the quantity of sights Great Britain had to offer American vacationers. Ogilvy, however, was not interested in quantifying Britain's landmarks but in animating the fantasies Americans had about Britain. He recognized that a powerful photograph not only documented what a place looked like but overlaid it with narratives of consumer desire.[67] It introduced the elements of time and materiality by imparting a message fundamental to selling tourist travel: what's pictured is real and can be seen in person. Ogilvy called these types of photographs "mouth watering images." For him, the image acted as a snare: it piqued the reader's wanderlust and triggered a visceral response.[68] In this regard, destination photographs needed a quality closer to what Barthes called the punctum. For Barthes, the punctum was the idiosyncratic detail that "rises from the scene, shoots out of it like an arrow, and pierces" the viewer to communicate in a subjective manner the photographic medium's fundamental message—"that-has-been." Pricked by the punctum, the viewer could understand that at one time and place the depicted subject was undeniably a part of the material world. Ogilvy viewed photographs in much the same manner and sought out images that pricked through the page to convey the scene's fundamental materiality—the cathedral, campus, or village pictured was a real place that the reader could corporeally experience.[69]

Copy compounded this effect by hailing readers in the present tense. As one ad described the experience of entering a cathedral town, "The first thing you notice is the peace. It isn't a dumb silence but a gentle harmony of sounds. The whirr of a lawnmower. The slippered footsteps of devout men. The creak of praying oaks." Another asked readers: "Where else could you be but London?" Above, a candidly snapped photo showed the royal party settling into their seats before the start of a play. "The present tense is the potent sense," *Printers' Ink* columnist Hal Stebbins observed of the ad. "People may believe in the hereafter but they live in the here-and-now. So whatever is happening to the lives of the people in your copy is happening *now*."[70] Working in combination, image and copy depicted touristic fantasies, like sitting next to the queen of England at a West End performance, as having all the materiality of the immediate moment in the reader's life. Operating on the same premise, the agency advised against scenes including tourists because they were already occupied. "We would rather create a marvelous setting," OBM explained, "which we invite the reader to fill."[71] Again, the most important message the photograph could convey was that the scene could be materially experienced. "People dream about visiting far-away places," Ogilvy wrote. "Your advertisements should convert their dreams into action—transforming potential energy into kinetic energy."[72]

Doyle Dane Bernbach (DDB), another agency in the vanguard of advertising's "creative revolution," adhered to the same principles in its campaign for the French Government Tourist Office (FGTO) in the early 1960s. "There is probably no area of public persuasion more suited to the creation of images than that of foreign travel and tourism," the bureau's public relations head explained of its advertising push. "The very motivation of public interest in travel is based on the conjuring of mental pictures of far-off places and distinctive ways of life."[73] Like the BTA campaign, the French bureau's photocentric ads were meant to create an atmosphere that lured the reader into the scene. In one celebrated instance, which Ogilvy later cited as the best travel ad he had seen, an old man and a young boy were pictured cycling down a tree-lined provincial road. Presumably returning home from the market, the cyclists carried two loaves of bread fastened to a rack behind them. "Next time you take a vacation," the headline suggested, "uncomplicate your life." Throughout the short blurb of copy, readers were addressed in the present tense: "You can shed your coat and tie, here. You can bicycle and keep your dignity. You can learn all there is to know about wine and cheese and bouillabaisse. You can fall in love, here. You can even stay forever."[74]

Like the BTA campaign, the ad relied on telltale symbols of national identity—berets, bread, bicycles—to mark the experience as quintessentially French. But also like the BTA ads, it went beyond evoking what Barthes might have called Frenchicity to convey a fundamental materiality. "Who can look at this tranquil country scene without longing to be there, cycling along that open road, befriended by cool green trees," Stebbins of *Printers' Ink* asked. Each ad in the series, he continued, "'puts you there.'"[75] By putting the reader "there," BTA and FGTO advertising communicated that the mythic settings of travel fantasies really did exist; they presented images that readers could recognize as both stills from past daydreams and glints of future memories. The new aesthetic was a far cry from the generic mountains, skylines, and cheesecake illustrations of the 1940s. No longer an advertising backwater, the most sophisticated destination ads were by 1960 at the industry's leading edge. In a changing consumer culture, the ads capitalized on the promise of meaningful, therapeutic experience that lay at the heart of service spending. By putting the viewer in the frame, the new tourism advertising told a story of journeys taken and dreams fulfilled that linked vacation travel with personal narratives of becoming.

Status and Segmentation

OBM's campaigns for Great Britain and Puerto Rico signaled a growing sophistication in destination advertising in another way: they reflected the growing tendency in marketing circles to divvy up demographically similar groups based on different motivations and desires. Echoing motivational research's call for a more qualitatively rich understanding of consumer behavior, OBM research director Myron J. Helfgott argued in a 1956 address: "The division of the population on the basis of personality dimensions may well be more relevant, and more discriminating than the traditional sociological definition we usually employ." The shared "emotional variables" that constituted a particular group, Helfgott explained, could be translated into symbols and themes that spoke to those defining traits.[76] Because OBM was attuned to the link between tourism and consumer fantasy, it recognized that not everyone traveled for the same reasons. Rather, different groups were spurred by different desires. Some went for fun, some for refinement, some for status, and so on. The agency's geographic renderings grew directly out of these imagined motivations. This meant that the landscape presented in an advertisement had to look like somewhere that could sate the desires attributed to the targeted group.

In the case of Great Britain, the nation had to appear desirable to the broad middle-income market—many of whom were traveling abroad for the first time. Ogilvy recognized that this group was ultimately drawn by the iconic sights they associated with the British Isles. But he also understood that tapping into popular knowledge could be a two-edged sword. If it allowed the agency to reference positive stereotypes, it also activated negative ones. In particular, OBM worried about two persisting points of notoriety—Britain's dreary climate and "excruciatingly awful" food. The familiar problem of "climate prejudice" was handled by banning any overcast settings from campaign imagery.[77] Ogilvy's nuanced way of looking at audiences led him to recognize that the second point of notoriety, Britain's infamous cuisine, could actually be used as a selling point. Knowing that many Americans feared the mysteries of Continental dining, he theorized that the familiarity of British food might actually make it more appealing to the novice traveler targeted by the BTA.

"Roast beef is the British ace of spades, which no French chef can trump," Ogilvy proclaimed in 1954. For American tourists on their first trip abroad and worried about snails hidden under exotic sauces, the traditional Sunday roast was a known quotient.[78] For Ogilvy and the BTA, the dish provided a way to allude to the cultural uncertainty that awaited first-time travelers in a more alien environment. In this regard, roast beef offered a line directly into the insecurities that middle-class tourists might feel about going abroad. A total lack of familiarity with the menu meant more than not being able to anticipate what would appear on the plate. Certainly there was the stress that came with ordering an expensive meal that proved unappetizing. But more than that, there was the specter of flubbing names, ordering the wrong types of dishes, and, more generally, looking foolish. The whole experience was metonymic for the disorientation and powerlessness a newcomer could feel in an unreadable cultural milieu. A later study by motivational research firm Social Research, Inc. called this tourism dynamic "fear of the unknown."[79]

With travel anxieties in mind, OBM crafted an ad built around a close-up photograph of a traditional roast, headlined: "The Roast Beef of Old England Is Back." The enormous hunk of beef, which, as one *New Yorker* critic pointed out, was preposterously large for an English roast, served as a symbol of both abundance and cultural familiarity. Copy explained that many tourists "appreciated the fact that the British don't disguise their dishes with indigestible sauces—or charge you outrageous prices. . . . There's an advantage, too, in being able to read your menu without the aid of a dictionary. You know exactly what you're ordering. And you can ask your waiter's advice without the embarrassment of a foreign language." Recognizing the food angle as fertile ground, Ogilvy revisited it over the rest of the decade. In 1957, he asked copywriter Clifford Field to create a follow-up that played on the same misgivings about "rich, complicated foreign sauces." Meanwhile, the agency reran the roast beef ad and created others, such as a "Traveler's Guide to Good Food in Britain."[80]

The English language provided another pipeline into deep-seated anxieties. Ogilvy asked his copywriters to play up the language angle, stressing that "you feel *at home* in Britain." One 1953 ad was built around the tagline "English Spoken Here."[81] "Their customs are different and fascinating," another copy idea noted. "But they talk your language (English) and they welcome American visitors with heart-warming friendliness and disarming informality." Ogilvy later wrote that, for Americans, fear was the second-biggest obstacle to foreign travel. "Fear that they won't be able to communicate," he argued. "Fear that they will lose their money. Fear of the foreigners. . . . Fear of the food. Do your best to allay these fears."[82] A common language and familiar cuisine offered soothing notes of familiarity. Directed at the right crowd, they could mark Great Britain as somewhere that offered the cachet of foreign travel without the embarrassments of fumbled phrases and scoffing waiters.

In taking this approach, OBM recognized that while many American vacationers were crossing the Atlantic by the 1950s, only some were uneasy about what awaited them on the other side. Well-to-do Americans who had vacationed overseas for years knew what to expect. The new "market of low-budget travelers," or those for whom foreign travel had only recently become affordable, did not.[83] Ads that touched on food and language anxieties were aimed at this heterogeneous group. They rested on a baseline assumption that novice travelers were especially status conscious and well aware of foreign travel's prestigious connotations.

For marketers in search of psychic factors that might spur a first-time trip to Europe, a desire to take part in rituals of upward mobility was one of the easiest motivations to spot. First, status anxiety seemed to be on the tip of nearly every social observer's tongue at midcentury. But just as important, foreign travel had long been a quintessential "leisure class" activity. OBM copywriters were repeatedly instructed to delicately work "prestige" into their appeals. In particular, copy directed toward "non-travelers" and "home-minded people" could highlight "the experiencing of some unique event that can be *retold* to homebound friends and is important and related to their 'prestige' feeling about European travel."[84] The agency's attempts to drench a British vacation with status connotations did not go unnoticed by savvy observers. The critic who took OBM to task for its oversized roast beef was even more put off by its description of Yorkshire pudding—a working-class side dish dressed up in the ad as a "patrician popover."[85]

Others in the industry drew the same connections, contrasting "travel centered" people, who were pleasure oriented and "worldly," with their "home centered" counterparts. The latter were as a rule much more sensitive to what others thought of them. "When these people travel," the Opinion Research Corporation reported in a 1962 study, "they do partly for the value that the trip will have for them after they get home in enhancing their position with their peers." The report suggested that advertisers mine this vein by emphasizing "what fun" new travelers would have recounting their experiences to friends at home. SRI laid out a similar profile of the "non-traveler" in a report for the P&O-Orient Lines in 1964, describing this group of consumers as eager to travel but fearful of rejection by their worldly, but "cold and distant," shipmates.[86]

Ogilvy, for his part, was not always certain how to address the diverse middle-income group. "The *new* travel market was brought up on funny papers—not Winnie the Pooh," Ogilvy lamented in 1957. "The new travel market has never read Ivanhoe."[87] Much of Ogilvy's success had come from his masterful understanding of the middlebrow imagination. The BTA campaign's Olde Curiosity Shoppe curios—literary references, historical sights, archetypal figures—came from the same symbolic universe as the dashing counts and imperial naval officers Ogilvy enlisted in other campaigns. As one *Harper's* profile duly observed, the Hathaway Man and Commander Whitehead were "contrasting studies in cosmopolitan elegance."[88] All reflected a middlebrow aesthetic that equated culture and pleasure with education and refinement. Ogilvy was less fluent, however, in the argot of mass culture. Motivational appeals that spoke to general desires, while subtly treading on common fears, provided a way to address the enigmatic mass market. Familiar food and a recognizable language offered a narrative of reassurance. For those contemplating a virgin trip abroad, OBM ventured that this was a powerful selling point.

Affluent tourists, on the other hand, accustomed to travel and eager to distance themselves from those who were not, could be addressed though a different body of symbols. This was exactly the stratum that OBM hoped to lure to Puerto Rico. On top of the campaign's genteel themes, the agency used the island's rum campaign, which it also held, to promote it as a distinctly highbrow vacationland. Beleaguered executives and socialites, highball in hand, were pictured lounging aboard sailboats or on sandy beaches while headlines explained that they picked up an affinity for Puerto Rican rum while on vacation. The connection between rum and tourism was strong enough by 1959 that a *New Yorker* cartoon could allude to a missing young socialite last spotted in one of Ogilvy's ads. "There was a photograph of Rodney, and the ad said he was very fond of Puerto Rico and rum," his mother explained. Similarly, the industrial arm of Operation Bootstrap plugged the island's recreational pleasures, selling the leisured way of life transplanted businesspeople could expect to find there. "The Executive Life in Puerto Rico," one ad announced. It pictured a stylish white woman standing statuesquely on a beach as a middle-aged companion let the surf wash over him.[89]

The agency's depiction of Puerto Rico stemmed directly from Ogilvy's image of what kinds of tourists he thought it was in the island's best interests to attract. "You cannot *accommodate,* you do not *want,* millions of blousy blonds from Hoboken or Chicago," he implored. Instead, the island should pursue "the best type of visitors at all times. . . . Tourists who will understand and respect Puerto Rico; tourists who will behave decently; tourists who will spend money."[90] Ogilvy's derisive attitude toward "vulgar tourists" was rooted in a snootiness that reared itself throughout his career. It echoed charges from across the ideological spectrum that mass tourism defiled, or, to borrow a term from Bernard DeVoto, "Coney Islanded," every place it touched.[91] By the postwar era, Florida had largely replaced Coney Island as the apogee of mass tourism. *Fortune,* which had been a breeding ground of sorts for mass culture critiques, maligned the Sunshine State as "a spell compounded of fantasy and mendacity and modern plumbing."[92] Miami Beach in particular was Ogilvy's favorite analogy, and he routinely warned against transforming Puerto Rico into another one. "If you swamp Puerto Rico with Miami Beach types," he cautioned one official, "your children will live to regret it."[93] But aside from Ogilvy's snobbery, his admonitions also grew from a fine-grained view of consumer culture that led him to differentiate between segments of the same broad demographic. Splintering the market in this manner meant evoking highly particular travel fantasies. In the case of Puerto Rico, it meant conjuring a dreamscape that could lure a junior executive while keeping his "blousy" stenographer at bay. Casal's cello, like a Sunday roast, would attract only certain people.

Into the mid-1960s, tourism remained a booming part of the advertising industry. Visually, the sleek, modern format that OBM introduced had become the default as dozens of travel marketers featured large, colorful, and mythically tinged photographs to lure visitors. The look had become so standard that Ogilvy suggested it might be time to try something new.[94] The agency stuck with its trademark look, but there were important changes afoot in tourism advertising. In the mid-1960s, a number of areas began spot advertising on television. France and Jamaica, both handled by DDB, led the way, pouring much of their ad budgets into television commercials in key local markets like New York, Chicago, and Miami. The agency's TV spots added sound and motion to the thematic appeals laid out in the print campaigns. Jamaica's ads, for instance, featured an infectious "electrifying, rhythmic beat."[95]

The great import of the new tourism advertising—pioneered in the campaigns for Great Britain, Puerto Rico, France, and a handful of other places—was not so much the sophisticated tone and modernized look but the larger aesthetic it introduced. The campaigns helped to standardize a type of marketing that focused on the therapeutic and experiential nature of tourism.

Instead of dangling a hodgepodge of generic lures in front of consumers, the ads told stories of personal development and idealized lives. Discussing travel writing in 1958, the novelist Paul Bowles observed that in the age of mass tourism the nature of the reader's geographic curiosity "has shifted from the place to the effect of the place upon the person." The same could be said of destination advertising. The new tourism ads held out the lure of settings where readers could imagine themselves experiencing the things they wanted out of life and developing into the kinds of people they wanted to be.[96] That might mean seeing hallowed tombs at Westminster Abbey, cycling through Provence, hearing cello music pour from a San Juan hacienda, or even laying poolside at Miami Beach. All spoke to different desires and senses of the self. And each one, marketers recognized, resonated with the daydreams of a specific segment of the larger vacationing public. While the campaigns spoke to different groups, they shared a recognition that the most powerful lure was a flattering reflection of the traveler him- or herself. One especially powerful reflection, the authentic self, would become particularly visible in the years to come.

6 GOING OFF THE BEATEN PATH
Authentic Places and the End of an Era

As the 1950s drew to a close, *Life* devoted an issue to the fast-changing face of American leisure. Russell Lynes, editor of *Harper's Magazine* and author of an earlier, famed table of highbrow, lowbrow, and middlebrow interests, revisited the topic to create a typology updated for the new decade. Lynes classified the recreational pursuits of the "Aristocrats," "Upper Bourgeois," "Lower Bourgeois," and "Peasants," noting their tastes and preferences in eighteen areas ranging from reading matter to vacationing. The author maintained that whether you rated as an aristocrat or a peasant had less to do with your wealth, background, or occupation than the zeal with which you pursued your leisure interests and the amount of deference you paid to "experts" in those areas. According to Lynes, aristocratic vacationers were "Discoverers of Little-Known Islands," always on the lookout for pristine areas. Upper-bourgeois tourists were "Museum and Cathedral Chasers," while their lower-bourgeois counterparts scrambled through "12 Countries in Three Weeks." The former spent a week learning the nuances of a single cathedral town, while the latter were whisked through whole countries so quickly they could barely remember where they were. Peasants, or those who "couldn't care less" about making their "leisure original or constructive," were "World and Other Cruise Takers."[1]

Lynes was not alone in commenting on Americans' changing vacations habits—especially the move toward an "off-the-beaten-path" sensibility. In a 1961 cover story, *Time* noted the same shift. "Having succeeded the British as the world's most relentless travelers," the newsmagazine noted, "Americans are becoming increasingly jaded with the major tourist encampments." The article laid out a narrative of postwar vacationing in which American travelers first flocked to Britain and France, then on to Italy and Spain, and finally on to the Caribbean. The crowd caught up with them at each spot, though, and by the early 1960s, trendsetters were squeezed to the far ends of the earth—Tahiti, Fiji, India, Nepal, Thailand, Kenya, Zanzibar, Antigua, the Greek Isles, and other novel destinations. Six weeks later, *Newsweek* also featured a cover story on the topic: "Summertime '61: Vacations Off the Beaten Track." As the decade wore on, the off-the-beaten-path narrative continued to gain steam.[2]

"Searching for Some Fresh Identity"

As Lynes and others had sensed, many Americans' travel tastes had started to change by the late 1950s. Some people were simply looking for new places to go. Others hoped to get away from crowds that, for them, had grown unbearable at popular sites. One *Atlantic Monthly* correspondent complained of being so "hemmed in by hundreds of thousands of half-familiar faces and seersucker suits" that "there are times when you can't see the Europeans for the Americans." Bernard DeVoto vowed to never again write about New England's vacation charms after viewing the summer crowds in 1955, calling the coast of Maine "a jerry-built, neon-lighted, overpopulated slum."[3] Exasperated with the crowds streaming into Washington, D.C., for the city's annual Cherry Blossom Festival, one newspaper editor issued a call to chop the trees down. "Hordes of tourists trample us natives into a pulp," he railed. "Savage children from the hinterland hurl bowls of food at you, flying elbows tattoo your ribs, people from Dubuque shout greetings . . . to people from Walla Walla." This sort of antitourist screed was partly rooted in mass culture critiques. But it also pointed to a backlash that had made its way into the larger travel boom narrative.[4]

American Express first noticed its clients in Europe going off the well-worn circuit in the mid-1950s when they started renting cars to escape the crowds. In the world of guidebooks, Arthur Frommer's *Europe on $5 a Day* appeared in 1957 and soon became a bible for young Americans looking to "rough it" across Europe. Domestically, vacation mecca Miami Beach saw a rash of empty hotel rooms in the late 1950s for the first time since the war. Industry watchers speculated that the missing tourists had moved on to the Caribbean. New visitors to the islands were lured by plummeting airfare, tropical beaches, and brand-new resorts constructed with middle-income Americans in mind.[5] The tourist migration was partly the product of waning prejudices toward areas outside Western Europe. "People with money and plenty of time to travel seem to be thinking in broader terms today than they did 10 or 15 years ago," Thomas Cook & Son president Edward O'Connor observed in 1959, attributing part of that change to "broader views on questions of race and color." *Harper's*, by the late 1950s, reported sightings of midwestern housewives as far away as Istanbul.[6]

Shifting vacation patterns also owed much to structural changes in the tourist industry. The Caribbean migration, in particular, was part of a larger phenomenon that saw well-financed developers undertake colossal projects to turn remote areas into mass-marketed tourist destinations. The first to appear was animation mogul Walt Disney's Orange County, California, theme park, Disneyland, which opened to great fanfare in 1955. Meticulously engineered, the resort was designed to offer middle-class families refuge from the uncertainties of modern life in the park's idealized landscapes, modeled after Disney's films and television programs. The exponentially more ambitious Walt Disney World, created as an independent vacation destination to offer tourists an even more elaborately self-contained universe, followed in 1971, rising out of the central Florida wilderness.[7] Similarly, Vail, Colorado, which debuted in 1962, was the product of a six-year endeavor to build a ski destination from scratch. Previously, ski areas had been developed out of rural mountain towns and appealed to an eclectic mix of ski enthusiasts and the glitterati. Vail, however, was designed from the ground up for upper-middle-class people who had little ski experience but nevertheless yenned for a vacation home. Industry observers looked admiringly across the Atlantic, as well, marveling at the success of Club Méditerranée's Tahitian-themed resort chain, which by the mid-1960s numbered eighteen sites. In one regard, these developments harkened back to the railroad's resort-building efforts at the turn of twentieth century. The new developers differed from their predecessors in two important ways, though. They were transnational in scope and targeted a mass market rather than the genteel travelers sought by the railroads. "We produce vacations just as another firm, might produce, say, automobiles," Club Med president Gilbert Trigano glibly explained.[8]

While some vacationers wanted to escape the crowds, others explicitly wanted to escape the standardizing aesthetics of mass tourism. Exclusive Caribbean resorts became a favorite with wealthy vacationers who, according to New York City travel agent Hans Helbing, "want more than anything else to relax and escape typical resort atmosphere." Jet travel and a state-of-the-art runway made Tahiti a popular destination with affluent tourists in search of unsullied places. But as one travel agent warned in 1960, "If you want to see it the way it was when Gauguin lived there you absolutely have to go this year. Next year: Howard Johnson's." Similarly, the cartoon illustrating Lynes's island-hopping aristocrats noted that "of course, when the tourists find it, it'll be ruined."[9] Such observations reflected a mounting sense of dread among travel enthusiasts and elites. The prospect of a blaze-orange roof towering over the Tahitian palms may have been a stretch, but it spoke to worries that an industrialized multinational tourist trade now reached into even the most far-flung places, transforming their landscapes with remarkable speed. The subset of romantic travelers chronicled by writers like Somerset Maugham and Paul Bowles in the 1940s could always find a Himalayan mountain or Saharan desert in which to seek refuge. But even these remote locales, observers lamented, were being drawn into the industry's orbit. By 1967, Pan Am had built a hotel in Samoa to house American tourists and had two more under construction in Tahiti and New Zealand.[10]

Viewed in this light, travel took on the quality of a race against time: no matter how far afield one went, mass tourism's homogenizing agents were never far behind. And with the blueprints for jumbo jets, or "cattle cars" as some critics called them, on drafting boards at Boeing, the stakes were never higher.[11] With so much of the globe already swallowed up, self-stylized travelers, or those who recognized that travel's etymological roots lay in the term "travail," as mass tourism critic Daniel Boorstin insisted, could view their travels as quests to experience what few authentic places still remained. The spread of this antitourist sentiment signaled a changing stance among many observers toward the desirability of technological progress and easy mobility. Whereas for decades social commentators had largely celebrated the modernizing thrust of a rapidly growing transport system, the off-the-beaten-path narrative recast modern travel infrastructure as a pernicious force, little by little destroying authentic places. Such concerns continued to build, and by the mid-1970s the British scholars Louis Turner and John Ash could liken the global tourist trade to "King Midas in reverse," seeing in it "a device for the systematic destruction of everything that is beautiful in the world."[12]

Although there were travelers who sought out fresh areas and experiences from the earliest days of tourism, notions of authenticity were a minor theme throughout most of the postwar vacation boom. By the late 1950s, however, concerns about authenticity were far more common. *Holiday*, for instance, devoted theme issues to Africa and the South Pacific for the first time in 1959 and 1960. In both cases, the magazine glowingly portrayed the regions as outside the circuit of modern life. "The Pacific," the editors noted, "is a treasure house of romance. Its tropical islands spell escape, languor, peace to the discipline-weary man of the West."[13] *Time* remarked in its 1961 cover story that "apart from seeking new horizons merely because they are there, U.S. travelers seem to be searching for some fresh identity with the elemental life and with the far past. They search for remnants of ancient civilizations, for the humbling majesty of raw, rugged nature, and for the mystique of island living—a symbolic as well as a genuine detachment from the rest of the world."[14]

Marketers recognized the growing attraction of the authentic and helped inflate its appeal. Ogilvy, who knew full well that tourist travel was especially sensitive to fashions, recognized by the late 1950s that "fundamental" sights and cultural familiarity might not offer the same draw they once did. Rather, novelty and fun were surpassing custom and refinement as the primary motivations to go abroad. OBM had found great success with Great Britain's "cottage and smocks" image in the 1950s; but to many tourists in the next decade, especially young travelers, those traits meant stodginess, not charm. A 1961 planning document noted that the "young like fun, and Britain may be thought of as deficient in fun." The very fact that English was spoken there made it less "adventurous."[15] Around this time, Ogilvy began considering a host of new ideas about how to recast Britain as a fun destination. After meeting with the secretary of the Parliamentary Committee on Tourism, W. R. Reese-Davis, in 1960, he reported that Britain's relaxed sex mores might be an affective appeal. Summarizing Reese-Davis's suggestions, Ogilvy wrote that "men travelling alone have a lonely time in New York because this city is so puritanical. In London there are at least 50 first class dancing places where the girls talk English and will not only drink with you, but sleep with you. This could be made into a tremendous attraction for American tourists, although Mr. Reese-Davis volunteered that we might encounter some difficulty in projecting the idea in advertisements." Boosters have often tried to turn locals into tourism industry ambassadors.[16] Reese-Davis' misogynistic ideas went well beyond this kind of mobilization, though, identifying British women themselves as amusements.

Ogilvy eventually decided against courting the youth market with sex appeals. "You make a mistake if you assume that students cross the Atlantic to visit discotheques," he argued in 1966. "They want to see how your people live, not your imitation American swingers, but your real people." But although they were ultimately rejected, Reese-Davis's suggestions speak to the extent to which social norms were changing in the early 1960s. By then, the British capital was turning into the "Swinging London" that would fully flower by mid-decade. Ogilvy was eager to sell the city's dynamism in BTA ads, recognizing that it could attract the younger crowd. But, as he reported to his brother Francis, his hands were tied "because it is the policy to get American tourists out of London, where there aren't enough hotels."[17] Even still, Ogilvy was very open to moving away from the antiquarian image sown over the previous ten years.[18] That picture of Britain had been designed with a mass market in mind, which, by the late 1950s, Ogilvy was sure would never materialize.[19] A new image could reposition Britain toward the young travelers and others who were most interested in finding a good time and experiencing a sense of discovery.[20]

As OBM's hand-wringing indicated, tourism image shapers faced a new fork in the road by the early 1960s. One option was to hold on to a waning norm of sightseeing travel that had combined genteel touring with a modern leisure sensibility. This direction lent itself to traditional appeals because it emphasized a familiar circuit of "fundamental" sights. Each had to be seen in order to complete the rite of passage a tour represented. In Ogilvy's words, the trip was about collecting clichés. Seeing Britain meant seeing castles, cottages, and London landmarks. These ideas were grounded in a tradition that linked cultural pilgrimage with social mobility by way of education and refinement. The burgeoning alternative celebrated more therapeutic notions of unique experience and personal fulfillment. "The fundamental element" within this new type of tourism, historian Ellen Furlough has observed, "was the imperative to pay, in all senses, attention to the self, a perspective in tandem with the emergent mythology of consumerist self-fabrication." Geographic representation within this context would need to tap into desires for personal realization. As one agency man urged in 1964, the industry needed to treat consumers as "emotional [sic] complex, thinking individuals" who traveled to find self-fulfillment.[21] Travel was an opportunity for personal expression. Moreover, it was a brief interlude in life that allowed individuals to see themselves as independent entities, liberated from the external pressures and social conditions that cramped their style in everyday life. Given the opportunity to throw off these burdens, therapeutic travelers could seek out places that allowed them to develop from within as individuals.

According to this new logic, instead of castles, seeing Britain might mean a quiet, contemplative journey into a remote district not yet discovered by the masses. And while Ogilvy backed away from selling young women, others in the trade seized on the therapeutic appeals of sex and other hedonistic themes. DDB, for instance, included a bikini-clad beachgoer in a 1960 gallery of French types, each signifying a different city along a trek through France. Shot from behind to emphasize her rear end, the shapely young blonde—in an obvious double entendre—represented the seaside town "Nice." The National Tourist Office of Greece, a country closely associated with the "off-the-beaten-path" trend, combined sex appeal with cultural tourism in an award-winning international campaign applauded by *Printers' Ink* in the early 1960s. Created by Coleman, Prentis & Varley International, one ad showed two scantily clad models resting peacefully on the rugged beaches of Rhodes. With no one else in sight, the image alluded to the timeless and unspoiled enclave, outside modernity's orbit and free of its stifling conventions. In another installment, a mysterious nude figure wearing a mask and shot from afar could be seen balancing atop a pile of ruins. The surreal photograph appeared like something out of a dream, blending symbols of antiquity, mythological adventure, and hedonistic excess.[22] This new, sex-laden brand of advertising was not simply a nod to the cheesecake imagery that graced plumbers' calendars and low-budget travel ads of old. While they certainly relied on a similar visual appeal, the new tourism campaigns placed sex within a narrative of touristic quest and self-discovery. No destination was more associated with this dynamic than Club Med, which by the 1960s was attracting great attention in the United States. Premised on furnishing a Robinson Crusoe–like experience, Club Med's island and desert resorts offered a "complete rupture," as one host described it, from "everyday life." And as *Life* noted in 1966, the club's basic marketing appeal was the prospect of regeneration: "that man can be reborn on vacation—even to changing himself from a cringing mouse into the likes of Lawrence Arabia." Such dramatic transformations could occur, though, only outside the standard sightseeing circuit, where traditional aims of refinement and status seeking seemed to no longer hold sway.[23]

The antitourist pitch grew louder over the 1960s, especially in the advertising efforts of distant vacation spots. The Australian National Travel Association, for example, taunted readers in 1961, remarking that "Only One Person in a Hundred Should Vacation in Australia," then asking, "Is that Person You?" In a similar challenge, the India Tourist Office cheekily featured an image of the Venetian canals in a 1965 ad. "Lovely. Everyone knows," it read. Beneath appeared a photo of the floating palaces of Udaipur and the tagline: "Lovely. Heaven only knows." Each area made remoteness a selling point, issuing a challenge to the subset of affluent people who fancied themselves adventurous. The tourist boards of Colombia, Ecuador, Peru, and Venezuela may have been the most overt when they teamed up in 1965 to brand themselves "the Difficult Countries." Framing the region as the ultimate escape, they goaded magazine readers to "Visit the Difficult Countries before Conrad Hilton Does." "We felt there must be people around . . . who would be bored to take just another trip to Miami or Europe," a representative of the agency behind the campaign explained.[24] Roughing it led travelers to seek out places farther and farther afield. In New York City, travel agent Lars-Eric Lindblad set up a specialty shop offering adventure vacations to Antarctica, Mongolia, and deep into the Amazon Basin. And by the mid-1970s, the writer Paul Theroux could report running into young American travelers scattered across dusty villages in Iran and Afghanistan. At around the same time, the U.S. State Department found it necessary to warn young American tourists of the strict drug laws and brutal prisons they could expect to find at off-the-beaten-path destinations—an image later immortalized in the film *Midnight Express* (1978).[25]

The self-realization trend extended to domestic vacationing as well. The *Saturday Evening Post* reported in 1957 that farm vacations were becoming increasingly attractive to Americans who wanted to pay homage to "the self-reliance and self-sufficiency that America stands for." *Look* ran a 1958 photo-essay profiling advertising executive Tom Buck, who eschewed a traditional holiday by taking his family on a sixteen-day trek, via covered wagon, from Morristown, New Jersey, to Pennsylvania Dutch country. The journey was a strenuous one, and Buck lost fifteen pounds by its end.[26] Taken as a whole, the off-the-beaten-path ads and articles showed a group of Americans willfully rejecting the standard vacation options of the day. But beyond ennui, they suggested a growing urge among some to bow out of the travel circuits that had given rise to industrial society and been central to conceptions of cultural modernity. Going off the beaten path spoke to a romantic instinct that there were still authentic places out there beyond the tourism industry's homogenizing reach—places where visceral experiences could trigger moments of self-realization. "Looking for yourself?" the New Zealand Government Tourist Office asked Americans in 1971. "Try Looking in New Zealand." Such appeals were in some ways a high-modern reincarnation of earlier antimodern sentiments.[27] What differed, though, were the elements the narrative brought together. Native Americans, no longer so exotic, were replaced by Amazonian tribal people; Ayer's Rock stood in for El Capitan. And whereas the earlier version promised awakening from modernity's lulling comforts, high-modern antimodernism offered fun unfiltered through the institutions of mass culture. Perhaps most important, the animating impulse behind the journey had shifted from steeling oneself to finding oneself. Whether that involved trekking through Greece or wading in a tropical lagoon, the objective was the same: the authentic experience and its validation of one's life as irreducibly unique.

The Decline of Mobility Culture

The life-stylization trends playing out in the early 1960s were one indication that a distinct era in travel was coming to a close. Another was that the U.S. government began to disincentivize foreign tourism for the first time since World War II. In 1961, duty-free limits were dramatically lowered from $500 to $100. This represented a major policy shift, as a decade earlier the ceiling had been raised to stimulate American spending abroad.[28] Simultaneous with this policy change was the first initiative to stoke foreign travel *to* the United States when Dwight Eisenhower declared 1960 "Visit the United States of America" year. The federal government's newfound commitment to the domestic trade had been spurred by cries that the biggest chunk of the $3.5 billion trade deficit was constituted by a widening "travel gap." By that point, American tourists overseas were outspending visitors to the United States by $1.1 billion.[29] At the time, the nation was spending less to promote its tourist trade abroad than Finland and Pakistan. And not surprisingly, such lackluster efforts yielded few visitors. While over 1.6 million Americans traveled outside North America in 1960, the United States hosted only 602,000 vacationers that year. Stepping up promotions, according to "Visit the U.S.A." champions, would help close the overall balance of payments. The initiative was poorly funded in 1960 but got a three-million-dollar boost the following year when Congress created the U.S. Travel Service—this time housed in the Department of Commerce—to run tourist offices and promotional campaigns overseas. Having established its flair for tourism advertising, OBM handled duties for Great Britain, Germany, and France, with a series of ads modeled directly after the BTA campaign. This time, though, they were graced by scenes of a mythic United States, such as a riverboat steaming down the Mississippi.[30] When the "travel gap" began to widen again in the mid-1960s, the Johnson administration lent its weight to a "Discover America" campaign intended to keep American tourist dollars at home. In 1968, the administration went further, launching an official "See America" effort that combined advertising abroad with a threatened international-travel tax at home.[31]

Perhaps the clearest sign that a distinct moment in travel was ending could be seen only in retrospect: the bold predictions bandied about in the press and industry journals stopped coming to fruition. For decades, commentators had boasted of coming innovations and social trends that would revolutionize travel habits. While some of the most farfetched predictions, such as mass markets for personal planes, did not work out, the overall picture of travel in the near future was, for the most part, realized. In the 1910s and 1920s, industry boosters talked of mass automobile ownership. In the 1930s and early 1940s, speculation shifted to a booming airline industry. And in the late 1940s and early 1950s, it moved to the coming jet age. Each technology eventually reached a mass market. Commentators of the late 1950s and early 1960s speculated with as much fervor about the next revolution in travel— supersonic transport (SST). In a 1960 forum on tourism in the new decade, a group of *Saturday Review* commentators spoke with utter certainty about "the coming supersonic age" and the "Supersonic Sixties." That same year *Fortune* called SST the "next step to instant travel."[32]

At the time, the American, British, French, and Soviet aviation industries were launching ambitious programs to introduce the first commercial SST aircraft. These planes would fly at speeds of up to eighteen hundred miles per hour, making it possible to cross the Atlantic in an afternoon's time. The Soviets and Americans eventually abandoned their projects in the 1970s. The American project partly fell victim to public protest over the thunderous noise and uncertain environmental consequences of SST. The Soviets' entry was plagued by mechanical problems. The British and French found success working together, though. Unveiling the Concorde in 1973, the jet was celebrated as a technological marvel. Yet as a mode of transport, it never reached beyond the superwealthy. More than anything else, the plane became synonymous with the transatlantic "Champagne Set," with roundtrip tickets costing as much as twelve thousand dollars in the early 2000s.[33] In this sense, SST was more emblematic of tourism's Victorian past than of its present or future: a throwback to a Veblenesque era when leisure travel was an elite privilege. In 2003, Air France and British Airways, no longer able to afford maintenance and turn a profit, grounded the planes. In a column for the *New York Times,* screenwriter Larry Gelbart wrote what was both a fond farewell to the Concorde and a eulogy for an earlier optimism. "As a boyhood fan of such interplanetary travelers as Buck Rogers and Flash Gordon," Gelbart wrote, "I never dreamed that the future might arrive during my lifetime. It makes me especially sad to see that part of the future disappear." Buck Rogers–like visions of total mobility resurface from time to time in the occasional news story about the nascent space tourism trade. Yet accounts of maverick millionaires paying fortunes (the going rate in 2008 was thirty million dollars) for passage into space read as much like stories torn from decades-old science fiction volumes as glimpses at the future.[34]

Another set of predictions stopped panning out as well in the early 1960s. For the previous half century, successive waves of the labor force had won paid vacations. The length of those vacations got longer and longer, too, with each decade. In 1961, average vacation times for blue-collar workers had reached two weeks and for white-collar workers had risen to almost three. Vacation times appeared as though they would only continue to climb. One sociologist predicted that workers would enjoy nearly seven weeks a year by the end of the century. From the vantage point of the early 1960s, the prediction did not look far fetched. The number of labor contracts that offered senior workers four weeks of vacation had doubled to a third between 1957 and 1961. The Steelworkers, United Autoworkers, and United Packinghouse Workers all pushed for sabbatical plans during that period, ranging from a twelve-month vacation after seven years of service to thirteen weeks after five years.[35] But extended vacations would never become a reality. Rather, vacation allotments would essentially freeze at their 1960s levels. In 2010, the average number of paid vacation days for private sector workers in their first year of service was just under two weeks (nine days). For those with ten years of service it was just over three weeks (seventeen days). And for workers with twenty-five years of service at a company, it averaged just under four weeks (nineteen days).[36]

While the postwar travel culture *Holiday* helped to construct underwent massive transformations in the 1960s, the magazine itself changed dramatically as well. *Holiday* continued on through the decade, with its circulation topping the one million mark for the first time in 1964. Advertisers still looked fondly on the publication, too. David Ogilvy, Leo Burnett, Raymond Rubicam, and nine other Madison Avenue luminaries took the unusual step of praising *Holiday*'s selling powers under Ted Patrick's watch in a full-page *New York Times* ad in 1964.[37] But the management situation at the Curtis Publishing Company, which had entered a downward spiral that would unceremoniously kill the media giant by decade's end, made it difficult for *Holiday* to run as smoothly as it had in the 1950s. The company's new head of editorial content allegedly resented Patrick and worked behind the scenes to oust him. The *New York Times* ad, written by Ogilvy, was intended to make sure this did not happen. To add to workplace politics, Curtis senior management began imposing restrictive editorial guidelines.[38] The publisher announced in a mailing to advertisers in 1962 that its magazines were recasting themselves as "the voice and conscience of the competitive enterprise system." Ogilvy, for one, was given "the creeps" by the shift and queried Patrick on what that might mean for *Holiday*, signing off "God help you." Patrick responded, agreeing that the policy's "smug chauvinism" bothered him too. Two months later, Ogilvy was helping Patrick seek employment elsewhere, personally inquiring with top executives at American Express.[39] The period was a difficult one for Patrick personally as well. He lost his two closest companions—his wife and his dog—in close succession. Shortly after, Patrick passed away unexpectedly after a brief bout with hepatitis in March 1964.[40]

Patrick's death had a profound impact on *Holiday*. Curtis executives installed an underwhelming new editor, Don A. Schanche, and before the year was out, the magazine's longtime staff had made a dramatic exit. Patrick's four top deputies submitted their letters of resignation in unison that December. Two more top editors resigned within a week. In a show of solidarity, a roster of fifty-six distinguished contributors, including Slim Aarons, Elliott Erwitt, Arnold Newman, William Golding, Arthur Miller, William Manchester, and John Steinbeck, took out a half-page ad in the *New York Times* to salute them.[41] Schanche was soon relieved, and Caskie Stinnett, a writer and editor for the *Saturday Evening Post*, took over the magazine. While the circulation held steady, *Holiday* went adrift editorially. The humorist S. J. Perelman, once a frequent contributor, saw the late 1960s *Holiday* as an unfortunate cross between *Esquire* and *Playboy*.[42]

By that time, the Curtis Publishing Company was in serious financial straits, losing $73 million between 1961 and 1968. A new chairman, Martin S. Ackerman, responded by liquidating the company and shutting down the *Saturday Evening Post* in 1968. Ackerman was soon ousted, and after a legal fight, Curtis regained ownership of *Holiday* in 1970. The magazine was cut to nine issues a year, and its pages were resized to a standard eight-by-eleven-inch format.[43] Indianapolis businessman Beurt R. SerVaas took control of Curtis in 1970 and attempted to reenergize the company's publications, restarting the *Saturday Evening Post* with moderate success. But *Holiday* lost money and saw its circulation dwindle. In 1977, it was sold to the Long Island publisher of *Travel* magazine. The new *Travel-Holiday* was shuffled around the publishing industry, changing hands from Reader's Digest Inc. to Hachette Filipacchi, before being retired in 2003.[44]

The *Holiday* of the mid-1960s onward was a shell of its postwar self, and its position in the magazine industry was filled by a number of new titles. Cowles Communications, publishers of *Look*, started *Venture* magazine in 1964. The title was never profitable, though, and was closed down seven years later. Tellingly, many *Holiday* veterans reconvened at what would develop into the most prominent of the new titles, *Travel and Leisure*.[45] The American Express–owned magazine started off as a publication for the company's affluent credit card holders and soon developed into a traditional magazine. *Outside, Adventure/Travel*, and a number of other specialty publications followed in the mid-1970s. A host of new travel magazines—Condé Nast's *Traveler*, Arthur Frommer's *Budget Travel*, and *National Geographic Traveler*—appeared in the 1980s and 1990s to reach various segments of the tourist market.[46] While some of these publications have been successful, none occupies a significant place within the broader culture. Each could be one of the hundreds of narrowly tailored titles that blanket today's magazine racks. In this regard, they do exactly what magazines are supposed to do in the contemporary media landscape: deliver a well-defined segment of consumers with a shared set of interests and values. *Holiday* played a pivotal role in introducing this function into the media industry and broader consumer culture. But it was born of a very different era, when big glossy magazines had dominated national advertising. Sneaking in just before the emergence of television, *Holiday* was a bridge between the spectacular publications that dominated the first half of the century and the specialized titles that thrived after television. Readers paged through the magazine each month to find stories by Hemingway and photos by Cartier-Bresson. But as they did, marketers were also picturing these readers in new ways, defining them as types whose interests spoke volumes about their buying habits.

The magazine medium's visual nature is what motivated publishers to cover travel in such detail. But television could lay claim to the same virtues as magazines—visuals and a large national audience—with the added benefits of sound and motion. What television could not offer in the 1950s and early 1960s was the color and size that tourism marketers coveted. Yet the magazine monopoly over these virtues would be short lived, lost with the introduction of color TV in the 1960s.[47]

Mass magazines did not die out solely because of television, though. While TV did rob them of their greatest attribute, more sweeping changes were transpiring that rendered mass audiences, according to the new marketing calculus, less appealing in general. As industry analyst Peter B. B. Andrews argued in a 1953 *Printers' Ink* report, "Much has been written about the great post-war growth of the middle-class market. . . . No less sensational, however, is the phenomenal growth of the top-class market, those with disposable incomes of $10,000 a year and over. The top-class market, contrary to some misconceived beliefs, has been growing rapidly in recent years."[48] By the second half of the 1950s, the notion that specialized markets offered better prospects than mass markets was gaining steam.[49] As *Business Week* explained in 1959, "We may have passed the time when the number of people able and ready to buy a particular kind of product was limited to such an extent that mass production—with all its economies—was possible only by restricting choices offered. A car was a car, with little functional variation. Now, though, there are groups of people large enough and rich enough to support mass output of specialized products."[50] And as the business world thought more and more in terms of specialty markets, media companies increasingly saw their role in terms of sorting audience groups into smaller and smaller boxes. "I see a continuation of the current trend to less shotgun, more rifle shooting," publisher Gardner Cowles predicted in 1970.[51]

By that point, specialization could be understood by Madison Avenue's big-picture thinkers as part of a much larger social transformation through which a white-collar professional stratum would pull away from the middle-income pack in the decades to follow. This "new class" of well-educated bureaucrats, engineers, doctors, professors, lawyers, scientists, consultants, and others working in skilled professions would soon constitute perhaps a third of the market and command up to 70 percent of its spending power. And as DDB creative executive E. B. Weiss warned in 1971, the new class would have a voracious appetite for services and little tolerance for mass appeals.[52] A therapeutic ethos of absolute individualism was key to understanding this group. As Foote, Cone & Belding president John O'Toole explained, "Young people, and not-so-young people, are stating with growing volume and clarity, 'I am a unique and special individual. Pay some attention to my needs.'" The trick for manufacturers and retailers going forward was to cater to the diverse and dynamic tastes of consumers who understood themselves as creative beings, managing a lifelong project of personal development. Within this environment, the most desirable consumers situated buying and spending within an existential "process of 'becoming,'" as a pair of marketing professors described it.[53] Increasingly, then, each purchase, no matter how trivial, would become an opportunity for creative expression as consumers selected whatever option most spoke to their individual sense of self. For Weiss, this development meant an across-the-board "end of the staple," or one-size-fits-all product. "Fractionate or perish may be too dramatic," he observed, "but with each passing year it tends to become less dramatic and more of a blunt fact of marking life."[54]

Media specialization, as marketers understood it, was a means of accelerating this process by straining the affluent from the comfortable. From their perspective, there were two steps to market segmentation—a carving-up process and a sifting-out process. In the first, audiences were divided by interest. In the second, they were divided by buying power and consumer ethos. And for many advertisers, the second step was more important because it allowed them to reach those free spenders willing to pay a premium for products that somehow contributed to their core concept of self. The industrialized specialty foods that began appearing on magazines pages in the late 1950s offer a window into this process. The processed foods giant General Foods, for example, began running full-page, color advertisements for its international-delicacy line in *Holiday* in 1957. The "Gourmet Foods" campaign promoted products such as Numaki spread, a Japanese blend of chicken livers and water chestnuts, and Café Diable, a flammable Spanish desert. These sorts of foods had a natural appeal to well-traveled cosmopolitans, along with the not-so-well-traveled who nevertheless understood themselves as cosmopolitan types. But they had limited appeal to the vast majority of middle-income Americans at a time when culinary adventurousness had little draw, even among many of those who had vacationed abroad.[55] *Holiday* played a pivotal role in the shift toward the niche marketing logic that made it worthwhile for a company like General Foods to market Numaki spread in the first place. The magazine represented the early convergence of institutional marketing power, systematic research, and an increasingly rationalized service sector. Magazines dating from the nineteenth century had catered to specific interests, such as science or hunting. Nevertheless, there was a qualitative difference, in terms of social and economic impact, between a specialized publication produced by an industry giant like the Curtis Publishing Company and one issued from the industry's fringes, just as there was a difference between General Motors and a craft builder producing specialized motorcars. These types of large institutional players had access to cutting-edge research, production technologies, distribution networks, and promotional machinery unavailable to smaller players. Indeed, they used the tools of corporate marketing power not so much to cater to some existing, but unmet, demand for specialty items, as to systematically cultivate lucrative specialty markets.

Market research has rendered the media industry perhaps the most astute observer of slow-building, but momentous, shifts in American culture. When media companies identify and act on a social trend, as the Curtis Publishing Company did with mass tourism, they step out of their role as observer and begin to actively reshape that phenomenon. First, they produce a body of narratives and imagery that help frame the terms of discussion. And second, their actions transform business operations within the industries involved. Advertising vehicles, when successful, grow markets, changing them in the process; moreover, they enable industry players to adopt new marketing strategies that determine which products are brought to market in the first place. Thus symbolic dynamics and business dynamics merge to reshape trends and spawn new ones. Media companies navigate their way through this complex process in a way that is both deliberative and blind. In the former sense, they doggedly pursue greater advertising revenue. But in the latter, they pay little attention, if any at all, to the desirability of the social changes they set in motion. This combination of sheer will and utter obliviousness can have ironic consequences. *Holiday*, a magazine launched in response to egalitarian trends and designed to spur interest in distant lands, in the end helped show other media how to carve up society and put up blinders to a wider world.

Holiday caught the tail end of another early to mid-twentieth century current in American culture—the middlebrow media intended to gently introduce novices to the more noteworthy things in life, as sanctified by experts, whether it be good books, informed discourse, or tourist travel.[56] As with other middlebrow texts, *Holiday*'s image of culture was aspirational: great works, if properly appreciated, could broaden an individual's perspective. That valorization originated with experts, rather than lay audiences, because only they had the training and enlightened sensibility to recognize what was truly exemplary. Certain writers, photographers, and other artists, according to this view, were simply better and had more significant things to say. A degree of familiarity with sophisticated works and activities allowed ordinary Americans, who were curious but not necessarily well educated, to feel connected to a dynamic, refined aesthetic and glean a sense of distinction from it. *Holiday*'s vision of the middlebrow extended beyond travel to blanket culture as a whole. The magazine, for example, annually gave out *Holiday* awards, modeled after the *Michelin Guide*'s star ratings, to a handful of U.S. restaurants. Restaurateurs considered it an honor and a valuable marketing opportunity.[57] So while the magazine was not above running an article every now and then on burgers or beer, Patrick would never have dreamed of bestowing a *Holiday* award on a burger and beer joint.

Combining spectacular imagery, good writing, and a middlebrow sensibility was a good way to reach a massive, if not quite mass, audience throughout much of the twentieth century. Magazine publishers recognized as much. By midcentury, they also knew that boosting the tourist trade could help them tap into a thriving set of advertising sectors. It would be mistake, though, to see the vacation boom as simply a mirage conjured up by advertisers, publishers, and ideologues. The postwar years were a cultural moment in which vacations and mobility captivated the public imagination. This sense of fascination showed itself in works ranging from *North by Northwest* at movie theaters to Kay Thompson's pint-sized tourist, *Eloise*, on children's bookshelves. For editors like Ted Patrick, it seemed natural that if people had the time and money to see the larger world out there, they would want to. And when people were homebound, the next best thing was to imaginatively visit those places in the "lorelei of all media."[58] Genuine excitement thus converged with marketing strategy to frame the world in magazine pages through the eyes of the middle-class American tourist, producing catalogs of places out there to one day be experienced firsthand.

When taken as a larger body of popular geography, travel content metaphorically suggested a world of possibilities within reach of a mass mobile public. In this regard, the entire notion of a travel boom reflected the egalitarian assumptions that underpinned much of American culture at the time. When observers celebrated mass tourist travel as a social achievement, they were lauding a collective, rather than individual, experience. The sense of pride attributed to mass leisure helps us understand what many midcentury Americans felt it meant to live in a modern, industrial democracy. Among other things, citizenship meant that leisure experiences long monopolized by the few were quickly becoming an expectation of the many. This view, of course, ignored the poverty that persisted in rural and urban slums. And it overlooked the humiliating barriers African Americans and other minorities encountered. But throughout the ranks of the white middle-income masses,

Americans enjoyed a standard of living that was utterly without precedent. While this gave free enterprise ideologues powerful fodder for public relations campaigns, it also allowed ordinary people to live comfortably and travel to the places they had always wanted to see. Mass tourism also carried the tantalizing prospect of sowing global consciousness. As with paid vacation plans, the diplomatic aspects of international tourism were seized upon by policymakers as a way of solidifying American capitalism and wooing Cold War allies. But for many people who had witnessed two world wars in thirty years and faced the threat of nuclear annihilation, international camaraderie did not seem so much a lofty ideal as a necessity.

The ease with which egalitarian and utopian sentiments slid away from vacation culture, however, raises questions about the capacity of consumer outlets to bring about and sustain progressive change.[59] Despite the excitement, hopes, and rhetoric surrounding the travel boom, vacationing from the start was situated at the individual level within a framework of consumer entitlement and Cold War exceptionalism. Vacations were not just a chance to expand one's geographic horizons or exercise authority over one's time; they were manifestations of American economic and technological power. These narratives of prosperity and mobility merged to suggest that American culture uniquely afforded opportunities for individual development through leisure and consumption. Given the cost of travel and the sense that it was an opportunity to splurge, Americans understandably pursued the vacations that best fit their tastes and interests.[60] Advertisers cultivated this outlook, tailoring depictions of place around more and more idiosyncratic desires, expectations, and fears. While diversification in the industry yielded a wider range of options, it also splintered the sense of a shared vacation culture. Less the story of a budding industrial folkway by the 1960s, vacations instead began to tell postindustrial stories of authentic places and episodes of self-realization. In its myriad niche forms, tourist travel over the decades to follow resumed its place as a powerful, but now more nuanced, symbol of privilege and distinction.

EPILOGUE

From National Folkway to Personal Quest

Midcentury American tourist culture helped set the stage for larger structural adjustments to the global economy in the early 1970s and the more fragmented culture that has come with it.[1] The tendency to group consumers in terms of leisure and lifestyle interests helped convince businesses that instead of scattering shot at the mass market, they were better off targeting especially desirable niches. As *Sports Illustrated* executive Richard Neale succinctly put it in 1956: "Some people are more important than others."[2] Or put another way, it paid to screen out the bleacherites, blousy blonds, and backyard barbequers. Writing off the mass market cut the legs out from under Keynesian economics. According to its fundamental precepts, ensuring economic growth meant ensuring that consumer demand followed an ever upward trajectory, which would in turn generate rising levels of production. Good wages and ample free time, equitably distributed, were the motors that made the system go. For Keynesians, consumption was thus a means of achieving a wide range of desirable social goals like full employment, mass affluence, and a more egalitarian social order. What marketers eventually found, though, was that this consumer-centric system could create corporate wealth just as effectively, or maybe even better, when shorn of its social vision: concentrated affluence worked just as well as mass affluence. The same went for leisure. When the bottom strata of spending fell off, the "important" ones on top could pick up the slack. In this way, the marketing world's discovery of niches and lifestyles dovetailed with the business world's larger push to reassert control over the post–New Deal political economy. Indeed, the new marketing paradigm offered a model for a consumer society purged of the expensive labor concessions, like long vacations, that were becoming expectations of the good life.

For the tourism industry, giving up on the mass market for extensive travel meant that, in the long term, not as many people would need the time for lengthy trips. And not surprisingly, vacation time has contracted in the decades since the economics of corporate prerogative unseated Keynesianism in the 1970s. Put in perspective, expanding vacation times were among the first of many perks to go as employers grabbed for greater authority over employment terms. The "Great American Two Weeks" isn't what it once was; it isn't even two weeks anymore for many Americans, especially those in the now dominant service sector.[3] In 2010, one out of four Americans in the service industries failed to receive any paid vacation time at all. Within this wildly diverse classification, which includes everyone from financial advisers to fast food cooks, workers in low-wage sectors like retail, leisure and hospitality, and administrative and waste services accounted for 57 percent of those without vacations. In a sad but paradoxical twist to the industry's rise, only one of two workers in the leisure and hospitality trade receive paid vacation days themselves.[4] In telling contrast, 95 percent of workers remaining in the manufacturing sector in 2010 still earned paid vacations. Also by comparison, every worker throughout Western Europe, Scandinavia, Australia, and much of industrialized Asia statutorily earned at least a full month's vacation—a leave period enjoyed by only a sliver of the American workforce. In the United States, the only group that receives comparable time is employees with more than twenty years at the same workplace.[5]

The international disparity in vacation time separates middle-income Americans not only from their contemporaries in similar societies but from their parents and grandparents as well. In the past forty years, a decent standard of living has been redefined in ways that exclude lengthy opportunities to venture far outside work's grasp. The Wal-Mart cashier on a two-week jaunt through Europe has no place in the postindustrial order, even theoretically. For that matter, the ground occupied by the footloose teacher and middle manager has grown perilously thin, too. Yet for their predecessors in midcentury department stores, offices, classrooms, and factories, "two weeks with pay" made perfect sense. Even if relatively few made such journeys, the prospect struck observers as realistic and desirable in the context of industrial modernity. Perhaps most important, it passed as common sense that the chance to get away for a while was a legitimate expectation of working life in an affluent, democratic society; free time was one's rightful due for contributing to the commonwealth.

Holiday was not aimed at the blue-collar and lower-middle-class Americans who brought up the rear of the mass market. The magazine's interest in that group's travel habits went little beyond its symbolic value. Rather, marketers like the Curtis Publishing Company and David Ogilvy had their sights on those individuals scattered throughout the top half who considered travel central to their core sense of being. But although lower-middle-income Americans at midcentury weren't targeted, their contemporaries today live in a consumer culture that has been remade by the targeting process: one of endless variety for a leisured professional class and fading possibilities for those who serve them. As the anthropologist Sidney Mintz has written, "People live inside the time they think they have."[6] The new scarcity of free time, in this way, is part of a larger ratcheting back of living standards for much of the American populace—a cleaving of the midcentury vacationing public in two that has placed upper-income free spenders on one side and time-minding penny pinchers on the other. If the structural upheavals of postindustrialization were not enough, the end of the Cold War removed any incentive for showing off middle-income tourists as testaments to the managerial largesse built into American capitalism.

With little time to stray too far, it is not surprising that Americans are seldom characterized in terms of wanderlust anymore. Free time, or the lack thereof, explains only so much, though, not accounting for the many Americans who could see the world, even if in small increments, but lack the inclination to. If marketers cleaved top from bottom, they also exploded the top into countless pieces. Thus the dampening of American wanderlust also owes much to how sightseeing tourism has been redefined in this fractured context. Consumer culture in the late twentieth century proved fallow ground for an exploratory mind-set, as Americans were encouraged to train their sights inward. Tourism marketers were among the first to systematically cultivate this therapeutic mind-set. Much of travel's appeal, savvy marketers recognized, rested on fantasies of transcending the pack and affirming one's individuality. Although this was not the only way to sell tourism, marketers seized on it as the best way to sell the distant travel that notions like wanderlust had spoken to. New places provided the stage for processes of becoming as travelers sought out the transformative experiences that would bring their idealized selves closer into being. In the decades since, this experiential ethos has drifted across the broader spectrum of social life. It emphasizes a view of identity forged through immersion in unique leisure pursuits, rather than the common bonds of citizenship and a shared cultural milieu. Ironically, this development has made geographic curiosity just another indicator of consumer behavior, no different from an interest in marathon running or bow hunting. Each is a skeleton key to a larger set of preferences, tendencies, and values for marketers, hawking everything from cell phones to senatorial candidates, to build a sales pitches around.

But an interest in other people and places is not just a lifestyle indicator.

While the tourist imagination inevitably refracts its subjects through one ideological prism or another, at times radically distorting people and places, it nevertheless turns one's sights outward to the presence of a broader social world and other ways of being in it. It is in this regard that Americans' conspicuous absence from the global tourism circuit has been framed as an abdication of responsibility. "What are the costs of this for American's [sic] view of the world and for U.S. diplomacy?" *Time* and CNN's *Global Public Square* asked readers in 2011. Fairly or not, the view from abroad is that Americans are geographically unimaginative and disinclined to engage with a globalized world their nation has exerted unmatched power in shaping. "We're not a travel culture," was the exasperated explanation offered by one industry watcher.[7] Although low passport rates and stereotypes of American parochialism overlook the millions of Americans who do travel, as well as the millions more who would like to, they still highlight a resurgent isolationism that midcentury observers were sure the jetliner had finished off. According to this dubious rhetoric, a lapsed passport and willful disengagement from the world can be taken as patriotic point of pride; a well-inked passport, on the other hand, raises the specter of misplaced loyalties or an elitist disconnect from the tastes, values, and aspirations of ordinary folk. Thus the rule of thumb for image-conscious political figures today is to plan trips stateside. "Nantucket is delightful, Minnesota is great, even Florida in August isn't so bad," former presidential press secretary Ari Fleischer explained. "Just don't cross any international borders."[8]

The idea that seeing new places is of little interest to most Americans outside a nomadic professional class stands in stark contrast to the mass mobile culture many observers saw on the horizon at midcentury. Yet it is also the logical outgrowth of the market segmentation, experiential consumerism, and postindustrial service economy that tourism marketing helped usher into place. Each in its own manner has pivoted American culture inward, celebrating the unique interest, solitary act of self-realization, and pleasures of personal catering. Tracing tourism's path from national folkway to personal quest illuminates how the new marketing logic's atomizing thrust foreshortened the egalitarian potentials of postwar affluence. Knocking the dust off old terms like "wanderlust" and "two weeks with pay" uncovers the public desires for intercultural contact and free time that were also central to what vacationing meant a half century ago. It explains how John Steinbeck could survey the crowds of tourists abroad in 1956 and remark: "This is the Great American dream . . . to travel, to see the world."[9] And it provides a glimpse at an alternative, less parochial, and more equitably leisured vision of American affluence.

NOTES

ABBREVIATIONS

AB   Anita Brenner Papers, Harry Ransom Center, University of Texas, Austin
AC   Advertising Council Records, John W. Hartman Center for Sales, Advertising, & Marketing History, Duke University Rare Book, Manuscripts and Special Collections Library, Durham, N.C.
BTA British Travel Association
CM   Carson McCullers Papers, Harry Ransom Center, University of Texas, Austin
CPC Curtis Publishing Company Records, ca. 1887–1960, Rare Book & Manuscript Library, University of Pennsylvania, Philadelphia
DO   David Ogilvy Papers, Manuscript Division, Library of Congress, Washington, D.C.
EE   Eliot Elisofon Papers, Harry Ransom Center, University of Texas, Austin
JG   John Graves Papers, Harry Ransom Center, University of Texas, Austin
JJ   James Jones Papers, Harry Ransom Center, University of Texas, Austin
JW   John Wanamaker Collection, Historical Society of Pennsylvania, Philadelphia
JWP Jerome Weidman Papers, Harry Ransom Center, University of Texas, Austin
JWT J. Walter Thompson Company Papers, John W. Hartman Center for Sales, Advertising, & Marketing History, Duke University Rare Book, Manuscripts and Special Collections Library, Durham, N.C.
NWR Nancy Wilson Ross Papers, Harry Ransom Center, University of Texas, Austin
PRC Commonwealth of Puerto Rico
RL   Richard Llewellyn Papers, Harry Ransom Center, University of Texas, Austin

INTRODUCTION

1. Alfred Hitchcock, "Hitchcock Trailer: A Guided Tour with Alfred Hitchcock," *North by Northwest,* DVD, directed by Alfred Hitchcock (Burbank, CA: Warner Bros., 2004); Alfred Hitchcock, *North by Northwest* (Los Angeles: Metro-Goldwyn-Mayer, 1959). *Saturday Review* called films with these sorts of backdrops "travelogues-with-plots." See "Baedeker from the Balcony," *Saturday Review,* October 20, 1956, 47. On the term "vacationscape," see Orvar Löfgren, *On Holiday: A History of Vacationing* (Berkeley: University of California Press, 1999), 93.

2. On Keynesianism, see Alan Brinkley, *The End of Reform: New Deal Liberalism in Recession and War* (New York: Vintage, 1996), and Daniel T. Rodgers, *Atlantic Crossings: Social Politics in the Progressive Age* (Cambridge, MA: Harvard University Press, Belknap Press, 1998). On the emergence of a New Deal coalition premised on rising living standards, see Lizabeth Cohen, *Making a New Deal: Industrial Workers in Chicago, 1919–1939* (Cambridge: Cambridge University Press, 1990); Meg Jacobs, *Pocketbook Politics: Economic Citizenship in Twentieth-Century America* (Princeton, NJ: Princeton University Press, 2005); Thomas Sugrue, *The Origins of the Urban Crisis: Race and Inequality in Postwar Detroit* (Princeton, NJ: Princeton University Press, 1996); and Jefferson Cowie and Nick Salvatore, "The Long Exception: Rethinking the Place of the

New Deal in American History," *International Labor and Working-Class History* 74, no. 3 (Fall 2008): 3–32. On midcentury consumer culture, see Lizabeth Cohen, *A Consumers' Republic: The Politics of Mass Consumption in Postwar America* (New York: Vintage, 2003); Gary Cross, *An All-Consuming Century: Why Commercialism Won in Modern America* (New York: Oxford University Press, 2000); Andrew Hurley, *Diners, Bowling Alleys, and Trailer Parks: Chasing the American Dream in Postwar Consumer Culture* (New York: Basic Books, 2001); Shelley Nickles, "More Is Better: Mass Consumption, Gender, and Class Identity in Postwar America," *American Quarterly* 54, no. 4 (December 2002): 581–622; Elaine Tyler May, *Homeward Bound: American Families in the Cold War Era*, rev. ed. (New York: Basic Books, 1999); and Thomas Frank, *The Conquest of Cool: Business Culture, Counterculture, and the Rise of Hip Consumerism* (Chicago: University of Chicago Press, 1997). On vacations and consumer culture, see Susan Session Rugh, *Are We There Yet? The Golden Age of American Family Vacations* (Lawrence: University Press of Kansas, 2008); Bryant Simon, *Boardwalk of Dreams: Atlantic City and the Fate of Urban America* (New York: Oxford University Press, 2004); Shelley Baranowski and Ellen Furlough, introduction to *Being Elsewhere: Tourism, Consumer Culture, and Identity in Modern Europe and North America*, ed. Shelley Baranowski and Ellen Furlough (Ann Arbor: University of Michigan Press, 2001), 1–31; and Michael Berkowitz, "A 'New Deal' for Leisure: Making Mass Tourism during the Great Depression," in Baranowski and Furlough, *Being Elsewhere*, 125–40. On Fordism, see David Harvey, *The Condition of Postmodernity: An Enquiry into the Origins of Cultural Change* (Oxford: Blackwell, 1990), 125–40; Eric Hobsbawm, *The Age of Extremes: A History of the World, 1914–1991* (New York: Vintage, 1996), 263–77; and Jackson Lears, "Reconsidering Abundance: A Plea for Ambiguity," in *Getting and Spending: European and American Consumer Societies in the Twentieth Century*, ed. Susan Strasser, Charles McGovern, and Matthias Judt (Cambridge: Cambridge University Press, 1998), 457–58.

3. Much of the white-collar workforce received paid vacations by the 1920s, and they were written into the blue-collar contracts in large numbers for the first time in the 1930s and early 1940s. "The Expanding Vacation," *Fortune*, September 1961, 195–96. Also see Cindy Aron, *Working at Play: A History of Vacations in the United States* (New York: Oxford University Press, 1999), and Berkowitz, "'New Deal' for Leisure," 187–91, 193–96.

4. Although the construction of shared temporal frameworks has been central to the development of consumer culture, it has received little attention from scholars. My approach here is influenced by Leigh Eric Schmidt, *Consumer Rites: The Buying and Selling of American Holidays* (Princeton, NJ: Princeton University Press, 1995) and Arjun Appadurai, *Modernity at Large: Cultural Dimensions of Globalization* (Minneapolis: University of Minnesota Press, 1996), 66-85.

5. Christopher Endy, *Cold War Holidays: American Tourism in France* (Chapel Hill: University of North Carolina Press, 2004), 112–18, 137–49; Christina Klein, *Cold War Orientalism: Asia in the Middlebrow Imagination, 1945–1961* (Berkeley: University of California Press, 2003), 103–13; William D. Patterson, "In Defense of the Tourist," *Saturday Review*, January 12, 1957, 16.

6. Edith Efron, "That Persistent Traveler—the American," *New York Times Magazine*, July 7, 1946, 85.

7. For a good example of this historical narrative, see Foster Rhea Dulles, "A Historical View of Americans Abroad," *Annals of the American Academy of Political and Social Science* 368 (November 1966): 11–20.

8. Daniel T. Rodgers, *The Work Ethic in Industrial America, 1850–1920* (Chicago: University of Chicago Press, 1979); Michael O'Malley, *Keeping Watch: A History of American Time* (Washington, DC: Smithsonian Institution Press, 1990); John F. Kasson, *Amusing the Million: Coney Island at*

the Turn of the Century (New York: Hill and Wang, 1978); Catherine Cocks, *Doing the Town: The Rise of Urban Tourism in the United States, 1850–1915* (Berkeley: University of California Press, 2001); Lary May, *Screening Out the Past: The Birth of Mass Culture and the Motion Picture Industry* (Chicago: University of Chicago Press, 1980); Kathy L. Peiss, *Cheap Amusements: Working Women and Leisure in Turn-of-the-Century New York* (Philadelphia: Temple University Press, 1986); David Nasaw, *Going Out: The Rise and Fall of Public Amusements* (New York: Basic Books, 1993); Elliot J. Gorn and Warren Goldstein, *A Brief History of American Sports* (Urbana: University of Illinois Press, 2004); Warren James Belasco, *Americans on the Road: From Autocamp to Motel, 1910–1945* (Cambridge, MA: MIT Press, 1979); Clifford E. Clark Jr. "Ranch House Suburbia: Ideals and Realities," in *Recasting America: Culture and Politics in the Age of Cold War*, ed. Lary May (Chicago: University of Chicago Press, 1989), 171–91; Lawrence Culver, *The Frontier of Leisure: Southern California and the Shaping of Modern America* (New York: Oxford University Press, 2010); Aron, *Working at Play*.

9. Foster Rhea Dulles, *America Learns to Play: A History of Popular Recreation, 1607–1940* (1940; Gloucester, MA: Peter Smith, 1959), 365; "The New Leisure," *Holiday*, March 1956, 35.

10. Paul F. Douglass, "Foreword," *Annals of the American Academy of Political and Social Science* 313 (September 1957): ix.

11. David Reisman, Nathan Glazer, and Reuel Denney, *The Lonely Crowd: A Study of the Changing American Character*, abridged ed. (Garden City, NY: Doubleday Anchor, 1953); Martha Wolfenstein, "The Emergence of Fun Morality," *Journal of Social Issues* 7, no. 4 (1951): 22; Martha Gellhorn, "An Odd, Restless, Beautiful Country," *New Republic*, August 4, 1947, 27.

12. Wolfgang Schivelbusch, *The Railway Journey: The Industrialization of Time and Space in the Nineteenth Century* (Berkeley: University of California Press, 1986); Stephen Kern, *The Culture of Time and Space, 1880–1918* (Cambridge, MA: Harvard University Press, 2003); Joseph J. Corn, *The Winged Gospel: America's Romance with Aviation* (1983; Baltimore: Johns Hopkins University Press, 2002); Susan Schulten, *The Geographical Imagination in America, 1880–1950* (Chicago: University of Chicago Press, 2001); David E. Nye, *American Technological Sublime* (Cambridge, MA: MIT Press, 1994).

13. Jack Scott, "The Romantic Places to Go," *Cosmopolitan*, March 1958, 26; James L. Bossemeyer, "Travel: American Mobility," *Annals of the American Academy of Political and Social Science* 313 (September 1957): 114.

14. Phil Gustafson, "I Rode the Jetliner to Africa and Back," *Saturday Evening Post*, December 6, 1952, 125; Bernard Foley, "They Showed Me a New America," *American Magazine*, October 1948, 34, 147–48.

15. "Blue Ribbon Summer," *Holiday*, August 1952, 23; "The S.S. United States," *Life*, July 21, 62, 59; "Scenic Way to California," Burlington, Rio Grande, Western Pacific (1949), Ad*Access—Ad #T2412, John W. Hartman Center for Sales, Advertising & Marketing History, Duke University Rare Book, Manuscripts and Special Collections Library, library.duke.edu/digitalcollections/adaccess/.

16. My thinking here has been shaped by the works of theorists who have identified notions of modernity as rooted in the social, cultural, and economic dimensions of time-space compression. See Harvey, *Condition of Postmodernity*; Fredric Jameson, "Postmodernism, or the Cultural Logic of Late Capitalism," *New Left Review* 146 (July–August 1984): 59–72; Appadurai, *Modernity at Large*; and Anthony Giddens, *The Consequences of Modernity* (Stanford, CA: Stanford University Press, 1990). On movement as the central organizing concept of modernity, see Zygmunt Bauman, *Postmodernity and Its Discontents* (New York: New York University Press, 1997). On modernity, movement, and networks of mobility, see John Tomlinson, *The Culture*

of Speed: The Coming of Immediacy (London: Sage, 2007); John Urry, *Mobilities* (Cambridge, UK: Polity, 2007); Cotten Seiler, *Republic of Drivers: A Cultural History of Automobility in America* (Chicago: University of Chicago Press, 2008); Jeremy Packer, *Mobility without Mayhem: Safety, Cars, and Citizenship* (Durham, NC: Duke University Press, 2008); Karal Ann Marling, *As Seen on TV: The Visual Culture of Everyday Life in the 1950s* (Cambridge, MA: Harvard University Press, 1994), 164–201; Michael Sorkin, "See You in Disneyland," in *Variations on a Theme Park: The New American City and End of Public Space*, ed. Michael Sorkin (New York: Hill and Wang, 1992), 212–21; and Annabel Jane Wharton, *Building the Cold War: Hilton International Hotels and Modern Architecture* (Chicago: University of Chicago Press, 2001).

17. On magazines and cultural narrative, see Carolyn Kitch, *Pages from the Past: History and Memory in American Magazines* (Chapel Hill: University of North Carolina Press, 2005), 17. On postwar magazines and American culture, see James L. Baughman, *The Republic of Mass Culture: Journalism, Filmmaking, and Broadcasting in America since 1941* (Baltimore: Johns Hopkins University Press, 1992); Wendy Kozol, *Life's America: Family and Nation in Postwar Photojournalism* (Philadelphia: Temple University Press, 1994); *Looking at Life Magazine*, ed. Erika Doss (Washington, DC: Smithsonian Institution Press, 2001); Sheila Webb, "The Tale of Advancement: Life Magazine's Construction of the Modern American Success Story," *Journalism History* 32 (2006): 2–12; Joanne P. Sharp, *Condensing the Cold War: Reader's Digest and American Identity* (Minneapolis: University of Minnesota, 2000); Joanne Meyerowitz, "Beyond the Feminine Mystique: A Reassessment of Postwar Mass Culture, 1946–1958," *Journal of American History* 79 (March 1993): 1455–82; Eva Moskowitz, "'It's Good to Blow Your Top': Women's Magazines and a Discourse of Discontent," *Journal of Women's History* 8, no. 3 (Fall 1996): 66–98; David Abrahamson, *Magazine-Made America: The Cultural Transformation of the Postwar Periodical* (Cresskill, NJ: Hampton Press, 1996); and Elizabeth Fraterrigo, *Playboy and the Making of the Good Life in Modern America* (New York: Oxford University Press, 2009).

18. Richard Ohmann, *Selling Culture: Magazines, Markets, and Class at the Turn of the Century* (New York: Verso, 1996); Janice Cohn, *Creating America: George Horace Lorimar and the Saturday Evening Post* (Pittsburgh: University of Pittsburgh Press, 1989); Carolyn Kitch, *The Girl on the Magazine Cover: The Origins of Visual Stereotypes in American Mass Media* (Chapel Hill: University of North Carolina Press, 2001); Ellen Gruber Garvey, *The Adman in the Parlor: Magazines and the Gendering of Consumer Culture, 1880s to 1910s* (New York: Oxford University Press, 1996); Matthew Schneirov, *The Dream of a New Social Order: Popular Magazines in America, 1893–1914* (New York: Columbia University Press, 1994); Jennifer Scanlon, *Inarticulate Longings: The Ladies' Home Journal, Gender and the Promise of Consumer Culture* (New York: Routledge, 1995); Helen Damon-Moore, *Magazines for the Millions: Gender and Commerce in the Ladies' Home Journal and the Saturday Evening Post* (Albany: State University of New York Press, 1994).

19. My understanding of sightseeing tourism versus recreational tourism is influenced by Löfgren, *On Holiday*, and Harvey Levenstein, *We'll Always Have Paris: American Tourists in France since 1930* (Chicago: University of Chicago Press, 2004), xi–xii. On sightseeing, also see Judith Adler, "Origins of Sightseeing," *Annals of Tourism Research* 16, no. 1 (1989): 7–29, and Dean MacCannell, *The Tourist: A New Theory of the Leisure Class* (1976; Berkeley: University of California Press, 1999).

20. Theodor W. Adorno, "Free Time," in *The Culture Industry: Selected Essays on Mass Culture* (New York: Routledge, 2001), 190–91.

21. On tourism as a quest for authenticity, the classic arguments are MacCannell, *Tourist*, and Donald Horne, *The Great Museum: The Re-presentation of History* (London: Pluto Press, 1984). On authenticity and distinction, see Suleiman Osman, *The Invention of Brownstone Brooklyn: Gentrification and the Search for Authenticity in Postwar New York* (New York: Oxford University

Press, 2011); Sharon Zukin, *Naked City: The Death and Life of Authentic Urban Places* (New York: Oxford University Press, 2010); Bryant Simon, *Everything but the Coffee: Learning about America from Starbucks* (Berkeley: University of California Press, 2009); and Pierre Bourdieu, *Distinction: A Social Critique of the Judgment of Taste,* trans. Richard Nice (Cambridge, MA: Harvard University Press, 1984).

22. For similar approaches to popular geography, see Schulten, *Geographical Imagination in America;* Kristin L. Hoganson, *Consumer's Imperium: The Global Production of American Domesticity, 1865–1920* (Chapel Hill: University of North Carolina Press, 2007); Klein, *Cold War Orientalism;* Melani McAlister, *Epic Encounters: Culture, Media, and U.S. Interests in the Middle East, 1945–2000* (Berkeley: University of California Press, 2001); and Marguerite Shaffer, *See America First: Tourism and National Identity, 1880–1940* (Washington, DC: Smithsonian Institution Press, 2001). On symbols, patterns, and media culture, see Susan J. Douglas, "Does Textual Analysis Tell Us Anything about Past Audiences?" in *Explorations in Communication and History,* ed. Barbie Zelizer (New York: Routledge, 2008), 66–76; James W. Carey, *Communication as Culture: Essays on Media and Society* (New York: Routledge, 1989); James W. Carey, "The Problem of Journalism History," in *James Carey: A Critical Reader,* ed. by Eve Stryker Munson and Catherine A. Warren (Minneapolis: University of Minnesota Press, 1997), 86–94; Raymond Williams, *Marxism and Literature* (New York: Oxford University Press, 1977), 133; and Clifford Geertz, "Ideology as a Cultural System," in *the Interpretation of Cultures: Selected Essays* (New York: Basic Books, 1973), 193–229.

23. Edward W. Said, *Culture and Imperialism* (New York: Vintage, 1994); Raymond Williams, *The Country and the City* (New York: Oxford University Press, 1973).

24. Jackson Lears, "Making Fun of Popular Culture," *American Historical Review* 97, no. 5 (1992): 1422–24. Also see David Paul Nord, "A Plea for Journalism History," *Journalism History* 15, no. 1 (1988): 8–15, and Timothy Havens, Amanda D. Lotz, and Sierra Tinic, "Critical Media Industries Studies: A Research Approach," *Communication, Culture and Critique* 2, no. 2 (June 2009): 234–52.

25. David Ogilvy, *Confessions of an Advertising Man* (New York: Ballantine, 1963), 122.

26. John Urry, *The Tourist Gaze* (London: Sage, 1990); Hal K. Rothman, "Selling the Meaning of Place: Entrepreneurship, Tourism, and Community Transformation in the Twentieth-Century American West," *Pacific Historical Review* 65, no. 4 (1996): 525–57; Hal K. Rothman, *Devil's Bargains: Tourism in the Twentieth-Century American West* (Lawrence: University Press of Kansas, 1998); Christine M. Skwiot, "Itineraries of Empire: The Uses of U.S. Tourism in Cuba and Hawaii, 1898–1959" (PhD diss., Rutgers University, 2002); Susan G. Davis, "Landscapes of the Imagination: Tourism in Southern California," *Pacific Historical Review* 68, no. 1 (1999): 173–91. On the production of globalized space and economic power, see Neil Smith, *American Empire: Roosevelt's Geographer and the Prelude to Globalization* (Berkeley: University of California Press, 2003).

27. James W. Cook, "The Return of the Culture Industry," in *The Cultural Turn in U.S. History: Past, Present, and Future,* ed. James W. Cook, Lawrence B. Glickman, and Michael O'Malley (Chicago: University of Chicago Press, 2007), 308.

28. Bauman, *Postmodernity and Its Discontents,* 83–94. A "sensation-seeking life" is mentioned on page 92.

29. Cohen, *Consumers' Republic,* 292–344; Joseph Turow, *Breaking Up America: Advertisers and the New Media World* (Chicago: University of Chicago Press, 1997); Richard S. Tedlow, *New and Improved: The Story of Mass Marketing in America* (New York: Basic Books, 1990); Abrahamson, *Magazine-Made America*. On gated communities, see Simon, *Boardwalk of Dreams,* 196–216.

30. The sociologist Juliet B. Schor has called this American consumer culture's work-and-

spend cycle. See *The Overworked American: The Unexpected Decline of Leisure* (New York: Basic Books, 1993). DuPont vacation figures are cited on page 32.

31. International figures from 2007 study by the Mercer human resources consulting firm. Cited in Jeanne Sehadi, "Who Gets the Most (and Least) Vacation," CNNMoney.com, June 14, 2007, money.cnn.com/2007/06/12/pf/vacation_days_worldwide/#table; Olivera Perkins, "Smartphones Let You Take Work Anywhere, That's a Problem," *Plain Dealer* (Cleveland), July 27, 2009, A1; Scott W. Campbell and Yong Jin Park, "Social Implications of Mobile Telephony: The Rise of Personal Communication Society," *Sociology Compass* 2, no. 2 (2008): 372–87; Rebecca Ray and John Schmitt, *No-Vacation Nation* (Washington, DC: Center for Economic and Policy Research, 2007), 1; "Take Back Your Time," timeday.org/default.asp.

32. On outbound tourism expenditures, see United Nations World Tourism Organization, *UNWTO World Tourism Barometer*, April 2010, 8. For recent population figures, see the "United States," "Germany," and "United Kingdom" entries in the Central Intelligence Agency, *CIA World Factbook*, cia.gov/library/publications/the-world-factbook/geos/us.html.

33. Jeffrey Bartholet, "A Team of Expatriates," *Newsweek*, January 17, 2009; Jane L. Levere, "Scrambling to Get Hold of a Passport," *New York Times*, January 23, 2007.

34. Horace Sutton, "Travelers Raise the Storm Signal," *Saturday Review*, January 12, 1957, 19; Joseph Wechsberg, "The American Abroad," *Atlantic Monthly*, November 1957, 265.

CHAPTER ONE

1. Foster Rhea Dulles, *America Learns to Play: A History of Popular Recreation, 1607–1940* (1940; Gloucester, MA: Peter Smith, 1959), 319. For a similar narrative of steady, mounting progress, see Sidney G. Watson, "From Class to Mass: The Evolution of Travel," *Current History*, May 1939, 60.

2. "Vacations: America's Summer Travelers Take Many to Grand Canyon," *Life*, August 5, 1940, 59. Radio personality Larry Nixon, host of WNEW's "The Travel Man," put it more succinctly: "You don't have to be rich to enjoy your vacation in America." Larry Nixon, *American Vacations* (Boston: Little, Brown, 1939).

3. "American Tourism Heads for Top," *Business Week*, May 18, 1940, 24. Also see G. R. Stahl, "This Vacation Business," *Barron's*, February 22, 1937, 19; "America's Ready for Travel Boom," *Business Week*, December 2, 1939, 16–17; James A. Wales, "Advertising Lifts Travel from the Slumps," *Advertising and Sales*, August 1938, 38. Shelley Baranowski and Ellen Furlough point out that by 1940 the tourism industry was on par with the oil, lumber, and auto manufacturing fields. See their introduction to *Being Elsewhere: Tourism, Consumer Culture, and Identity in Modern Europe and North America*, ed. Shelley Baranowski and Ellen Furlough (Ann Arbor: University of Michigan Press, 2001), 15; "Six Billion Dollar Travel Budget Creates Unique Marketing Problem," *Sales Management*, June 15, 1940, 42; Albert K. Dawson, "The Recreation Industry," *Survey Graphic*, March 1938, 184.

4. "Travel Pickup," *Business Week*, July 28, 1934, 28; "U.S. on the Move," *Printers' Ink*, August 2, 1934, 54; "Travel—One Business That's Up," *Business Week*, June 4, 1938, 13.

5. On getting and spending as folkways, see Charles F. McGovern, *Sold American: Consumption and Citizenship, 1890–1945* (Chapel Hill: University of North Carolina Press, 2006). On vacationing and liminal experience, see Victor W. Turner and Edith Turner, *Image and Pilgrimage in Christian Culture* (New York: Columbia University Press, 1978), 1–39; Victor W. Turner, "Variations on a Theme of Liminality," in *Secular Ritual*, ed. Sally F. Moore and Barbara G. Myerhoff (Amsterdam: Van Gorcum, 1977), 36–52; and Erik Cohen, "Tourism as Play," *Religion* 15 (1985): 291–304.

6. Cindy Aron, *Working at Play: A History of Vacations in the United States* (New York: Oxford University Press, 1999), 244; Neil Harris, "On Vacation," in *Resorts of the Catskills* (New York: St. Martin's Press, 1979), 101–8; "Vacations with Pay," *Factory Management and Maintenance*, June 1935, 248; "Two Weeks or Bust," *Outlook*, June 19, 1923, 657.

7. "More Paid Vacations in 1936," *Forbes*, May 1, 1936, 18; "Bigger and Better Vacations," *Management Review* 27, September 1938, 306; "Trends in Company Vacation Policies," *Management Review* 29, May 1940, 174; U.S. Bureau of Labor Statistics, *How American Buying Habits Change* (Washington, DC: U.S. Government Printing Office, 1959), 199; "Vacations: 1942," *Business Week*, May 3, 1942, 57; Michael Berkowitz, "A 'New Deal' for Leisure: Making Mass Tourism During the Great Depression," in Baranowski and Furlough, *Being Elsewhere*, 191–93; "Another 'Hidden' Raise," *Business Week*, November 13, 1943, 103.

8. Roy Rosenzweig, *Eight Hours for What We Will: Workers and Leisure in the Industrial City, 1870–1920* (New York: Cambridge University Press, 1983); Lawrence B. Glickman, *A Living Wage: American Workers and the Making of Consumer Society* (Ithaca, NY: Cornell University Press, 1997), 99–107; Michael O'Malley, *Keeping Watch: A History of American Time* (Washington, DC: Smithsonian Institution Press, 1990), 256-262.

9. George H. Copeland, "The Vacation Scene—Second War Summer," *New York Times*, June 13, 1943, SR3; "Go to the Speed Boat Races at Detroit," *New York Times*, August 21, 1927, XX17; David William Moore, "'Two Weeks'—or Bust!" *Outlook*, August 29, 1923, 669; Helen Bell Grady, "Two Weeks for Mother—with Pay," *American Home*, August 1939, 38. On shared temporal frameworks, see Eviatar Zerubavel, *Hidden Rhythms: Schedules and Calendars in Social Life* (Chicago: University of Chicago Press, 1981), 14; Pierre Bourdieu, *The Logic of Practice* (Stanford, CA: Stanford University Press, 1990), 80–111; and E. P. Thompson, "Time, Work-Discipline, and Industrial Capitalism," *Past and Present* 38, no. 1 (December 1967): 56–97.

10. Ethel Romig Fuller, "Prayer for the Vacations of Young Office Workers," *Independent Woman*, July 1939, 178.

11. Wales, "Advertising Lifts Travel from Slumps," 36.

12. Kenneth T. Jackson, *Crabgrass Frontier: The Suburbanization of the United States* (New York: Oxford University Press, 1985), 161; Warren James Belasco, *Americans on the Road: From Autocamp to Motel, 1910–1945* (Cambridge, MA: MIT Press, 1979); Robert S. Lynd and Helen Merrell Lynd, *Middletown: A Study in Modern American Culture* (New York: Harvest Books, 1929), 260, 262–63.

13. "American Tourism Heads for the Top," 20; U.S. Bureau of Labor Statistics, *Family Expenditures in Selected Cities, 1935–1936: Travel and Transportation* (Washington, DC: U.S. Government Printing Office, 1940), 3; U.S. Bureau of Labor Statistics, *How American Buying Habits Change*, 184; American Automobile Association, *Americans on the Highway: A Survey of Recent Trends in Tourist Travel* (Washington, DC: AAA, 1940), 6.

14. "The Great American Roadside," *Fortune*, September 1934, 53–54.

15. Anne Cameron, "A Vacation Tour through the National Parks," *Saturday Evening Post*, August 12, 1933, 14.

16. Sidney Drake, "The Fine Art of Adventuring," *Holiday* (AAA), October 1930, 15; Horace Coon, *100 Vacations Costing from $50 to $500: A Consumer's Guide to Holiday Spending* (New York: Doubleday, Doran and Co., 1939), 1; "Horizons and Holidays," *Holiday* (AAA), November 1930, 9.

17. "Save to Travel Clubs Flourish," *Travel Talks*, May 1925, 16; "Vacations," *Nation*, August 17, 1932, 137.

18. Lorraine Coons and Alexander Varias, *Tourist Third Cabin: Steamship Travel in the Interwar Years* (New York: Palgrave, 2003), 14, 16–18; Mark Rennella and Whitney Walton, "Planned Serendipity: American Travelers and the Transatlantic Voyage in the Nineteenth and Twentieth

Century," *Journal of Social History* 38 (2004): 365–83; Christopher Endy, *Cold War Holidays: American Tourism in France* (Chapel Hill: University of North Carolina Press, 2004), 16; Horace Sutton, *Travelers: The American Tourist from Stagecoach to Space Shuttle* (New York: William Morrow and Co., 1980), 190.

19. Donald J. Bush, "Streamlining and American Industrial Design," *Leonardo* 7, no. 4 (1974): 313–14.

20. Joseph J. Corn, *The Winged Gospel: America's Romance with Aviation* (1983; Baltimore: Johns Hopkins University Press, 2002), 16; Kathleen Barry, *Femininity in Flight: A History of Flight Attendants* (Durham, NC: Duke University Press, 2007); T. A. Heppenheimer, *Turbulent Skies: The History of Commercial Aviation* (New York: John Wiley and Sons, 1995), 36, 63–64. Only 2.2 percent of people flew for business that year and an even smaller group flew for pleasure (Research Department of the Curtis Publishing Company); *Saturday Evening Post Aviation Survey* (Philadelphia: Curtis Publishing Company, 1946), 35, box 109, CPC.

21. Marylin Bender and Selig Altschul, *Chosen Instrument: Pan Am Juan Trippe, the Rise and Fall of an American Entrepreneur* (New York: Simon and Schuster, 1982); "Pan American, Airways," *Fortune*, April 1936, 176.

22. Rosalie Schwartz, *Flying Down to Rio: Hollywood, Tourists, and Yankee Clippers* (College Station, TX: Texas A&M University Press, 2004). Interwar genre films are described in Roger Dooley, *From Scarface to Scarlet: American Films in the 1930s* (New York: Harcourt Brace Jovanovich, 1979). Grand Central Station opening quoted in Gerald Nachman, *Raised on Radio* (New York: Pantheon, 1998), 431.

23. Susan Schulten, *The Geographical Imagination in America, 1880–1950* (Chicago: University of Chicago Press, 2001), 204–28; "Baedeker of Business in New York," *Fortune*, July 1939, 109.

24. Roland Marchand, *Creating the Corporate Soul: The Rise of Public Relations and Corporate Imagery in American Big Business* (Berkeley: University of California Press, 1998), 291–311; David E. Nye, *American Technological Sublime* (Cambridge, MA: MIT Press, 1994), 203–224; Christina Cogdell, "The Futurama Recontextualized: Norman Bel Geddes's Eugenic 'World of Tomorrow,'" *American Quarterly* 52, no. 2 (June 2000): 225–36; Grover Whalen, "What the Fair Means to Business and Industry," *New York World's Fair Bulletin*, June 1937, box 44, folder 40, JW.

25. John Dos Passos, *U.S.A.: The Big Money* (1937; Boston: Houghton Mifflin, 1963), 493–94.

26. "Advertising for Tourist Business," *Printers' Ink*, January 11, 1934, 61.

27. "Save-to-Travel New Banking Plan" and "The Bower Savings Bank Is the First to Offer a Save-to-Travel Club," *Travel Talks*, January 1925, 10, 16.

28. M. Zenn Kaufman, "Travel Now—Pay Later," *Advertising and Selling*, March 31, 1932, 27, 46; "If Credit's Good, You Travel on It," *Business Week*, May 11, 1940, 24.

29. S. W. Holland to W. L. Nevin, June 24, 1929; T. A. Pendergast to W. L. Nevin, August, 7, 1930; "A Service That Will Make Your Travel Care-Free (1929)," all in box 44, folder 14, JW; "Flying on Credit," *Business Week*, February 22, 1941, 32; "Travel on Bamberger," *Business Week*, March 15, 1941, 69.

30. "Winter Tide of Travel in Full Swing" *Travel Talks*, January 1925, 3; Don Thomas, "Sixteen Years of Resort Advertising," *Printers' Ink Monthly*, May 1937, 19. Also see Franklin Snow, "A Challenge for Travel Advertising," *Advertising and Selling*, March 28, 1935, 26; Kaufman, "Travel Now—Pay Later," 47; George C. Warren, "New Jersey's Official 'Sales Force,'" *Public Opinion Quarterly* 2, no. 3 (July 1938): 487.

31. Hiram Motherwell, "The American Tourist Makes History," *Harper's Monthly*, January 1929, 72.

32. Wales, "Advertising Lifts Travel from the Slumps," 36; "California Sells Travel

Dreams Now . . . to Be Realized Post War," *Printers' Ink*, March 19, 1943, 36; Ann Bradshaw, "A $216,000,000 Industry: California's Reward for Faith in Advertising," *Sales Management*, February 1, 1938, 26; "Advertising for Tourist Business," 60–61; "Pennsylvania Advertising Results," *Printers' Ink*, November 17, 1939, 88; Berkowitz, "'New Deal' for Leisure," 198; Thomas, "Sixteen Years of Resort Advertising," 63.

33. "The Road to Yesterday," *Printers' Ink Monthly*, March 1932, 48; "Why Southern California's All-Year-Club Increased Its Advertising," *Printers' Ink*, March 24, 1932, 25; Berkowitz, "'New Deal' for Leisure," 200.

34. "Cheap as Staying Home, Travel Builds for Future," *Business Week*, July 13, 1932, 22; "Depression as Advertising Theme of Steamship Campaign," *Printers' Ink*, April 27, 1933, 51.

35. Kay Winn, "How and Why States Advertise," *Advertising and Selling*, September 24, 1936, 25; "Travel Pickup, 28."

36. On recreation as a social and economic good, see Neil M. Maher, *Nature's New Deal: The Civilian Conservation Corps and the Roots of the American Environmental Movement* (New York: Oxford University Press, 2008). On identity, place, and the parks, see John Bodnar, *Remaking America: Public Memory, Commemoration, and Patriotism in the Twentieth Century* (Princeton, NJ: Princeton University Press, 1992), 173–76, 195; Berkowitz, "'New Deal' for Leisure," 200–203; Bureau of Labor Statistics, *How American Buying Habits Change*, 186; Hal K. Rothman, *Devil's Bargains: Tourism in the Twentieth-Century American West* (Lawrence: University Press of Kansas, 1998), 157.

37. Warren I. Susman, "The Culture of the Thirties," in *Culture as History: The Transformation of American Society in the Twentieth Century* (New York: Pantheon, 1984), 154; Robert L. Dorman, *The Revolt of the Provinces: The Regionalist Movement in America, 1920–1945* (Chapel Hill: University of North Carolina Press, 1993), 23–25; Michael C. Steiner, "Regionalism in the Great Depression," *Geographical Review* 73, no. 4 (1983): 430–46, 432.

38. Federal Writers' Project, *Philadelphia: A Guide to the Nation's Birthplace* (Harrisburg: Pennsylvania Historical Commission, 1937), vii; Marguerite S. Shaffer, *See America First: Tourism and National Identity, 1880–1940* (Washington, DC: Smithsonian Institution Press, 2001), 206.

39. Frederick Gutheim, "America in Guide Books," *Saturday Review of Literature*, June 14, 1941, 4, 15; Federal Writers' Project, *Arizona: A State Guide* (New York: Hastings House, 1940), xix; Federal Writers' Project, *Florida: A Guide to the Southernmost State* (New York: Oxford University Press, 1939), 297; Federal Writers' Project, *Philadelphia*, 441; Federal Writers' Project, *A Vacation Guide to Custer State Park in the Black Hills of South Dakota* (Hermosa, SD: Custer State Park Board, 1938), 5.

40. See Maren Stange, *Symbols of Ideal Life: Social Documentary Photography in America, 1890–1950* (New York: Cambridge University Press, 1989), 89–131; James Curtis, *Mind's Eye, Mind's Truth: FSA Photography Reconsidered* (Philadelphia: Temple University Press, 1989), 3–20, 34–44; Alan Trachtenberg, "The FSA File: From Image to Story," in *Lincoln's Smile and Other Enigmas* (New York: Hill and Wang, 2007), 293; and Lawrence W. Levine, "The Historian and the Icon: Photography and the History of the American People in the 1930s and 1940s," in *The Unpredictable Past: Explorations in American Cultural History* (New York: Oxford University Press, 1993), 274–77. Also see William Stott, *Documentary Expression and Thirties America* (New York: Oxford University Press, 1973). Stryker quoted in Curtis, *Mind's Eye*, viii.

41. Maher, *Nature's New Deal*, 115–50.

42. Berkowitz, "'New Deal' for Leisure," 203–4.

43. Charles W. Stokes, "Europe Calls on America," *Advertising and Selling*, April 29, 1931, 30; James M. Campbell, "Tourisme: A Billion Dollar Industry," *Advertising and Selling*, March 6, 1929,

52. Also see F. W. Ogilvie's "Tourist Traffic," in *Encyclopaedia of the Social Sciences*, vol. 14, ed. Edwin R. A. Seligman and Alvin Johnson (New York: Macmillan, 1931).

44. Desmond Holdridge, "We Need a Tourist Dollar," *Survey Graphic* 30 (December 1941): 716; Ellen Furlough, "Making Mass Vacations: Tourism and Consumer Culture in France, 1930s to 1970s," *Comparative Studies in Society and History* 40 (1998): 254–59; Shelley Baranowski, "Strength through Joy: Tourism and National Integration in the Third Reich," in Baranowski and Furlough, *Being Elsewhere*, 213–36, 216.

45. Ogilvie, "Tourist Traffic," 661.

46. Dane York, "The Florida of the North," *American Mercury*, July 1930, 275–80. Also see George Patullo, "Lords of the World's Wealth," *Saturday Evening Post*, June 6, 1925, 158.

47. Berkowitz, "'New Deal' for Leisure," 197; C. A. Kirkpatrick and G. B. Brown, "The Sovereign State Turns Barker," *Journal of Marketing* 3, no. 1 (July 1938): 77; Robert Huse, "Regional Development and the New England Council," *Public Opinion Quarterly* 2, no. 3 (July 1938): 422; Bernard B. Smith, "Our International Money's Worth," *Harper's*, October 1944, 416.

48. John Morton Blum, *V Was for Victory: Politics and American Culture during World War II* (San Diego, CA: Harcourt Brace, 1976), 92–94; "The Expanding Vacation," *Fortune*, September 1961, 195–96; Joseph S. Zeisel, "The Workweek in American Industry, 1850–1956," in *Mass Leisure*, ed. Eric Larrabee and Rolf Meyersohn (Glencoe, IL: Free Press, 1958), 152; "Trends in Vacation Policies," *Management Review* 34, no. 6 (June 1945): 222.

49. Quoted in George L. Fichtenbaum, *Passport to the World: The History of ASTA* (Alexandria, VA: American Society of Travel Agents, 1990), 36.

50. Hazel Kyrk, "Consumers and the War," *Consumer Problems in Wartime*, ed. Kenneth Dameron (New York: McGraw-Hill, 1944), 30; Leland J. Gordon, *Consumers in Wartime: A Guide to the Family Economy in Emergency* (New York: Harper and Bros., 1943), 25; Faith M. Williams, "The Standard of Living in Wartime," *Annals of the American Academy of Political and Social Science* 229 (September 1943): 117–18.

51. Blum, *V Was for Victory*, 95–97; Lizabeth Cohen, *A Consumers' Republic: The Politics of Mass Consumption in Postwar America* (New York: Vintage, 2003), 69–70; "Expanding Vacation," 196.

52. Alastair Cooke, *The American Home Front, 1941–1942* (1941–42; New York: Atlantic Monthly Press, 2006), 212–15; Don McFadden and "unnamed farmer," oral histories in Studs Terkel, *"The Good War": An Oral History of World War Two* (New York: New Press, 1984), 146, 311. Also see Richard R. Lingeman, *Don't You Know There's a War On? The American Home Front, 1941–1945* (New York: G. P. Putnam's Sons, 1970), 269–322.

53. E. DeAlton Partridge and Nell C. Partridge, "Recreation in Wartime," in *Consumer Problems in Wartime*, ed. Kenneth Dameron (New York: McGraw-Hill, 1944), 637, 637–49.

54. "Vacations: 1942"; "Vacation Debacle," *Business Week*, May 8, 1943, 89–90; "Vacation at Home," *Business Week*, May 22, 1943, 86–87; "It's Hard on Parks," *Business Week*, June 19, 1943, 33–34; "Wartime Living: Vacation Days," *Time*, June 8, 1942, 18; "Resorts Go to War," *Business Week*, August 12, 1944, 38–42; Demaree Bess, "Four Continents in Four Days," *Saturday Evening Post*, June 19, 1943, 44.

55. Joseph B. Eastman, "Don't Travel Now," *Rotarian*, June 1943, 7; "Vacationers—World Is at Your Doorstep," *Philadelphia Evening Bulletin*, July 10, 1943, 12B; Partridge and Partridge, "Recreation in Wartime," 651; "Here's the Best Buy for Your Vacation," *New Yorker*, May 5, 1942, 46; Harold I. Ickes, "Ickes Sees Curtailed Park Use," *New York Times*, July 4, 1943, X11. For more on the ODT, see Bradley Flamm, "Putting the Brakes on Non-Essential Travel: 1940s Wartime Mobility, Prosperity, and the US Office of Defense," *Journal of Transport History* 27, no. 1 (March 2006): 71–92.

56. Mercedes Roseberry, *This Day's Madness: A Story of the American People against the*

Background of the War Effort (New York: Macmillan, 1944), 212–13; Henry F. Pringle, "The War Agencies," in *While You Were Gone: A Report on Wartime Life in the United States*, ed. Jack Goodman (New York: Simon and Schuster, 1946), 181.

57. James A. Maxwell and Margaret N. Balcom, "Gasoline Rationing in the United States, I," *Quarterly Journal of Economics* 60, no. 4 (August 1946): 564. The redeployment of troops to the Pacific in 1945 finally forced many vacationers off the trains. "Sheer discomfort," Pringle explained, "began to deter civilian travel where appeals to patriotism had failed." Pringle, "War Agencies," 181–82.

58. Alan Brinkley, *The End of Reform: New Deal Liberalism in Recession and War* (New York: Vintage, 1996), 189–92, 235–64; Diana Rice, "In the Field of Travel," *New York Times*, November 28, 1943, X12.

59. Diana Rice, "In the Field of Travel," *New York Times*, October 29, 1944, X9; "Survey Covers 12 Questions about Post-War Travel," *Printers' Ink*, June 22, 1945; "Canadians to Woo Tourists—U.S. Cities Also Courting Visitors," *Printers' Ink*, October 13, 1944, 44; "Extensive Tourist Ad for Florida," *Printers' Ink*, December 15, 1944, 52; "Mr. & Mrs. America to Become Globe Trotters after the War," *Sales Management*, April 15, 1945, 102; Coert Du Bois, *Caribbean Tourist Trade: A Regional Approach* (Washington, DC: Anglo-American Caribbean Commission, 1945), 9, 24–26.

60. "Britain Wants Tourists," *Printers' Ink*, October 13, 1944, 44; Endy, *Cold War Holidays*, 35.

61. "Pullman-Standard Announces Travel Modernization Program," *Printers' Ink*, February 23, 1945, 50; "Astra-Dome Railroad Cars Envisioned for Post-War," *Printers' Ink*, March 23, 1945, 57; "Customers Polled," *Business Week*, October 7, 1944, 96–97; Diana Rice, "In the Field of Travel," *New York Times*, August 6, 1944, X7; Bender and Altschul, *Chosen Instrument*, 382–94.

62. Boyden Sparkes, "Revolution in the Air," *Saturday Evening Post*, September 25, 1943, 28–29, 44–46; Wesley Price, "I'll Get in My Little Plane and—Zip!" *Saturday Evening Post*, October 7, 1944, 9–11, 70. A June 1945 *Printers' Ink* market report on private planes wondered whether the "millions of returning servicemen, particularly those in the air forces," would make "the family airplane . . . an immediate reality." Harold E. Greene, "Private Aviation Growth Depends on Aggressive Merchandising," *Printers' Ink*, June 1, 1945, 21–22, 94–98; Marion White, "The World Is Waiting for the Tourist," *Independent Woman*, March 1945, 81.

63. Boyden Sparkes, "The Coming Boom in Vacations," *Saturday Evening Post*, August 5, 1944, 29, 47–52.

64. McGovern, *Sold American*; Robert B. Westbrook, "Fighting for the American Family: Private Interests and Political Obligations in World War II," in *The Power of Culture: Critical Essays in American History*, ed. Richard W. Fox and T. J. Jackson Lears (Chicago: University of Chicago Press, 1993), 213–15; Cohen, *Consumers' Republic*, 69–75. On what Paul Fussell has called the "ideological vacuum," or sense among GIs that they were mainly fighting to simply get back home again, see *Wartime: Understanding and Behavior in the Second World War* (New York: Oxford University Press, 1989), 129–43.

65. Sparkes, "Coming Boom in Vacations," 29.

66. F. M. Reck, "Tomorrow We'll Go Places," *Better Homes and Gardens*, June 1943, 72.

67. On notions of consumer republicanism, see McGovern, *Sold American*, 204–8, 284–300, 327–65.

68. Reck, "Tomorrow We'll Go Places," 72; "Tomorrow the World Is Yours!" *New Yorker*, May 29, 1943, 63; "The Family with Everywhere to Go," *Time*, March 12, 1945, 51.

69. Joseph C. Goulden, *The Best Years: 1945–1950* (New York: Atheneum, 1976), 91; Harold J. Ickes, "Space for Play," *Holiday*, May 1946, 36; Philip Newill and Phyliss Newill, "Carefree Car Travel," *Holiday*, April 1946, 86.

70. "Exodus, 1946," *Holiday,* July 1946, 99; "Midsummer," *Life,* August 12, 1946, 34.

71. "Timetable for Vacation Plans," *Better Homes and Gardens,* May 1946, 14. Also see "Vacations: The Gold Rush of '46," *Newsweek,* June 24, 1946, 70; Edith Efron, "That Persistent Traveler—the American," *New York Times Magazine,* July 7, 1946, 85; J. Frank Beaman, "Time to Play," *Holiday,* May 1946, 17.

72. "Announcing Look at America," *Look,* February 5, 1946, 19; Ickes, "Space for Play," 33.

73. "V-E Day, V-J Day, and Soon V-W Days!" Burlington Lines (1945), T2865, and "You've Earned This Celebration!" Greyhound (1945), Ad*Access—Ads # T2865 and T2717, John W. Hartman Center for Sales, Advertising & Marketing History, Duke University Rare Book, Manuscripts and Special Collections Library, library.duke.edu/digitalcollections/adaccess/.

74. "Super-Colossal," *Time,* July 1, 1946, 20; "Life Goes on a 'Happiness Tour,'" *Life,* July 22, 1946, 97; "Tourist Florida," *Life,* February 4, 1946, 48; "Innocents Abroad," *Time,* August 5, 1946, 40; Tom Bernard, "Vacations—American Plan," *American Magazine,* Vacation Issue 1947, 32; "Vacations: The Gold Rush of '46," 70.

75. Goulden, *Best Years,* 93; "Holiday Mood," *Business Week,* February 15, 1947, 19; Fichtenbaum, *Passport to the World,* 53; "Holiday News," *Holiday,* October 1946, 8; "Just Pack Your Bags But," *Time,* April 1, 1946, 80; "Tourists Again," *Business Week,* May 11, 1946, 22; "Vacations: The Gold Rush of '46," 70.

76. Meg Jacobs, "'How about Some Meat?' The Office of Price Administration, Consumption Politics, and State Building from the Bottom Up, 1941–1946," *Journal of American History* 84, no. 3 (December 1997): 937–41; Goulden, *Best Years,* 105–7.

77. On the 1946 strikes and shortages, see Cohen, *Consumers' Republic,* 108, 153; John T. Patterson, *Grand Expectations: The United States, 1945–1974* (New York: Oxford University Press, 1996), 43–44; Goulden, *Best Years,* 108–31; J. Frank Beaman, "OPA on Vacation," *Holiday,* June 1946, 21; and "A Hard Place to Get Away From," *Business Week,* March 30, 1946, 19.

78. "What 1946 Vacationist Faces: Shortages, Crowds, High Prices," *U.S. News and World Report,* March 29, 1946, 40; Louisa M. Constock, "Tomorrow's Traveler Can Take It Easy!" *Better Homes and Gardens,* August 1946, 38; "Resort Bites Tourist," *Printers' Ink,* December 7, 1945, 80; "What's Wrong with the Airlines?" *Fortune,* August 1946, 73; Wesley Price, "Why Air Passengers Get Mad," *Saturday Evening Post,* October 19, 1946, 12.

79. "Florida Won't Hold Back Ads," *Printers' Ink,* February 1, 1946, 140; "Travelers' Travail," *Life,* November 18, 1946, 38.

80. Jacobs, "'How about Some Meat?'" 912.

81. Frederick C. Otham, "The Turn of the Worm," *Holiday,* June 1946, 80; Duncan Hines and Frank J. Taylor, "How to Find a Decent Meal," *Saturday Evening Post,* April 26, 1947, 18, 102, 99.

82. Bill Mauldin, "Check th' tires . . . ," in *Back Home* (New York: William Sloane Associates, 1947), 151.

CHAPTER TWO

1. Robert B. Westbrook, "Fighting for the American Family: Private Interests and Political Obligations in World War II," in *The Power of Culture: Critical Essays in American History,* ed. Richard W. Fox and T. J. Jackson Lears (Chicago: University of Chicago Press, 1993), 195–221; Alan Brinkley, *The End of Reform: New Deal Liberalism in Recession and War* (New York: Vintage, 1996), 186–94; Charles F. McGovern, *Sold American: Consumption and Citizenship, 1890–1945* (Chapel Hill: University of North Carolina Press, 2006), 301–65; Lizabeth Cohen, *A Consumers' Republic: The Politics of Mass Consumption in Postwar America* (New York: Vintage, 2003), 69–75.

2. Address by Donald M. Hobart given to the American Marketing Association, "Planning

a Holiday," May 23, 1946, 2, box 152, folder 144, CPC; "Magazine X," *Tide*, February 8, 1946, 40; "Holiday," *Tide*, February 22, 1946, 42.

3. David Abrahamson, *Magazine-Made America: The Cultural Transformation of the Postwar Periodical* (Cresskill, NJ: Hampton Press, 1996), 37–43; Elizabeth Fraterrigo, *Playboy and the Making of the Good Life in Modern America* (New York: Oxford University Press, 2009).

4. On mass magazines and the rise of consumer culture, see Helen Damon-Moore, *Magazines for the Millions: Gender and Commerce in the Ladies' Home Journal and the Saturday Evening Post* (Albany: State University of New York Press, 1994); Richard Ohmann, *Selling Culture: Magazines, Markets, and Class at the Turn of the Century* (New York: Verso, 1996); Janice Cohn, *Creating America: George Horace Lorimar and the Saturday Evening Post* (Pittsburgh: University of Pittsburgh Press, 1989); Matthew Schneirov, *The Dream of a New Social Order: Popular Magazines in America, 1893–1914* (New York: Columbia University Press, 1994); Ellen Gruber Garvey, *The Adman in the Parlor: Magazines and the Gendering of Consumer Culture, 1880s to 1910s* (New York: Oxford University Press, 1996); and Christopher P. Wilson, "The Rhetoric of Consumption: Mass-Market Magazines and the Demise of the Gentle Reader, 1880–1920," in *The Culture of Consumption: Critical Essays in American History, 1880–1980*, ed. Richard Wightman Fox and T. J. Jackson Lears (New York: Pantheon, 1983), 39–64. On the rise of a mass consumption economy, see Susan Strasser, *Satisfaction Guaranteed: The Making of the American Mass Market* (Washington, DC: Smithsonian Books, 1989); Pamela Walker Laird, *Advertising Progress: American Business and the Rise of Consumer Marketing* (Baltimore: Johns Hopkins University Press, 1998); Jackson Lears, *Fables of Abundance: A Cultural History of Advertising in America* (New York: Basic Books, 1994); William Leach, *Land of Desire: Merchants, Power and the Rise of a New American Culture* (New York: Vintage, 1993); and McGovern, *Sold American*.

5. Damon-Moore, *Magazines for the Millions*, 1–2.

6. Butler quoted in Donald M. Hobart, ed., *Marketing Research Practice* (New York: Ronald Press Co., 1950), 4. On the development of Curtis's market-research arm, see Douglas B. Ward, "Tracking the Culture of Consumption: Curtis Publishing Company, Charles Coolidge Parlin, and the Origins of Market Research, 1911–1930" (PhD diss., University of Maryland, College Park, 1996). On the development of market research more generally, also see Lawrence C. Lockley, "Notes on the History of Marketing Research," *Journal of Marketing* 14, no. 5 (April 1950): 733–36; Wroe Alderson, "Charles Coolidge Parlin," *Journal of Marketing* 21, no. 1 (July 1956): 1; McGovern, *Sold American*, 31–36; James Beniger, *The Control Revolution: Technological and Economic Origins of the Information Society* (Cambridge, MA: Harvard University Press, 1986), 381; Strasser, *Satisfaction Guaranteed*, 149–53.

7. Department Stores Lines quoted in Hobart, *Marketing Research Practice*, 6–7.

8. Ward, "Tracking the Culture of Consumption"; Lockley, "Notes on the History of Marketing Research," 734–35; Alderson, "Charles Coolidge Parlin," 1–3.

9. Ward, "Tracking the Culture of Consumption," 204.

10. See Olivier Zunz, *Why the American Century?* (Chicago: University of Chicago Press, 1998), 61; Beniger, *Control Revolution*, 337, 376–89; Strasser, *Satisfaction Guaranteed*, 148–61; Susan Douglas, *Listening In: Radio and the American Imagination* (New York: Times Books, 1999), 124–60; Sarah E. Igo, *The Averaged American: Surveys, Citizenship, and the Making of a Mass Public* (Cambridge, MA: Harvard University Press, 2007), 109–18, 148; Roland Marchand, *Advertising the American Dream: Making Way for Modernity, 1920–1940* (Berkeley: University of California Press, 1985), 72–80; Thomas A. Stapleford, "Market Visions: Expenditure Surveys, Market Research, and Economic Planning in the New Deal," *Journal of American History* 94, no. 2 (September 2007): 438–44.

11. Marchand, *Advertising the American Dream*, 25–83; Hobart, *Marketing Research Practice*, 135.

12. Virgil D. Reed, "Marketing Research: The Base on Which Selling Plans and Policies Must Build," *Printers' Ink*, October 31, 1947, 64.

13. Beniger, *Control Revolution*, 310–13; Mildred Parten, *Surveys, Polls, and Samples: Practical Procedures* (New York: Harper and Bros., 1950), 37–38; Henry G. Weaver, "Consumer Research and Consumer Education," *Annals of the American Academy of Political and Social Science* 182 (November 1935): 93–100, 95. Weaver, GM's director of Customer Research, quotes Sloan in the article.

14. James Playsted Wood, "Donald M. Hobart," *Journal of Marketing* 26, no. 1 (January 1962): 79–80; "What the End of the War Means to . . . ," *Printers' Ink*, August 24, 1945, 21.

15. Reed, "Marketing Research," 74; Wilford L. White, "Marketing Research," *Annals of the Academy of Political and Social Science* 209 (May 1940): 189.

16. Wood, "Donald M. Hobart," 79–80.

17. Donald M. Hobart, "The Value of Consumer Purchase Surveys to Management," *Journal of Marketing* 4, no. 1 (July 1939): 23; Donald M. Hobart, "Occupational Classification for Market Research," *Journal of Marketing* 7, no. 4 (April 1943): 367. Hobart's deputy, Wroe Alderson, also wrote on the subject. See "Market Classification of Families," *Journal of Marketing* 6, no. 2 (October 1941): 143. Hobart's textbooks were *Marketing Research Practice* and Donald M. Hobart and James Playsted Wood, *Selling Forces* (New York: Ronald Press, 1953).

18. Wood, "Donald M. Hobart," 79–80; Donald M. Hobart, "Dynamic Marketing: Economic Hope of the Future," 1954, 9, box 151, folder 121, CPC.

19. Hobart, "Planning a Holiday," 2; "Editorial: Premise for New Periodicals," *Printers' Ink*, August 24, 1945, 116.

20. Sixty-five percent expected to receive paid vacations that summer, and three-quarters expected to receive them after the war. Nine out of ten planned on using their vacation to travel. Thirty-four percent thought they would travel abroad. Nearly a fifth thought they would receive paid vacations in the wintertime, as well. Research Department, "A Survey of Vacation Travel," 1945, in *Digests of Principal Research Department Studies*, vol. 3: *1941–1945* (Philadelphia: Curtis Publishing Co., 1949), 159–60. Curtis's findings were echoed in another major postwar market study conducted by advertising agency Charles W. Hoyt, "Postwar Travel," *Tide*, May 15, 1945, 111.

21. Research Department, *Advertising Classification Analysis*, 1945, charts 62, 43–44, box 132, CPC. An estimated half of the recreation sector's $6.5 million went toward motion picture advertising, though. On transport, see charts 8, 63–64. Passenger travel ad spending was rolled into the "Travel and Accommodations" market, but generic transportation spending would have also included institutional ads that promoted the company or industry in general.

22. On *The Golden Opportunity*, see Donald M. Hobart, "Research Communication between Business and Colleges," *Journal of Marketing* 12, no. 1 (July 1947): 101; Hobart, *Marketing Research Practice*, 181; Research Department, *Saturday Evening Post Aviation Study*, 6–7, 35–36, 1946, box 109, CPC.

23. Hobart, "Planning a Holiday," 2.

24. Julius Weinberger, "Economic Aspects of Recreation," *Harvard Business Review* 15, no. 4 (Summer 1937): 448–63; C. A. Kirkpatrick, "Budgets for Promoting Pleasure Travel," *Printers' Ink Monthly*, August 1941, 61; "The Fortune Poll: The American Vacation," *Fortune*, July 1936, 158; Lawrence P. Lessing, "State of Florida," *Fortune*, February 1948, 66; American Automobile Association, *Americans on the Highway: A Report on Recent Trends of Tourist Travel* (Washington, DC: AAA, 1949), 6; C. Hartley Grattan, "The Economics of Holidays," *Harper's*, July 1950, 85–86.

25. Marion Clawson, "Statistical Data Available for Economic Research on Certain Types of Recreation," *American Statistical Association Journal* 54, no. 285 (March 1959): 281.

26. J. Frederic Dewhurst and Associates, *America's Needs and Resources: A New Survey* (New York: Twentieth Century Fund, 1955), 346.

27. "Tourist Cash Survey," *Business Week*, March 23, 1946, 116; Andrew M. Heath, "How New Hampshire Measures Her Vacation Business," *Printers' Ink*, December 28, 1945, 38; "Tourist Tabulations," *Business Week*, May 17, 1947, 18.

28. Donald M. Hobart, "Planning a Holiday," *Journal of Marketing* 12, no. 1 (July 1947): 48–49. Curtis acquired the name *Holiday* from the American Automobile Association.

29. "It Makes People Want Things," *Advertising Age*, April 8, 1946, 20; "It's No Holiday," *People*, May 1946, 14, all in box 167, folder 265, CPC. "More and More Advertising in Holiday," *Advertising Age*, June 10, 1946, 22.

30. Elmo Roper, "Classifying Respondents by Economic Status," *Public Opinion Quarterly* 4, no. 2 (June 1940): 271.

31. W. Lloyd Warner and Paul S. Lunt, *The Status System of a Modern Community* (New Haven: Yale University Press, 1942); W. Lloyd Warner, Marchia Meeker, and Kenneth Eels, *Social Class in America: A Manual of Procedure for the Measurement of Social Status* (Chicago: Science Research Associates, 1949); Burleigh B. Gardner, "The Anthropologist in Business and Industry," *Anthropological Quarterly* 50, no. 4 (October 1977): 171–72.

32. Paul F. Lazarsfeld, "The Psychological Aspect of Market Research," *Harvard Business Review* 34, no. 13 (October 1934): 54–71; Paul F. Lazarsfeld, "The Art of Asking Why," *National Marketing Review* 1, no. 1 (Summer 1935): 26–38; Charles Y. Glock and Francesco M. Nicosia, "Sociology and the Study of Consumers," *Journal of Advertising Research* 3, no. 3 (September 1963): 23–24; "Readership Surveys," *Tide*, July 1, 1945, 102; "Use Social Scientists, Harper Tells Agencies," *Advertising Age*, April 11, 1949, 1; "Market Research Now Directed at Motives," *Advertising Age*, October 17, 1949, 1; Ernest Dichter, *The Psychology of Everyday Living* (New York: Barnes and Noble, 1947); Ernest Dichter, "A Psychological View of Advertising Effectiveness," *Journal of Marketing* 14, no. 1 (July 1949): 61–66; Louis Cheskin and L. B. Ward, "Indirect Approach to Market Reactions," *Harvard Business Review* 26, no. 5 (September 1948): 572–80; "Market Research Nears New Era, Elder Tells AMA," *Advertising Age*, May 20, 1946, 92.

33. Don Thomas, "America's $6,000,000 Tourist Trade: Are You Getting a Share?" *Sales Management*, May 1, 1941, 24.

34. George A. Lundberg, Mirra Komarovsky, and Mary Alice McInerny, *Leisure: A Suburban Study* (New York: Columbia University Press, 1934), 21, 22. The authors also emphasized that "problems of leisure have meaning only against this background of life in general" (23). Edman quoted in discussion on p. 18.

35. George A. Lundberg, "Marketing and Social Organization," 1945, 25, box 151, folder 111, CPC.

36. Wroe Alderson, introduction to Lundberg, "Marketing and Social Organization," 6, box 151, folder 111, CPC.

37. Richard S. Tedlow, *New and Improved: The Story of Mass Marketing in America* (New York: Basic Books, 1990), 371–72; Cohen, *Consumers' Republic*, 293–309; Abrahamson, *Magazine-Made America*; Joseph Turow, *Breaking Up America: Advertisers and the New Media World* (Chicago: University of Chicago Press, 1997), 3, 18–54, 90–124.

38. John Bakeless, *Magazine Making* (New York: Viking Press, 1931), 250–51; Roland E. Wolseley, *The Magazine World: An Introduction to Magazine Journalism* (New York: Prentice Hall, 1951), 221–40; Ben Duffy, *Advertising Media and Markets*, 2nd ed. (New York: Prentice Hall, 1951), 118–22.

39. Duffy, *Advertising Media and Markets*, 32–33.

40. Bakeless, *Magazine Making*, 250–51; Wolseley, *Magazine World*, 233.

41. Phillips Wyman, *Magazine Circulation: An Outline of Methods and Meanings* (New York: McCall Co., 1936), 22. For representative articles, see "Readership Surveys," *Tide*, July 1, 1945, 102; "Mass Observation," *Tide*, July 1, 145, 106; and Edward L. Bernays, "Advertising Is behind the Times—Culturally," *Printers' Ink*, March 30, 1951, 25.

42. "How Does Holiday Get Such Amazing Results," *Advertising Age*, December 2, 1946, 10–11.

43. "Holiday Magazine Moves Merchandise," *Advertising Age*, July 21, 1947, 30–31. Curtis offered a similar explanation a year later as to why "some women are more responsive than others," noting that "Holiday stimulates them, puts them in a responsive state of mind." "Why Are Some Women More Responsive Than Others?" *Advertising Age*, June 7, 1948, 20–21.

44. "Vacation Haunts or Business Jaunts," *Printers' Ink*, May 1, 1953, 68; "America Is off Its Rocker!" *Printers' Ink*, Advertising Annual—1955, 185; "Holiday Sets Another Space Record . . . ," *Printers' Ink*, February 25, 1955, 59; "Holiday Takes Another Big Hop!" *Printers' Ink*, November 18, 1955, 45; "Some People Get Around in Grand Style," *Printers' Ink Advertisers' Guide for Marketing for 1956*, 167.

45. "Holiday Upsets One of the Oldest Theories in the Magazine Business," *Advertising Age*, December 6, 1948, 59; "Report from Holiday," *Advertising Age*, May 9, 1949, 14.

46. "BBDO Newsletter," *Printers' Ink*, April 24, 1953, 2; "Holiday Families . . . ," *Printers' Ink*, September 12, 1952, 113. Also see "Some People's Lives Are Brimful of Activity," *Printers' Ink*, October 21, 1954, 14; "Some People Have a Hand in More Activities Than Others," *Advertising Age*, April 25, 1955, 14.

47. David Reisman, Nathan Glazer, and Reuel Denney, *The Lonely Crowd: A Study of the Changing American Character*, abridged ed. (Garden City, NY: Doubleday Anchor, 1953); David Reisman and Eric Larrabee, "Autos in America," in David Reisman, *Abundance for What? And Other Essays* (1956; New York: Doubleday, 1964), 270–99.

48. Martha Wolfenstein, "The Emergence of Fun Morality," *Journal of Social Issues* 7, no. 4 (1951): 22.

49. "Curtis' 'Holiday' Will Take Liquor Ads," *Advertising Age*, October 6, 1947, 1; "Holiday," *Tide*, October 10, 1947, 34; "Holiday to Accept Liquor Ads Starting in January," *Printers' Ink*, October 10, 1947, 87; "'Holiday' Is Here," *Tide*, October 15, 1945, 68.

50. See Cohn, *Creating America*, and Damon-Moore, *Magazines for the Millions*.

51. Morris Livingston, "The Marketing Viewpoint in Planning for the Business Enterprise," *Journal of Marketing* 7, no. 4 (April 1943): 336; Dero A. Saunders and Sanford S. Parker, "$30 Billion for Fun," *Fortune*, June 1954, 234. On the importance of new markets, see Editors of Fortune, "The Changing American Market," in *The Changing American Market* (Garden City, NY: Hanover House, 1955), 13–30.

52. James Playsted Wood, *The Curtis Magazines* (New York: Ronald Press, 1971), 272–81; Matthew J. Culligan, *The Curtis-Culligan Story: From Cyrus to Horace to Joe: The Inside Story of the Decline of the Curtis Publishing Company* (New York: Crown, 1970), 163–65; Joseph C. Goulden, *The Curtis Caper* (New York: G. P. Putnam's Sons, 1965), 216.

53. "The Holiday Subscriber Family," "Highlights of Two Surveys among Holiday's Charter Subscribers and Newsstand Buyers," "Recreation Is Big Business," "The Holiday Newsstand Buyer Family," in *Digests of Principal Research Department Studies*, vol. 4: *1946–1949* (Philadelphia: Curtis Publishing Co., 1949), 23–26, 44, 78.

54. "Summary Findings of a Survey among New Holiday Subscribers January, February 1948," in *Digests of Principal Research Department Studies*, 4:109.

55. "The Post—An Alert and Active Market," in *Digests of Principal Research Department Studies*, 4:155–56.

56. Hobart, "Planning a Holiday," 4; Herbert C. Ludeke, "The Role of Research in the Editorial Reconversion Problems of a Magazine," *Journalism Quarterly* 25 (September 1948): 215.

57. Ludeke, "Role of Research," 215.

58. Hobart, "Planning a Holiday," 4; Hobart, *Marketing Research Practice*, 312, 310.

59. "It's No Holiday," 13–15; Hobart, "Planning a Holiday," 8.

60. Hobart, "Planning a Holiday," 5–6; U.S. Bureau of the Census, *Income and Expenditures Tables* (Washington, DC: U.S. Government Printing Office, 1949), 279–97. *Holiday* readers' average income placed them in the top 21 percent of the income bracket. Research Department, "The Holiday Subscriber Family," 1946, and "Highlights of Two Surveys among Holiday's Charter Subscribers and Newsstand Buyers," in *Digests of Principal Research Department Studies*, 4:6, 25–26; Hobart, "Planning a Holiday," 5–6; "Holiday Cashes Dreams for Dollars," *Sales Management*, June 15, 1946, 137.

61. Hobart, "Planning a Holiday," 8.

62. This paraphrase of May's remarks appeared in "Curtis' Holiday Format Prompted by Expected Recreation, Travel Upswing," *Printers' Ink*, February 22, 1946, 116.

63. Ibid.; "The Editorial Field of Holiday," *Printers' Ink*, December 21, 1945, 39.

64. On the emergence of middlebrow culture, see Joan Shelley Rubin, *The Making of Middlebrow Culture* (Chapel Hill: University of North Carolina Press, 1992), and Joanne P. Sharp, *Condensing the Cold War: Reader's Digest and American Identity* (Minneapolis: University of Minnesota Press, 2000). On the demarcation of cultural boundaries and taste levels, see Lawrence W. Levine, *Highbrow/Lowbrow: The Emergence of Cultural Hierarchy in America* (Cambridge, MA: Harvard University Press, 1988), and Paul DiMaggio, "Cultural Entrepreneurship in Nineteenth-Century Boston: The Creation of an Organizational Base for High Culture in America," in *Rethinking Popular Culture: Contemporary Perspectives in Cultural Studies*, ed. Chandra Mukerji and Michael Schudson (Berkeley: University of California Press, 1991), 374–97. On middlebrow reading as a cultural circuit, see Janice A. Radway, *A Feeling for Books: The Book-of-the-Month Club, Literary Taste, and Middle-Class Desire* (Chapel Hill: University of North Carolina Press, 1997), 168–76.

65. J. Frank Beaman, "Editorial: In Pursuit of Happiness," *Holiday*, March 1946, 3.

66. Lowell Thomas, "The World to Choose From," *Holiday*, July 1946, 43; Philip Newill and Phyllis Newill, "Carefree Car Travel," *Holiday*, April 1946, 86, 90. Also see Frederick C. Otham, "Round the World in Six Days," *Holiday*, March 1946, 19; Edward M. Strode, "Europe's Still There," *Holiday*, April 1946, 55; and Morris Fishbein, "It's Doctor's Orders," *Holiday*, March 1946, 52.

67. J. Frank Beaman, "Editorial: New Coins to Spend," *Holiday*, April 1946, 17; Malcolm S. Knowles, "Having Any Fun?" *Holiday*, June 1946, 14–17.

68. Jackson Lears, *Something for Nothing: Luck in America* (New York: Penguin, 2003), 6–10, 17–21, 231; Johann Huizinga, *Homo Ludens: A Study of the Play Element in Culture* (Boston: Beacon Press, 1950). Also see Roger Caillois, *Man, Play, and Games* (New York: Free Press, 1961).

69. Lears, *Something for Nothing*, 19.

70. Hobart, "Dynamic Marketing," 7.

71. Research Department, "The Holiday Subscriber Family," 1946, and "Highlights of Two Surveys among Holiday's Charter Subscribers and Newsstand Buyers," 23–26; Hobart, "Planning a Holiday," 5–6.

72. "ABC, Retailer Join Curtis in Holiday Promotion," *Printers' Ink*, May 24, 1946, 100; Hobart, "Planning a Holiday," 7.

73. "Philadelphia Project," *Time*, February 25, 1946, 58. James Playsted Wood, a Curtis executive and company historian, even characterized the magazine in its first months as reading "like a chamber of commerce brochure." Wood, *Curtis Magazines*, 187; "Holiday," *Tide*, February 22, 1946, 42; "Holiday Troubles," *Time*, July 8, 1946, 48.

74. "Curtis Counts Chips," *Business Week*, September 28, 1946, 47–48; "Magazine X," 40; "Holiday Troubles," 48; "Philadelphia Project." Beaman went on to put out another tourism magazine, the *Traveler*, published for distribution to hotels for their rooms and newsstands. See "The Traveler to Expand," *Printers' Ink*, June 22, 1951, 14.

75. Daniels quoted in Stephen Fox, *The Mirror Makers: A History of American Advertising and Its Creators* (New York: William Morrow & Co., 1984), 134–35; "What about Those Peaceway Ads?" *Printers' Ink*, December 14, 1945, 49; Wood, *Curtis Magazines*, 187; Kathryn News, "Edwin Hill ('Ted') Patrick," in *American Magazine Journalists, 1900–1960*, 2nd ser., ed. Sam G. Riley (Detroit: Gale Research, 1994), 219; "People," *Printers' Ink*, December 28, 1945, 73; "Ted Patrick Joins Curtis to Explore Pictorial Field," *Advertising Age*, December 24, 1945, 57.

76. "Holiday Troubles," 48; Beaman, "Editorial: In Pursuit of Happiness," 3.

77. "Holiday Troubles," 48.

78. "Curtis Counts Chips," 48; "Holiday Progress," *Tide*, October 18, 1946, 34; "Holiday Grows Up," *Tide*, October 25, 1946, 40, 44; "Happy Holiday," *Time*, March 3, 1947, 71–72.

79. "Holiday to Accept Liquor Ads Starting in January," 87; "Happy Holiday," 71–72.

80. E. B. White, "Here Is New York," *Holiday*, April 1949, 41; John Steinbeck, "In Quest of America," *Holiday*, July 1961, 27; John Steinbeck, "Part Two: In Quest of America," *Holiday*, December 1961, 60; "Happy Holiday," *Newsweek*, March 5, 1956, 78.

81. "Report from Holiday," *Advertising Age*, May 9, 1949, 14–15.

82. "Cowles Empire—a Magazine Phenomenon," *Business Week*, October 8, 1949, 31–34; "Flair Quits Next Month," *Printers' Ink*, December 8, 1950, 67; "Business Briefs," *Business Week*, December 9, 1950, 28; "Shorter and Shorter," *Business Week*, October 21, 1950, 54; "Business Briefs," *Business Week*, April 18, 1953, 34. *Quick* was sold to its staff and renamed *Tempo*.

83. Theodore B. Peterson, *Magazines in the Twentieth Century* (Urbana: University of Illinois Press, 1964), 107, 119; "Crowell-Collier to Publish International Magazine," *Printers' Ink*, March 29, 1946, 95; "19 Foreign Publishers Join New Crowell-Collier Venture," *Printers' Ink*, April 4, 1947, 101; "International Magazine," *Business Week*, April 5, 1947, 68.

84. "1946: Big Year for Advertising," *Business Week*, February 15, 1947, 70; "Another Big Year in '48," *Business Week*, February 21, 1948, 66.

85. "Is Video Pattern Emerging?" *Advertising Age*, December 6, 1948, 12; "1950 Looks Rosy for Ad Men," *Business Week*, February 11, 1950, 30; "Advertising Licks its Chops," *Business Week*, February 16, 1952, 152; "Advertising Outlook: Stable," *Business Week*, February 19, 1949, 83; "Magazines: Is TV a Real Threat?" *Business Week*, November 11, 1951, 120; "Magazines Undisputed Media Champ: MAB," *Advertising Age*, September 8, 1952, 84; "The Arithmetic of Magazine Advertising," *Printers' Ink*, September 18, 1953, 64.

86. "Magazines: Is TV a Real Threat?" 121; "'48 Media Products Continue '47 Downward Trend," *Printers' Ink*, August 27, 1948, 101; "Specialized Magazines May Fold Up If Postal Rates Increase, NPA Warns House," *Printers' Ink*, April 4, 1947, 95. Curtis, perhaps in a play to gain leverage in the debate, toyed with abandoning the U.S. Postal Service to develop a private delivery group of its own. "Curtis Executive Tells How Readers Prefer Newsstand Purchases," *Advertising Age*, March 21, 1949, 4; "Staff Report," *Printers' Ink*, September 7, 1951, 7; "Publishers Plan Educational Campaign," *Printers' Ink*, October 16, 1953, 12.

87. "Ad Prospects: Rosy or Just Laggard?" *Business Week*, February 13, 1954, 42.

88. James L. Baughman, *The Republic of Mass Culture: Journalism, Filmmaking, and Broadcasting in America since 1941* (Baltimore: Johns Hopkins University Press, 1992); Read H. Wright, "How Will Television Affect Advertising's Tomorrow?" *Printers' Ink*, September 26, 1952, 104.

89. "Splitting Country Gentleman," *Business Week*, June 18, 1955, 129; "Collier's Goes Biweekly in Circulation Battle," *Business Week*, May 16, 1953, 50; Peterson, *Magazines in the Twentieth Century*, 128; "Television's Gain Is Other Media's Loss," *Business Week*, April 9, 1955, 68.

90. "Unease on Magazine Row," *Business Week*, August 7, 1954, 63; Leo Bogart, "Magazines Adopting 'New Look' to Keep Pace with TV," *Media/Scope*, January 1957, 23; Karal Ann Marling, *As Seen on TV: The Visual Culture of Everyday Life in the 1950s* (Cambridge, MA: Harvard University Press, 1994), 51–59; Leo Bogart, "Magazines Lean toward Greater Diversification," *Media/Scope*, March 1957, 17.

91. Milton Moskowitz, "Ziff-Davis Head Sees Rosy Future for Specialized Magazine Titles," *Advertising Age*, August 8, 1955, 82.

92. "Television's Gain Is Other Media's Loss," 68; "Here's How Magazines Are Faring on the Touchy Circulation Front," *Tide*, November 20, 1954, 60; "Mags Facing Problems, but Most Are Happy," *Advertising Age*, January 21, 1957, 1; David M. Potter, *People of Plenty: Economic Abundance and the American Character* (Chicago: University of Chicago Press, 1954), 181.

93. "Magazine's Selective Punch," *Business Week*, May 5, 1956, 148; "Market Still Grows for Cars, Appliances, Homes, Home Improvements: Look Study," *Advertising Age*, April 30, 1956, 26; "'Reader's Digest' Reveals Results of Columbus Study," *Advertising Age*, October 26, 1959, 73; "Study Compares Quality, Buying Potential of Magazine and TV Audiences," *Media/Scope*, November 1959, 67; "Consumer Magazines Claim Top Half of U.S. Market," *Media/Scope*, December 1959, 74; " 'U.S. News' Says It Hits Well-Heeled Better," *Advertising Age*, February 15, 1960, 117; "Nielsen's Romance with Magazines," *Business Week*, July 15, 1961, 82. "Magazines Aim at Class Readership," *Business Week*, May 27, 1961, 101; "Magazine Industry Tackles Its Problems with a New Program," *Printers' Ink*, October 3, 1958, 12; "Here's How Magazines Are Faring," 60.

94. Roy E. Larson, "I Predict: Magazines Will Become Even More Important," *Printers' Ink*, December 27, 1957, 55.

95. "Magazine Paradox—Are They Thriving or Dying?" *Business Week*, January 19, 1957, 97

96. Hobart, "Dynamic Marketing," 10–11.

97. "Magazine Paradox," 97; "Editorial: Premise for New Periodicals," 116; "Should Advertisers 'Tailor' Ads for Special Audiences or Markets?" *Tide*, October 9, 1954, 54.

98. "Shaping a Magazine of the Wonderful Moneyed World of Sports," *Business Week*, August 7, 1954, 55; "Unease on Magazine Row," 63–64; "Magazine Paradox," 97.

99. "Power of Specialized Magazines," *Printers' Ink*, March 11, 1960, 21, 25. For similar, leisure-based explanations, see "Selective Magazines Experience Prosperity," *Media/Scope*, November 1957, 24, and "Publisher 'Pete' Petersen: He Found the Teenage Male Market," *Printers' Ink*, August 8, 1958, 41.

100. Abrahamson, *Magazine-Made America*, 37–43, 71–72.

101. "Power of Specialized Magazines," 30.

102. "Publisher 'Pete' Petersen," 43; "Since 'Hod Rod' Zoomed in '48, Petersen's Built 7-Book Entry," *Advertising Age*, April 21, 1958, 38.

103. Leo Bogart, "How to Use Magazine Readership Studies," *Printers' Ink*, August 6, 1954, 53; Ernest Dichter, "10 New Concepts in Media Research," *Media/Scope*, July 1959, 47; For an explanation of how motivational research built on traditional demographic study, see Perrin Stryker, "What's the Motive," in Editors of Fortune, eds., *The Amazing Advertising Business* (New York: Simon and Schuster, 1957), 67–68.

104. Bogart, "How to Use Magazine Readership Studies, 53.

105. Ibid.; Dichter, "10 New Concepts in Media Research," 47; "Media Letter," *Printers' Ink,* December 12, 1958, 27; Jerome Greene, "Some Psychological Traits of Media and Markets," *Media/Scope,* November 1959, 68.

106. Daniel Seligman, "The Ad Boom," in Editors of Fortune, *Amazing Advertising Business,* 93.

107. Leo Bogart, "Inside Market Research," *Public Opinion Quarterly* 27, no. 4 (Winter 1963): 563.

108. Daniel Horowitz, *The Anxieties of Affluence: Critiques of American Consumer Culture, 1939–1979* (Amherst: University of Massachusetts Press, 2004), 63. On SRI and Martineau, see Shelley Nickles, "More Is Better: Mass Consumption, Gender, and Class Identity in Postwar America," *American Quarterly* 54, no. 4 (December 2002): 581–622; Cohen, *Consumers' Republic,* 295–301.

109. Nelson N. Foote, "The Autonomy of the Consumer," in *Consumer Behavior: The Dynamics of Consumer Reaction,* ed. Lincoln H. Clark (New York: New York University Press, 1954), 15–24, 20. Emanuel Demby, "Psychographics and from Whence It Came," in *Life Style and Psychographics,* ed. William D. Wells (Chicago: American Marketing Association, 1974), 11–30; James H. Myers and Jonathan Gutman, "Life Style: The Essence of Social Class," in Wells, *Life Style and Psychographics,* 243–66.

110. Life Inc. research reported in "Magazine Opens New Market Study Service," *Printers' Ink,* March 20, 1959, 65.

111. "Sports Illustrated: A Lesson in How to Launch a Magazine," *Tide,* August 28, 1954, 40; H. H. S. Phillips Jr., "Memo from the Publisher," *Sports Illustrated,* August 16, 1954, 10.

112. "Shaping a Magazine of the Wonderful Moneyed World of Sports," 55–56.

113. Ibid.; "Sports Illustrated: A Lesson," 40; Richard L. Neale, "Story behind Time's New Sports Weekly," *Printers' Ink,* August 13, 1954, 52; "Memorandum," *Tide,* November 6, 1954, 67.

114. "The First 12 Weeks," *Tide,* November 20, 1954, 19; "Sports Illustrated," *Printers' Ink,* July 30, 1954, insert between pp. 16 and 17; "Attention . . . Sales at Work," *Printers' Ink,* October 8, 1954, 47.

115. "Sports Illustrated Promotes Sports in Tie-in with Suburban Shopping Centers," *Printers' Ink,* March 114, 1958, 60; Harry Phillips, "Memo from the Publisher," *Sports Illustrated,* November 15, 1954, 1.

116. Richard L. Neale, "Marketing a New Magazine," address to American Marketing Association, November 5, 1956, quoted in Roland E. Wolseley, *Understanding Magazines* (Ames: Iowa State University Press, 1965), 414.

117. Elihu Katz and Paul F. Lazarsfeld, *Personal Influence; The Part Played by People in the Flow of Mass Communications* (Glencoe, IL: Free Press, 1955).

118. Wolseley, *Understanding Magazines,* 267–68. Just after SI's launch in late summer 1954, advertising executive David Ogilvy characterized it as "looking sickly," predicting its imminent collapse. Six months later Ogilvy offered his kudos to publisher John Tibby, noting that the advertising trade had been wrong in predicting its failure. David Ogilvy to William S. Dietz, September 20, 1954, and David Ogilvy to John Tibby, March 17, 1955, both in box 26, Sports Illustrated folder, DO.

CHAPTER THREE

1. Carl L. Biemiller, "Dime-Bank Odyssey," *Holiday,* May 1946, 42, 44; Sam Huffman, "Pin

Money Paid Our Way to Europe," *American Magazine*, December 1951, 52; "Your Right to Be Restless," *Holiday*, April 1951, 30.

2. John T. Patterson, *Grand Expectations: The United States, 1945–1974* (New York: Oxford University Press, 1996); Lizabeth Cohen, *A Consumers' Republic: The Politics of Mass Consumption in Postwar America* (New York: Vintage, 2003), 112–29.

3. Eric Hobsbawm, *The Age of Extremes: A History of the World, 1914–1991* (New York: Vintage, 1996); Neil Smith, *American Empire: Roosevelt's Geographer and the Prelude to Globalization* (Berkeley: University of California Press, 2003); Christina Klein, *Cold War Orientalism: Asia in the Middlebrow Imagination, 1945–1961* (Berkeley: University of California Press, 2003); Christopher Endy, *Cold War Holidays: American Tourism in France* (Chapel Hill: University of North Carolina Press, 2004); Horace Sutton, *Travelers: The American Tourist from Stagecoach to Space Shuttle* (New York: William Morrow and Co., 1980), 215–218; Marylin Bender and Selig Altschul, *Chosen Instrument: Pan Am, Juan Trippe, the Rise and Fall of an American Entrepreneur* (New York: Simon and Schuster, 1982).

4. Alan Brinkley, *The End of Reform: New Deal Liberalism in Recession and War* (New York: Vintage, 1996); Kim Phillips-Fein, *Invisible Hands: The Businessmen's Crusade against the New Deal* (New York: W. W. Norton, 2009); Roland Marchand, *Creating the Corporate Soul: The Rise of Public Relations and Corporate Imagery in American Big Business* (Berkeley: University of California Press, 1998), 312–56; William L. Bird, *Better Living: Advertising, Media, and the New Vocabulary of Business Leadership, 1935–1955* (Evanston, IL: Northwestern University Press, 1999).

5. Kenneth T. Jackson, *Crabgrass Frontier: The Suburbanization of the United States* (New York: Oxford University Press, 1985); Lawrence Culver, *The Frontier of Leisure: Southern California and the Shaping of Modern America* (New York: Oxford University Press, 2010), 170–238; Elaine Tyler May, *Homeward Bound: American Families in the Cold War Era*, rev. ed (New York: Basic Books, 1999); Lynn Spigel, *Make Room for TV: Television and the Family Ideal in Postwar America* (Chicago: University of Chicago Press, 1992); Wendy Kozol, *Life's America: Family and Nation in Postwar Photojournalism* (Philadelphia: Temple University Press, 1994); Jane Sherron De Hart, "Containment at Home: Gender, Sexuality, and National Identity in Cold War America," in *Rethinking Cold War Culture*, ed. Peter J. Kuznick and James Gilbert (Washington, DC: Smithsonian Institution Press, 2001), 130–34. On white flight, see Thomas Sugrue, *The Origins of the Urban Crisis: Race and Inequality in Postwar Detroit* (Princeton, NJ: Princeton University Press, 1996). On the retreat from public amusements, see David Nasaw, *Going Out: The Rise and Fall of Public Amusements* (New York: Basic Books, 1993); Eric Avila, *Popular Culture in the Age of White Flight: Fear and Fantasy in Suburban Los Angeles* (Berkeley: University of California Press, 2004); Bryant Simon, *Boardwalk of Dreams: Atlantic City and the Fate of Urban America* (New York: Oxford University Press, 2004). As Elizabeth Fratterigo argues, much of the appeal of *Playboy* magazine in the 1950s and 1960s was the idealized picture of modern urban life it presented as an alternative to suburban domesticity. See *Playboy and the Making of the Good Life in Modern America* (New York: Oxford University Press, 2009), 80–104.

6. On notions that class had become an outmoded concept in postwar American culture, see Roland Marchand, "Visions of Classlessness, Quests for Dominion: American Popular Culture, 1945–1960," in *Reshaping America: Society and Institutions, 1945–1960*, ed. Robert H. Bremner and Gary W. Reichard (Columbus: Ohio State University Press, 1982), 163–90; Alan Brinkley, "The Illusion of Unity in Cold War Culture," in Kuznick and Gilbert, *Rethinking Cold War Culture*, 61–73. On the "middle majority," see Andrew Hurley, *Diners, Bowling Alleys, and Trailer Parks: Chasing the American Dream in Postwar Consumer Culture* (New York: Basic Books, 2001), 12.

7. Tom Bernard, "Vacations—American Plan," *American Magazine*, Vacation Issue, 1947, 32.

8. John Steinbeck, "The Yank in Europe," *Holiday,* January 1956, 25

9. Hubert Kelly, "Travelers Tell All," *American Magazine,* August 1949, 37.

10. Eleanor Phillips, "Come On, Girls—Paris Is Ours!" *Independent Woman,* March 1949, 80.

11. Irwin Shaw, "How to Live Abroad," *Holiday,* July 1951, 86–87; Gordon Gaskill, "Mr. Smith Goes to Europe," *American Magazine,* March 1950, 30; Juan Trippe, "Now You Can Take That Trip Abroad," *Reader's Digest,* January 1949, 69; "Your Right to Be Restless," 30.

12. "Homecoming Tourists Break Travel Record," *Life,* September 26, 1949, 38; H. W. Shane, "Letter from the Publisher," *Travel,* July 1955, 3; "Where to Go Vacationing," *Ebony,* July 1947, 14.

13. Matson Line, "Sailing Day," *Holiday,* September 1948, 90; Social Research, Inc., *P&O-Orient Lines in California: A Research Report* (1964), 36, box 57, folder P&O 1964, DO.

14. Trippe, "Now You Can Take That Trip Abroad," 70.

15. "Travel 1953," *Look,* December 30, 1952, 17; Carl L. Biemiller, "Our Wonderful Restlessness," *Holiday,* July 1952, 46.

16. "Biggest Year for Resorts," *Business Week,* June 10, 1950, 91; "More Time Off," *Business Week,* June 28, 1952, 154.

17. Robert M. Yoder and Don Tobin, "Two Weeks with Pay," *Saturday Evening Post,* July 3, 1948, 38; "The Great American Two Weeks," *Look,* June 15, 1954, 120; "Planning for Next Year's Vacation?" *The Eagle Speaks,* September 1951, 3, box 78, folder 2, JW; Eddie Cochran, *Summertime Blues,* Jerry Capehart and Eddie Cochran, Liberty Records, 1958.

18. "Notes on the Permanent Revolution," *Fortune,* August 1951, 64; George Soule, "The Economics of Leisure," *Annals of the American Academy of Political and Social Science* 313 (September 1957): 17.

19. "Innocents Abroad," *The Eagle Speaks,* September 1955, 5, box 78, folder 6, JW.

20. "Under the Sun: 365 with Pay," *Holiday,* August 1949 21; "A Year's Vacation," *Time,* June 22, 1953, 76.

21. "On the Move?" *The Eagle Speaks,* February 1955, 3, box 78, folder 6, JW; "A Country Day Livens Stay-Home Vacations," *Business Week,* August 7, 1954, 106, 108.

22. Roy Rosenzweig, *Eight Hours for What We Will: Workers and Leisure in an Industrial City, 1870–1920* (Cambridge: Cambridge University Press, 1983), 68–71; Jerome P. Bjelopera, *City of Clerks: Office and Sales Workers in Philadelphia, 1870–1920* (Urbana: University of Illinois Press, 2005), 107–10.

23. "Fort Wayne Flies to Paris," *Fortune,* June 1953, 111–12. *Newsweek* later reported that Communists they met in Italy were astounded by their capacity to vacation in Europe. "The 'Innocents'—1954," *Newsweek,* September 27, 1954, 96; Larry Sims, "90 Factory Women Off on Flight to See Europe," *Philadelphia Evening Bulletin,* July 26, 1953; "No Recession in Tourist Trade," *Business Week,* May 10, 1958, 78; "Trips for Toilers," *Newsweek,* August 4, 1952, 71.

24. "Havana Jaunt for 132, All on the Boss," *Life,* December 16, 1957, 125.

25. As Elizabeth Fones-Wolf has noted, the American System campaign was part of a larger public-relations effort mounted by business to resuscitate the "political language of the twenties, once again associating the American way with a harmonious, classless society, with nationalism, individual rights, free enterprise, and abundance rising from ever increasing productivity." Elizabeth Fones-Wolf, *Selling Free Enterprise: The Business Assault on Labor and Liberalism, 1945–1960* (Urbana: University of Illinois Press, 1994), 5.

26. Clark quoted in Robert Griffith, "The Selling of America: The Advertising Council and American Politics, 1942–1960," *Business History Review* 57, no. 3 (August 1983): 400; "Copy Theme for American System Campaign Ready This Month," *Printers' Ink,* June 13, 1947, 85.

27. *The Miracle of America,* Advertising Council, 1948, box 16, folder American Economic

System, 1948–51, AC; Griffith, "Selling of America," 402; "10 Prosperous Years Seen," *Philadelphia Evening Bulletin*, September 30, 1949.

28. "People's Capitalism: The Background—How and Why the Project Was Developed," n.d., box 31, folder People's Capitalism, 1956–59, AC; Advertising Council, *The American Roundtable Discussions on People's Capitalism at Yale University, New Haven, Connecticut, November 16 and 17, 1956* (New York: Advertising Council, 1957), 61, 5, 13. The digest was written up by David M. Potter.

29. "People's Capitalism Exhibit," typescript for exhibit (1956), box 31, folder People's Capitalism, 1956–59, AC; Advertising Council, *The American Roundtable Discussions*, 56, 59; Advertising Council, *The American Roundtable: People's Capitalism, Part II. An Inquiry into the Social and Cultural Trends in America under Our System of Widely Shared Material Benefits at the Yale Club, New York, New York, May 22, 1957* (New York: Advertising Council, 1958), 5.

30. Advertising Council, *American Roundtable: People's Capitalism, Part II*, 34.

31. U.S. Bureau of Labor Statistics, *How American Buying Habits Change* (Washington, DC: U.S. Government Printing Office, 1959), 216, 205; Shelley Nickles, "More Is Better: Mass Consumption, Gender, and Class Identity in Postwar America," *American Quarterly* 54, no. 4 (December 2002): 581–622.

32. Research Department, "Tourist and Vacation Advertising Expenditures in 1947," in *Digests of Principal Research Department Studies*, vol. 4: *1946–1949* (Philadelphia: Curtis Publishing Co., n.d.), 45.

33. C. Hartley Grattan, "The Economics of Holidays," *Harper's*, July 1950, 87; Dero A. Saunders and Sanford S. Parker, "$30 Billion for Fun," *Fortune*, June 1954, 234.

34. "More Fun for More Dollars," *Newsweek*, June 9, 1947, 68; "Vacation Gold in Them Thar Hills," *Business Week*, October 6, 1951, 118; "Biggest Season Yet: 55-Million Americans on the Move," *Business Week*, June 28, 1952, 150; "Economy-Size Vacations," *Business Week*, September 18, 1954, 29.

35. Peter B. B. Andrews, "Americans May Spend 12 Billion on Vacations This Year," *Printers' Ink*, April 27, 1951, 42; "Everyone's Going Someplace," *Business Week*, May 26, 1951, 44; "Florida Project Plays a New Trend in Vacations," *Business Week*, March 1, 1952, 75; Peter B. B. Andrews, "New Peaks for Vacation Travel Expenditures," *Printers' Ink*, May 23, 1952, 48, 60; Peter B. B. Andrews, "1953 Will Be Top Travel Promotion Year," *Printers' Ink*, May 1, 1953, 72; "No Recession in Tourist Trade," *Business Week*, May 10, 1958, 72; "Shorter Vacation Hops," *Business Week*, June 21, 1958, 33.

36. "The Vacation Business Is Booming As Never Before," *Newsweek*, July 3, 1950, 20; "Americans on the Move," *Newsweek*, July 2, 1951, 59; "American Tourists Are Spending $1,094,000,000," *Newsweek*, November 4, 1952, 75; "Americans Hit the Open Road: It's a Record Year for Travel," *Newsweek*, July 20, 1953, 70; "Booming Winter Travel: By Air, Land, and Sea," *Newsweek*, January 18, 1954, 78; "America on the Go: More People Going More Places," *Newsweek*, April 5, 1954, 57; "Big Rush to the Sun," *Newsweek*, January 17, 1955, 67; "Destination: Everywhere," *Newsweek*, April 4, 1955, 63.

37. "More Fun for More Dollars," 68, 70; "Florida Beckons," *Business Week*, January 8, 1949, 24; Andrew L. Yarrow, "The Big Postwar Story: The Big Postwar Story: Abundance and the Rise of Economic Journalism," *Journalism History* 32, no. 2 (Summer 2006): 66–69, 72.

38. Endy, *Cold War Holidays*, 143–44. Endy provides a brief but helpful discussion of the middle-class globetrotter as an overrepresented but ideologically powerful figure.

39. "Cold War: A Four-Color Duel," *Business Week*, July 28, 1956, 33–34; Harry Phillips, "Memo from the Publisher," *Sports Illustrated*, May 20, 1955, 10.

40. Survey Research Center, *The Travel Market, 1956* (University of Michigan: Institute for Social Research, 1957), 98, 103.

41. All quoted in ibid., 92–96, 103.

42. Ibid., 92–96.

43. John B. Lansing, *The Travel Market, 1958: A Report on the Vacation Travel, Travel Patterns and Attitudes of American Families* (University of Michigan: Institute For Social Research, 1958), 21, 22–23, 29–30.

44. Ibid., 30–33.

45. David Ogilvy to W. S. Blair, March 14, 1955, box 44, folder BTA January–July 1955, DO.

46. Bill Blair, "Comments on 'Potential Travel Market for Europe in the U.S.A'" (n.d.), 7, 11, box 45, folder BTA 1958–1960, DO; David Ogilvy to Roger Lloyd, August 31, 1959, box 45, folder BTA 1958–1960, DO.

47. "Railroad Travel Can Be Dressed Up, Sold through Advertising, Says C&O Chair," *Printers' Ink*, February 1, 1946, 91; Arthur Miller, *Death of a Salesman: Certain Private Conversations in Two Acts and a Requiem* (New York: Viking Press, 1949), 22.

48. Cotten Seiler, *Republic of Drivers: A Cultural History of Automobility in America* (Chicago: University of Chicago Press, 2008); John A. Kouwenhoven, *The Beer Can by the Highway: Essays on What's 'American' about America* (Garden City, NY: Doubleday and Co., 1961), 222–23.

49. "Americans on the Move," *Holiday*, July 1952, 33. Also see William Atwood, "A New Look at Americans," *Look*, July 12, 1956, 48; Biemiller, "Our Wonderful Restlessness," 46; "Publisher's Letter," *Time*, July 4, 1955, 7.

50. "The 121st Holiday," *Holiday*, March 1956, 32.

51. William D. Patterson, "Everyman, Everywhere," *Saturday Review*, October 12, 1956, 33; "Booming Winter Travel," 80; "For Women Only," *Look*, June 25, 1957, 94.

52. Arthur W. Baum, "Adventures in the Family Car," *Saturday Evening Post*, October 31, 1953; "Dude Ranch Vacations," *Look*, October 29, 1946, 68; "Travel and Vacation with Look," *Look*, January 1, 1952, 19. Also see "Time to Play," *Holiday*, May 1946, 17.

53. John Steinbeck, *Travels with Charley: In Search of America* (1962; New York: Penguin, 1986), 103–4; Foster Rhea Dulles, "A Historical View of Americans Abroad," *Annals of American Academy of Political and Social Science* 368 (November 1966): 12, 19.

54. John W. MacPherrin, "It's American to Travel," *American Magazine*, May 1954, 136; "Americans on the Move," *Holiday*, July 1952, 33; John Kord Lagemann, "The Glory Road," *Collier's*, March 26, 1949, 16, 34; John Kord Lagemann, "The Glory Road: Part II," *Collier's*, April 2, 1949, 33. For similar statements, see Biemiller, "Our Wonderful Restlessness," 46.

55. Jack Kerouac, *On the Road* (1957; New York: Penguin, 2003), 7–8.

56. Toni Robin, "America's Own Fashions," *Holiday*, July 1952, 105, 103.

57. "Tourist Visits Europe's Big Cities without Leaving U.S.," *Life*, January 10, 1949, 10; "Headstander Is Off Again," *Life*, October 24, 1949, 131. Also see "A Town on Tour," *Life*, February 21, 1955, 142–43; Cornelius F. Cronin Jr., "Vacation Afloat," *American Magazine*, February 1951, 84–85.

58. "Your Right to Be Restless," 30; Harry Dooley, "You Can Go Where You Please," *American Magazine*, March 1950, 132; Roger Angell, "Journey to Freedom," *Holiday*, November 1950, 24.

59. Sir William P. Hildred, "Very Suspicious Characters," *Saturday Evening Post*, December 7, 1946, 73, 74; "Holiday Invites You to Join a Crusade," *Holiday*, September 1946, 20; Henry A. Wallace, "Letters," *Holiday*, November 1946, 8. Also see "For a Fundamental Freedom," *Time*, July 4, 1955, 16.

60. "Ted Patrick," *Holiday*, May 1964, 37; "Place of the Month: United Nations," *Holiday*,

October 1955, 124–25; "Five Years of Holiday," *Holiday*, March 1951, 32; "Who and Where," *Holiday*, March 1956, 32; "The Small Voice of Peace," *Holiday*, August 1960, 27; Patterson, "Everyman, Everywhere," 33; William D. Patterson, "The Fifth Freedom: Travel," *Saturday Review*, March 15, 1952, 42. Also see the internationalist-tinged collection of *Holiday* essays *The World of Mankind* (New York: Golden Press, 1962).

61. Eric J. Sandeen, *Picturing an Exhibition: The Family of Man and 1950s America* (Albuquerque: University of New Mexico Press, 1995), 11–38; Peggy M. Von Eschen, *Satchmo Blows Up the World: Jazz Ambassadors Play the Cold War* (Cambridge, MA: Harvard University Press, 2004); Klein, *Cold War Orientalism*, 100–142, 29–32. On the World War II–era aversion to war by those directly impacted by it, see Paul Fussell, *Wartime: Understanding and Behavior in the Second World War* (New York: Oxford University Press, 1989), 269–90.

62. On modernism and technocracy, see Jackson Lears, *Something for Nothing: Luck in America* (New York: Penguin, 2003), and Suleiman Osman, *The Invention of Brownstone Brooklyn: Gentrification and the Search for Authenticity in Postwar New York* (New York: Oxford University Press, 2011). On the swinging pendulum of internationalism and nationalism, see David Harvey, *The Condition of Postmodernity: An Enquiry into the Origins of Cultural Change* (Oxford: Blackwell, 1990), 270–83, 36–38.

63. Wendell L. Willkie, *One World* (New York: Simon and Schuster, 1943), 202–3; David E. Nye, *American Technological Sublime* (Cambridge, MA: MIT Press, 1994), 62, 70–76, 201–3.

64. Norman Corwin to Bill Costello, June 14, 1946, in *Norman Corwin's Letters*, ed. A. J. Langguth (New York: Barricade Books, 1993), 94.

65. Norman Corwin, "Airborne," *Holiday*, August 1946, 49–50, 52. On romantic tourism and rhapsodizing in the nineteenth century, see Dona Brown, *Inventing New England: Regional Tourism in the Nineteenth Century* (Washington, DC: Smithsonian Institution Press, 1995), 15–40.

66. Walker Evans, "Over California," *Fortune*, March 1954, 105; Newman Bumstead, "A Map Maker Looks at the U.S.," *National Geographic*, June 1951, 705; "What Will It Be Like to Fly in a Jet," *Holiday*, April 1957, 12–13.

67. "Map Happy," *Holiday*, July 1951, 20.

68. William Atwood, "One Way to See the Biggest Prison in the World," *Look*, November 25, 1958, 45; Nate White, "'Nyet' to Tourists in Soviet Russia," *Reader's Digest*, December 1960, 98, 96; Eugene Lyons, "One Trip to Russia Doesn't Make an Expert," *Reader's Digest*, October 1959, 213. On the fierce anti-Communism that characterized postwar *Reader's Digest*, see Joanne P. Sharp, *Condensing the Cold War: Reader's Digest and American Identity* (Minneapolis: University of Minnesota, 2000).

69. Atwood, "One Way to See the Biggest Prison in the World, 45; Harry G. Nickles, "Holiday in Russia," *Holiday*, July 1955, 103. Also see "Bonjour Ivan," *Life*, October 10, 1955, 193; Fielding's anti-Communism is described in Neal Moses Rosendorf, "Be El Caudillo's Guest," *Diplomatic History* 30, no. 3 (June 2006): 393–95.

70. "The Rush to 'Out-of-the-Way' Europe," *Newsweek*, June 3, 1963, 69.

71. "Calling the Crack," *Newsweek*, May 12, 1952, 49; Leonard B. Boudin, "The Right to Travel: A Significant Victory," *Nation*, July 30, 1955, 95; "International Gag," *Nation*, January 15, 1955, 43; "The American Right to Travel Abroad," *New Republic*, July 4, 1955, 3; "Fly Your Kite, Foster," *New Republic*, September 19, 1957, 4; Joseph N. Welch, "A Citizen Criticizes," *Saturday Review*, January 11, 1958, 10; "The Right to Travel," *New Republic*, April 14, 1958, 6; "They May Not Travel," *New Republic*, December 18, 1961, 4; Henry Steele Commager, "A Nation of Travelers," *Saturday Review*, January 11, 1958, 24.

72. Rosendorf, "Be El Caudillo's Guest," 367–407; Horace Sutton, "Europe This Summer?"

Nation, May 17, 1947, 571; "Spain: American Tourists Rediscover Treasure of Color and History," *Life*, August 18, 1952, 50.

73. "World's Winter Wonderlands," *Newsweek*, January 18, 1954, 78; Nadine Gordimer, "Apartheid," *Holiday*, April 1959, 94. On apartheid and the Cold War relations between South Africa and the United States, see Hobsbawm, *Age of Extremes*, 40, 72, 131, 248.

74. "Atlantic Coast Has Most Negro Resorts," *Ebony*, July 1947, 16.

75. Susan Session Rugh, *Are We There Yet? The Golden Age of American Family Vacations* (Lawrence: University Press of Kansas, 2008), 80; Horace Sutton, "Vacations across the Color Line," *Saturday Review*, May 13, 1950, 40; Hollis Alpert, "Vacations for Every Purse," *New Republic*, July 7, 1947, 18.

76. On the *Green Book* and *Travelguide*, see Seiler, *Republic of Drivers*, 105–28; W. T. Lhamon Jr., *Deliberate Speed: The Origins of a Cultural Style in the American 1950s* (Washington, DC: Smithsonian Institution Press, 1990), 7, 76–86; "Auto Travel Is Best Way to Travel," *Ebony*, May 1948, 24. On the "hate stare," see John Howard Griffith, *Black Like Me* (New York: Signet, 1961), 50–51.

77. "Summercamps," *Ebony*, August 1947, 36, 36–40; "Florida Package Vacation," *Ebony*, April 1950, 61.

78. "Two GIs Go Back to Paris," *Ebony*, March 1947, 16; "Where to Vacation in California," *Ebony*, May 1948, 23; "Summer Resorts," *Ebony*, July 1949, 34; Harvey Levenstein, *We'll Always Have Paris: American Tourists in France since 1930* (Chicago: University of Chicago Press, 2004), 147–52.

79. "Art Student in Europe," *Ebony*, February 1949, 57; "Mexico," *Ebony*, October 1948, 13, 15.

80. "Vacation in the West Indies," *Ebony*, March 1951, 35; "Winter Vacations," *Ebony*, December 1953, 62; "Vacation in Nassau," *Ebony*, February 1953, 76.

81. "Atlantic Coast Has Most Negro Resorts," 16; "Skiing," *Ebony*, February 1949, 52–53.

82. "Why Resort Decided to Accept Negroes," *Ebony*, July 1953, 108; "Hotels on the Highway," *Ebony*, June 1955, 93, 96, 103.

83. Charles W. Lowery, "Letters," *Ebony*, May 1949, 9; Charles Muscovalley, "Letters," *Ebony*, September 1953; Mrs. Robert Ferguson, "Letters," *Ebony*, August 1955, 6.

84. "Engine Charlie," *Time*, October 6, 1961, 24. Wilson actually said, "For years I thought that what was good for our country was good for General Motors, and vice versa."

CHAPTER FOUR

1. Anita Brenner, "Mexican Fact and Fiction," *Holiday*, March 1947, 22, 25, 50; Trevor Christie to Anita Brenner, July 17, 1947, box 65, folder 2, AB; Alex Buelna to Laura Bergquist, March 31, 1947, box 29, folder 6, AB; Anita Brenner to Ik Shuman, March 29, 1947, box 65, folder 2, AB.

2. On tourism narratives and imagery as integral to the global tourism economy, see Edward M. Bruner, *Culture on Tour: Ethnographies of Travel* (Chicago: University of Chicago Press, 2005), 22;

3. On knowledge, fantasy, and imagined landscapes see, Edward Said, *Orientalism* (New York: Vintage, 1978); and Elizabeth Edwards, "Postcards from Another World," in *The Tourist Image: Myths and Myth Making in Tourism*, ed. Tom Selwyn (New York: John Wiley and Sons, 1996), 216. On guidebooks and ways of seeing, see Jan Palmowski, "Travels with Baedeker: The Guidebook and the Middle Classes in Victorian and Edwardian England," in *Histories of Leisure*, ed. Rudi Koshar (New York: Berg, 2002), 105–30, and Rudi Koshar, "'What Ought to Be Seen': Tourists Guidebooks in Modern Germany and Europe," *Journal of Contemporary History* 33, no. 3 (1998): 323–40.

4. Eric J. Sandeen, *Picturing an Exhibition: The Family of Man and 1950s America* (Albuquerque:

University of New Mexico Press, 1995), 11–38; Christina Klein, *Cold War Orientalism: Asia in the Middlebrow Imagination, 1945–1961* (Berkeley: University of California Press, 2003), 100–142, 29–32; David Harvey, *The Condition of Postmodernity: An Enquiry into the Origins of Cultural Change* (Oxford: Blackwell, 1990), 270–83, 36–38.

5. Dean MacCannell, *The Tourist: A New Theory of the Leisure Class* (1976; Berkeley: University of California Press, 1999), 13. Sociologist Judith Adler has called this "a double movement of projection and reinternalization" in "Travel as Performed Art," *American Journal of Sociology* 94, no. 6 (1989): 1376.

6. Orvar Löfgren, *On Holiday: A History of Vacationing* (Berkeley: University of California Press, 1999), 93; Bruner, *Culture on Tour*, 22, 198–199.

7. Kathryn News, "Edwin Hill ('Ted') Patrick," in *American Magazine Journalists, 1900–1960*, 2nd ser., ed. Sam G. Riley (Detroit: Gale Research, 1994), 219; "1961 P.A.T.A. Award Winners," *New York Times*, February 18, 1962, ADS18.

8. Lawrence R. Samuel, *Brought to You By: Postwar Television Advertising and the American Dream* (Austin: University of Texas Press, 2001), 192–94; "Pan American World Airways (December 1956)," 1, 7, J. Walter Thompson—Review Board Records, box 23, folder Meetings: Pan American Minutes, 1955–1956, JWT. United Airlines also eschewed network television advertising, with rare exceptions such as an NBC special about Hawaii, through the early 1960s. "Jet Age Media Strategy at United Air Lines," *Media/Scope*, May 1960, 106. Also see David Ogilvy, "How the New Tourism Can Be Sold," box 78, folder Speeches 1963–1968, 3, DO.

9. For representative examples, see "California Dude Ranch," *Ebony*, February 1947, 5; "Mexico in 1947," *Life*, April 24, 1947, 96; "Grand Canyon," *Life*, September 8, 1947, 74; "The New Riviera," *Life*, November 10, 1947, 137; "Life Takes a Cruise on the 'Corsair,'" *Life*, December 1, 1947, 153; John Kord Lagemann, "Beauty on a Bend," *Collier's*, January 31, 1948, 13; John K. Lagemann, "The Mermaid in the Bottle," *Collier's*, March 13, 1948, 26; J. Marshall, "Out Where the West Ends," *Collier's*, April 24, 1948, 22; John K. Lagemann, "They Cut Down the Old Pine Tree in Northern Michigan," *Collier's*, June 19, 1948, 70; "Vacation in Haiti," *Ebony*, July 1948, 52; "Mexico," *Ebony*, October 1948, 13; "Jamaica," *Ebony*, November 1948; "Caribbean Winter," *Life*, January 3, 1949, 37; "The Southwest," *Life*, March 14, 1949, 62; "Niagara Falls," *Life*, June 6, 1949, 76; "The Coast of Europe," *Life*, June 13, 1949, 62; "The Skyline Drive," *Life*, June 20, 1949, 72; "Yosemite," *Life*, July 25, 1949, 53; "Rome," *Life*, August 1, 1949, 45; "With Douglas in Iran," *Life*, August 15, 1949, 59; "Capri," *Life*, September 19, 1949, 74; "Caribbean Carnival," *Life*, March 13, 1950, 98; "Cape Vincent—Where the Fish Go to Bite," *Look*, May 23, 1950, 82; "U.S. Luxury Cruise Hits the Casbah," *Life*, April 3, 1950, 21; "Columbia River Holiday," *Look*, August 15, 1950; "Ozark Vacation," *Look*, August 29, 1950; "Life Visits a South American Riviera," *Life*, April 2, 1951, 120; "Arizona's Best Foot," *Life*, September 24, 1951, 97; "Life Goes on a Travel Agent's Dream Tour," *Life*, November 5, 1951, 160; "Mexico's Pet Volcano," *Life*, March 17, 1952, 58; "Refuge in Jamaica," *Look*, July 1, 1952, 54; "Spain: American Tourists Rediscover Treasure of Color and History," *Life*, August 18, 1952, 50; "Las Vegas," *Look*, November 4, 1952, 57; "The Rocky Sahara," *Life*, May 4, 1953, 36; "Colorado," *Look*, August 25, 1953, 31; "Jones Beach: Swimmin' Hole for Millions," *Look*, August 25, 1953, 92; "An Artist in Africa," *Life*, November 10, 1953, 109; "West Indies Escape," *Life*, January 1, 1954, 76; "The Rhine," *Life*, May 10, 1954, 94; "A Cook's Tour in Katmandu," *Life*, March 28, 1955, 43; "Mediterranean Leisure Land," *Life*, July 18, 1955, 81; "Back-Yard Vacation," *Look*, July 24, 1956; "The West Is a Way of Living," *Look*, September 18, 1956, 19; "Family Fun in Our Newest National Park," *Look*, November 13, 1956, 136; "A Tourist's Eye View of Manhattan," *Look*, February, 18, 1958, 34; "The Color That Is Rome," *Look*, August 5, 1958, 52.

10. *Look at the USA* (1947; Boston: Houghton-Mifflin, 1955); Carl Carmer, "Beautiful, but ...," *Saturday Revew,* October 18, 1947.

11. "Travelers Checks Cashed Here," *Time,* June 14, 1948, 23; "Fair and Warmer, South of the Border," *Time,* February 21, 1949, 35; "Tourist Outpost," *Time,* July 4, 1949, 28; "Dollars Abroad in a Tourist Tide," *Newsweek,* July 4, 1949, 28; "Festivaland," *Time,* July 2, 1951, 25; "Travel Posters," *Time,* May 5, 1952, 82; "Cruise Stopover," *Newsweek,* November 15, 1954, 60; "Moscow for the Tourist," *Time,* November, 28, 1955, 53.

12. Fill Calhoun to Ed Thompson, January 3, 1950, box 61, folder 3, EE.

13. Eliot Elisofon to Phil Wootton, September 27, 1957, box 62, folder 3, EE; Eliot Elisofon to Roy Mackland, October 6, 1958, box 27, folder 10, EE; "Rocky Sahara," 37.

14. Norman D. Ford, "Twenty New Budget Vacations," *Collier's,* June 10, 1955, 30; "Twenty Budget Vacations for 1956," *Collier's,* June 8, 1956, 28; "Fall Travel: Take an Autumn Leave," *Collier's,* September 28, 1956, 36; Norman D. Ford, "New Budget Winter Vacations," *Collier's,* January 4, 1957, 52; "Top 12 with Tourists," *Look,* January 1, 1952, 37; "Pacific Coast: The Eighth Wonder," *Look,* January 1, 1952, 20; "Everything under the Sun ... ," *Look,* January 1, 1952, 46; "Pleasure Hunting in the West Indies," *Look,* January 1, 1952, 48; "Canada for Skiing," *Look,* January 1, 1952, 42; Saul Steinberg, "And Europe," *Look,* January 1, 1952, 54; Arthur Rothstein, "The West by Family Car," *Look,* December 30, 1952, 18; "The Mediterranean," *Look,* December 30, 1952, 35; "Walter Winchell's New York," *Look,* January 12, 1954, 20; "Pacific Paradise," *Look,* January 12, 1954, 14; "Key Hopping," *Look,* January 12, 1954, 22; "The Sunny Southwest," *Look,* January 12, 1954, 26; "Guaymas of the Bay," *Look,* January 12, 1954, 29; "West Indies Ho!" *Look,* January 12, 1954, 42; "Haiti," *Look,* January 12, 1954, 45; "Herb Cohen's San Francisco," *Look,* January 12, 1954, 48; "Canada's Laurentians," *Look,* January 12, 1954, 50; "Central America," *Look,* January 12, 1954, 54; "Southern California," *Look,* January 12, 1954, 58.

15. James A. Linen, "Publisher's Letter," *Time,* July 4, 1955, 7; John W. McPherrin, "It's American to Travel," *American Magazine,* May 1954, 136. *American Magazine* directly contacted ad agencies to express its goals of stimulating travel. See Somerset R. Waters to A. Hewitt, March 22, 1951, box 1, folder American Magazine, DO. Also see Theodore F. Mueller, "Vacation Plans," *Newsweek,* April 11, 1955, 23.

16. Bert Steinhauser to Eliot Elisofon, June 3, 1959, box 62, folder 5, EE; "Pan American World Airways Script for System Sales Meeting," December 6, 1955, 21–23, box 23, folder Meetings: Pan American Minutes, 1955–1956, J. Walter Thompson—Review Board Records, JWT.

17. "Guide and Instructions to Canadian Club Photographers," box 14, folder 18, EE; "Early Times Expects Good Times with Liquor and Vacations," *Printers' Ink,* June 4, 1954, 30.

18. "I Wish I Were in Michigan," *Look,* July 28, 1953, 72.

19. "Wish You Were Here," *Printers' Ink,* August 19, 1955, 83–84.

20. Ibid.

21. Raymond Williams, *The Country and the City* (New York: Oxford University Press, 1973); Raymond Williams, *The Long Revolution* (New York: Columbia University Press, 1961), 47; Edward W. Said, *Culture and Imperialism* (New York: Vintage, 1994), 52, 78.

22. Pierre Bourdieu, *The Field of Cultural Production: Essays on Art and Literature* (New York: Columbia University Press, 1993).

23. "'Holiday' Is Here," *Tide,* October 15, 1945, 68.

24. "Introductory," *Magazine of Travel: A Work Devoted to Original Travels, in Various Countries, Both of the Old World and the New,* January 1857, v.

25. Frank Luther Mott, *A History of American Magazines* (Cambridge, MA: Harvard University

Press, 1938), 224–25; Theodore B. Peterson, *Magazines in the Twentieth Century* (Urbana: University of Illinois Press, 1964), 394. On the Bay View reading groups and the broader middle-class fascination with foreign travel at the turn of the century, see Kristin L. Hoganson, *Consumers' Imperium: The Global Production of American Domesticity, 1865–1920* (Chapel Hill: University of North Carolina Press, 2007), 153–208.

26. Ishbel Ross, "Geography Inc.," *Scribner's Magazine*, May 1938, 23; "National Geographic," *Tide*, December 20, 1946, 36. Also see Susan Schulten, *The Geographical Imagination in America, 1880–1950* (Chicago: University of Chicago Press, 2001), and Catherine A. Lutz and Jane L. Collins, *Reading National Geographic* (Chicago: University of Chicago Press, 1993).

27. On Victorian notions of exploration and discovery, see Mary Louise Pratt, *Imperial Eyes: Travel Writing and Transculturation* (London: Routledge, 1992), 201–5, and Michael F. Robinson, *The Coldest Crucible: Arctic Exploration and American Culture* (Chicago: University of Chicago Press, 2006).

28. "Henry Collins Walsh Joins Nomad Staff," *Journeys Beautiful*, February 1925, 5; "Henry C. Walsh, Explorer, Dead," *New York Times*, April 30, 1927, 19; cover, *Nomad*, December 1929; "Nomad Travel Club Dinners," *Journeys Beautiful*, October 1925, 30; "Answer the Call of the Wanderlust," *Journeys Beautiful*, November 1925, 53.

29. "Fix Date For Ocean Flight," *New York Times*, July 24, 1925, 13; "To Fly for $25,000 Prize," *New York Times*, August 13, 1925, 4. World Traveler acted as a liaison for French flying pioneers Paul Tarascon and Francois Coli in the mid-1920s. Coli would eventually crash into the North Atlantic just weeks before Charles Lindbergh made his historic journey. "Topics of the Times: Crippled Airmen to Fly the Atlantic," *New York Times*, October 7, 1926, 26; "Hope for Aviators Nears End in Paris," *New York Times*, May 15, 1927, 2; "New Yorker Gets Lost in a German Castle," *New York Times*, October 6, 1925, 2.

30. Howard Clark, "Notes of a Cosmopolite," *World Traveler*, February 1929, 20; "Automobile Salon: The Aristocracy of Motordom," *World Traveler*, February 1929, 9; Basil Woon, "The Europe of the Summer," *World Traveler*, March 1929, 17.

31. "So You're Going," *So You're Going News*, December 1936, 13; Florence Finch Kelly, "An Editor Takes to Travel," *New York Times*, May 6, 1934, BR19.

32. John M. Coward, "Selling the Southwestern Indian: Ideology and Image in Arizona Highways, 1925–1940," *American Journalism* 20 (Spring 2003): 13–31, 16–17; American Automobile Association, *Americans on the Highway: A Report on Recent Trends of Tourist Travel* (Washington, DC: AAA, 1949), 22; Peterson, *Magazines in the Twentieth Century*, 394.

33. Barbara Berglund, "Western Living Sunset Style in the 1920s and 1930s: The Middlebrow, the Civilized, and the Modern," *Western Historical Quarterly* 37, no. 2 (Summer 2006): 133–57; Diana Rice, "Random Notes for Travelers," *New York Times*, March 1, 1936, XX5; Philip H. Dougherty, "Advertising: Reader's Digest Acquisition," *New York Times*, December 19, 1986, D7.

34. Quoted in Kirk Polking, "Curtis," *Writer's Yearbook 1958*, 157, in box 152, folder 146, CPC. *Information Please!* was premised on ordinary listeners stumping the certified expert on a topic.

35. On Fadiman, see Joan Shelley Rubin, *The Making of Middlebrow Culture* (Chapel Hill: University of North Carolina Press, 1992); Janice A. Radway, *A Feeling for Books: The Book-of-the-Month Club, Literary Taste, and Middle-Class Desire* (Chapel Hill: University of North Carolina Press, 1997). Despite the offensive nature of terms like "lowbrow," "middlebrow," and "highbrow"—which were rooted in the racist pseudoscience of phrenology, or the study of skulls for signs of evolutionary development—"brow" remained a commonly used descriptor of cultural sophistication throughout the midcentury era. Thus "middlebrow" culture is not used here as

a pejorative term but to describe a type of media content often referred to as "middlebrow" at the time. On the development of "highbrow" and "lowbrow" discourse, see Lawrence W. Levine, *Highbrow/Lowbrow: The Emergence of Cultural Hierarchy in America* (Cambridge, MA: Harvard University Press, 1988), 221–27.

36. Jerome Weidman to Harry Sions, February 12, 1955, box 11, folder 2, JWP.
37. Polking, "Curtis," 15.
38. Malcolm Cowley, "The Magazine Story of the Year," *Holiday*, August 1954, 33.
39. Harry Sions to Sewell Haggard, May 4, 1950, box 11, folder 12, RL.
40. Alex Buelna to Laura Bergquist, March 31, 1947, box 29, folder 6, AB.
41. Richard Field to Anita Brenner, November 21, 1947, box 33, folder 7, AB.
42. Jack Kerouac to Sterling Lord, June 2, 1962, in *Selected Letters, 1957–1969/Jack Kerouac*, ed. by Ann Charters (New York: Viking, 1999), 338–39.
43. Harry Sions to Nancy Wilson Ross, August 1, 1956, box 75, folder 13, NWR.
44. Richard L. Field to Carson McCullers, June 17, 1953, box 27, folder 1, CM. The magazine would later go on to reject the story it solicited from McCullers.
45. Richard Llewellyn, "Wales," *Holiday*, May 1951, 87, 89; Richard L. Field to Richard Llewellyn, July 1, 1949, box 11, folder 12, RL.
46. Llewellyn, "Wales," 87, 89.
47. Ibid., 60–61.
48. Bruner, *Culture on Tour*, 22; Adler, "Travel as Performed Art," 1376.
49. Harry Sions to James Jones, February 9, May 11, 1956, box 53, folder 5, JJ.
50. Educational Bureau, *Case History of the New York Issue of Holiday* (Philadelphia: Curtis Publishing Co., 1959), 3, folder 33, MSS8AF, Wisconsin Historical Society, Madison, Wis.
51. Aubrey Menen, "A First Look at New York," *Holiday*, October 1959, 54; Educational Bureau, *Case History*, 7; Richard Llewellyn, "Untitled Article on Buenos Aires," 2, box 8, folder 7, RL; Harry Sions to Sewell Haggard, May 4, 1950, box 11, folder 12, RL.
52. John Schaffner to John Graves, May 29, December 4, 1958, box 5, folder 3, JG; John Graves, *Goodbye to a River* (New York: Knopf, 1960).
53. John Graves to John Schaffner, September 12, 1957, box 5, folder 3, JG; John Graves, "A Piece of a River; Shortened Revision of 19 April 1958," 13, box 5, folder 3, JG; John Graves, "Drifting down the Brazos," *Holiday*, November 1959, 36.
54. Percy Knauth to John Schaffner, March 31, 1958, box 5, folder 3, JG; Graves, "Drifting down the Brazos," 35.
55. Hubert Creekmore to John Graves, April 23, 1959, box 3, folder 5, JG; John Graves to Arnold Ehrlich, May 2, 1958, box 3, folder 5, JG; Graves, "Drifting down the Brazos," 36.
56. John Graves, "A Note," in *Goodbye to a River*, front matter.
57. Quoted in John D. Weaver, *Speaking of Holiday* 8, no. 5, May 1961, in box 97, folder 1, NWR.
58. Graves, "Piece of a River," 17. On violence and American frontier mythology, see Richard Slotkin, *Regeneration through Violence: The Mythology of the American Frontier, 1600–1860* (Norman: University of Oklahoma Press, 2000).
59. Graves, "Drifting down the Brazos," 37; Percy Knauth to John Schaffner, March 31, 1958, box 5, folder 3, JG; James Cerruti to John Graves, August 29, 1961, and James Cerruti to John Graves, December 13, 1961, both in box 5, folder 2, JG.
60. *Holiday* editors sent Carson McCullers a copy of Guthrie's "Montana" as an example of the kind of profile they were looking for. Richard Field to Carson McCullers, June 17, 1953, box 27, folder 1, CM; A. B. Guthrie Jr., "Montana," *Holiday*, September 1950, 36, 91.

61. James L. Baughman, *The Republic of Mass Culture: Journalism, Filmmaking, and Broadcasting in America since 1941* (Baltimore: Johns Hopkins University Press, 1992), 89; Dayton Kohler, "A. B. Guthrie, Jr. and the West," *English Journal* 40, no. 2 (February 1951): 68–69.

62. See Richard Slotkin, *Gunfighter Nation: The Myth of the Frontier in Twentieth-Century America* (New York: Atheneum, 1992); John G. Cawelti, *The Six-Gun Mystique* (Bowling Green, OH: Bowling Green University Popular Press, 1971); Earl Pomeroy, *In Search of the Golden West: The Tourist in Western America* (New York: Knopf, 1957), 73–111; T. J. Jackson Lears, *No Place of Grace: Antimodernism and the Transformation of American Culture, 1880–1920* (Chicago: University of Chicago Press, 1981), 123; and K. A. Cuordileone, "Politics in the Age of Anxiety: Cold War Political Culture and the Crisis in American Masculinity, 1949–1960," *Journal of American History* 87, no. 2 (September 2000): 515–45.

63. James Cerruti to John Graves, January 27, 1961, and John Graves to James Cerruti, January 31, 1961, both in box 1, folder 2, JG.

64. Nancy Wilson Ross to Louis Mercie and Frank Zachary, December 6, 1958, box 77, folder 6, NWR; Nancy Wilson Ross to Harry Sions, January 17, 1959, box 77, folder 5, NWR; Nancy Wilson Ross, "Portland," *Holiday*, May 1959, 161.

65. On Spock and Spillane, see Elaine Tyler May, *Homeward Bound: American Families in the Cold War Era*, rev. ed. (New York: Basic Books, 1999), 85–86, 141. On Packard, White, and self-help books, see Roland Marchand, "Visions of Classlessness, Quests for Dominion," in *Reshaping America: Society and Institutions, 1945–1960*, ed. Robert H. Bremner and Gary W. Reichard (Columbus: Ohio State University Press, 1982), 175–76.

66. Marchand, "Visions of Classlessness," 173–76. See, for example, David Reisman, Nathan Glazer, and Reuel Denney, *The Lonely Crowd: A Study of the Changing American Character*, abridged ed. (Garden City, NY: Doubleday Anchor, 1953); C. Wright Mills, *White Collar: The American Middle Class* (New York: Oxford University Press, 1956); "A Life Roundtable on the Pursuit of Happiness," *Life*, July 12, 1948, 94; and Richard Hofstadter, *The Paranoid Style in American Politics and Other Essays* (Vintage: New York, 1964).

67. John Graves to Arnold Ehrlich, December 30, 1960, and John Graves to Ruth Graves, February 27, 1961, both in box 1, folder 2, JG.

68. Educational Bureau, *Case History*, 3.

69. For an illuminating example of how photography and layout could overwhelm text in *Holiday*, see Nancy Wilson Ross to Harry Sions, October 11, 1958, box 77, folder 5, NWR; Nancy Wilson Ross to Rachel Griffin, December 9, 1958, box 77, folder 6, NWR; Nancy Wilson Ross to Jane Platt, December 18, 1958, box 77, folder 6, NWR; and Nancy Wilson Ross to John W. S. Platt, December 28, 1958, box 77, folder 6, NWR.

70. *Speaking of Holiday* 4, no. 11, November 1957, box 97, folder 1, NWR.

71. "Paris Portrait," *Holiday*, April 1953, 33; E. B. White, "Here Is New York," *Holiday*, April 1949, 34; Educational Bureau, *Case History*, 1.

72. Educational Bureau, *Case History*, 2.

73. Ibid., 2; "Facing New York," *Holiday*, October 1959, 49.

74. The Staff to Ted Patrick and Harry Sions, January 12, 1959, and Richard L. Field to Ted Patrick et al., March 31, 1958, memos reproduced in Educational Bureau, *Case History*, Exhibits E and C. For the evolution of stories and writers over the next fifteen months, see Exhibit D. Slim Aarons, "The Glittering Socialites," *Holiday*, October 1959, 74; Jack Kerouac, "The Roaming Beatniks," *Holiday*, October 1959, 82; Alfred Kazin, "Writing: The Voice of the City," *Holiday*, October 1959, 88; Francis Steegmuller, "A Stroll in the Art Galleries," *Holiday*, October 1959, 90; Kenneth Tynan, "The Dilemma of the Theater," *Holiday*, October 1959, 94; Kyle Crichton,

"Discovering New York Hotels," *Holiday*, October 1959, 117; "Holiday Handbook of New York Restaurants," *Holiday*, October 1959, 133.

75. The Staff to Ted Patrick and Harry Sions, January 12, 1959, memo reproduced in Educational Bureau, *Case History*, Exhibit E.

76. Susan Sontag, *On Photography* (New York: Farrar, Straus and Giroux, 1977), 97, 110.

77. "Architect," *Holiday*, October 1959, 61; "Poets Are Everywhere," *Holiday*, October 1959, 83.

78. Educational Bureau, *Case Study*, 10; Arnold Newman, "First Lady," *Holiday*, October 1959, 94–95. On Broadway as a collective dreamworld, see Neal Gabler, *Winchell: Gossip, Power and the Culture of Celebrity* (New York: Knopf, 1994), 87–91.

79. Educational Bureau, *Case Study*, 10.

80. Ibid., 9.

81. Marshall Berman, *All That Is Solid Melts into Air: The Experience of Modernity* (New York: Penguin, 1982), 299–308 (Moses quote, 301).

82. Arnold Newman, "City Planner," *Holiday*, October 1959, 50–51.

83. Berman, *All That Is Solid Melts into Air*, 307.

84. Ibid., 301; John Urry, *The Tourist Gaze* (London: Sage, 1990); Annabel Jane Wharton, *Building the Cold War: Hilton International Hotels and Modern Architecture* (Chicago: University of Chicago Press, 2001), 159–94.

85. Henri Cartier-Bresson, "Paris! City of Types," *Holiday*, April 1953, 49.

86. Henri Cartier-Bresson, "The Face of Europe," *Holiday*, January 1954, 36–37, 46–47, 32.

87. On the strands of postwar thought that converged to form this high modern ideology, see Olivier Zunz, *Why the American Century?* (Chicago: University of Chicago Press, 1998), xiv–xv; Suleiman Osman, *The Invention of Brownstone Brooklyn: Gentrification and the Search for Authenticity in Postwar New York* (New York: Oxford University Press, 2011); Alan Brinkley, *The End of Reform: New Deal Liberalism in Recession and War* (New York: Vintage, 1996), 265–68; Klein, *Cold War Orientalism*, 32; Jackson Lears, *Something for Nothing: Luck in America* (New York: Penguin, 2003), 237–38; Sontag, *On Photography*, 83–112.

CHAPTER FIVE

1. "Look, mister . . . ," *Advertising Age*, July 7, 1947, 12.

2. C. A. Kirkpatrick and G. B. Brown, "The Sovereign State Turns Barker," *Journal of Marketing* 3, no. 1 (July 1938): 80; Kay Winn, "How and Why States Advertise," *Advertising and Selling*, September 24, 1936, 25; Gay Cunningham, "$5,650,000 for State Advertising," *Advertising and Selling*, November 4, 1937, 28; C. B. Larrabee and Joel Lewis, "These Copy Ideas Can Draw Dollars," *Printers' Ink*, December 15, 1939, 11.

3. "The Road to Yesterday," *Printers' Ink Monthly*, March 1932, 48, 64; Ann Bradshaw, "A $216,000,000 Industry: California's Reward for Faith in Advertising," *Sales Management*, February 1, 1938, 26; Larrabee and Lewis, "These Copy Ideas Can Draw Dollars," 11; C. B. Larrabee and Joel Lewis, "More Copy Ideas That Draw Travel Dollars," *Printers' Ink*, December 22, 1939, 26.

4. Hugh De Santis, "The Democratization of Travel: The Travel Agent in American History," *Journal of American Culture* 1, no. 1 (1978): 4; Neil Harris, "On Vacation," in *Resorts of the Catskills* (New York: St. Martin's Press, 1979), 102.

5. Carolyn Kitch, "'A Piazza from Which the View Is Constantly Changing': The Promise of Class and Gender Mobility on the Pennsylvania Railroad's Cross-Country Tours," *Pennsylvania History* 72, 4 (2005): 507–29; Catherine Cocks, "The Chamber of Commerce's Carnival: City

Festivals and Urban Tourism in the United States, 1890–1915," in *Being Elsewhere: Tourism, Consumer Culture, and Identity in Modern Europe and North America*, ed. Shelley Baranowski and Ellen Furlough (Ann Arbor: University of Michigan Press, 2001), 91–94; Fred E. Dayton, "Advertising Vacations," *Printers' Ink*, April 7, 1909, 52; Marguerite S. Shaffer, *See America First: Tourism and National Identity, 1880–1940* (Washington, DC: Smithsonian Institution Press, 2001), 26–85.

6. Shaffer, *See America First*, 26–129.

7. "Advertising for Tourist Business," *Printers' Ink*, January 11, 1934, 64.

8. "Wish You Were Here," *Printers' Ink*, August 19, 1955, 83–84; Thomas Bulfinch, *The Age of Fable or Beauties of Mythology*, ed. Rev. J. Loughran Scott (Philadelphia: David McKay, 1898), 441–43. Mark Twain brought the Lorelei legend to American readers in a chapter of his *A Tramp Abroad* (1880). Later, the songwriting duo George and Ira Gershwin penned a Broadway version of the myth for the 1932 musical *Pardon My English*. Mark Twain, *A Tramp Abroad* (Hartford, CT: American Publishing Co., 1880), 140–49; *The Complete Lyrics of Ira Gershwin*, ed. Robert Kimball (New York: Knopf, 1993), 194.

9. F. W. Ogilvie, "Tourist Traffic," in *Encyclopaedia of the Social Sciences*, vol. 14, ed. Edwin R. A. Seligman and Alvin Johnson (New York: Macmillan, 1931), 663; Harvey Levenstein, *We'll Always Have Paris: American Tourists in France since 1930* (Chicago: University of Chicago Press, 2004), 7; Christopher Endy, *Cold War Holidays: American Tourism in France* (Chapel Hill: University of North Carolina Press, 2004), 58–59; James Buzard, "Culture for Export: Tourism and Autoethnography in Postwar Britain," in Baranowski and Furlough, *Being Elsewhere*, 301.

10. Aesop Glim, "German Travel Advertising," *Printers' Ink*, June 1934, 16–17, 48; Hiram Motherwall, "The American Tourist Makes History," *Harper's Monthly*, January 1929, 72; James M. Campbell, "Tourisme: A Billion Dollar Industry," *Advertising and Selling*, March 6, 1929, 52.

11. Don Thomas, "Sixteen Years of Resort Advertising," *Printers' Ink Monthly*, May 1937, 19; Robert Huse, "Regional Development and the New England Council," *Public Opinion Quarterly* 2, no. 3 (July 1938): 418, 422.

12. Don Thomas, "All-Year Club Seeks to Break Summer Vacation Habit," *Sales Management*, February 15, 1949, 106; Earl Pomeroy, *Into the Golden West: The Tourist in Western America* (New York: Knopf, 1957), 136–37; Larrabee and Lewis, "More Copy Ideas That Draw Dollars," 23.

13. James Beniger, *The Control Revolution: Technological and Economic Origins of the Information Society* (Cambridge, MA: Harvard University Press, 1986), 344–56; Jackson Lears, *Fables of Abundance: A Cultural History of Advertising in America* (New York: Basic Books, 1994), 191; Patricia Johnston, *Real Fantasies: Edward Steichen's Advertising Photography* (Berkeley: University of California Press, 1997), 155; George C. Warren, "New Jersey's Official 'Sales Force,'" *Public Opinion Quarterly* 2, no. 3 (July 1938): 489.

14. "Promotion of Florida as Year Round Vacation Site Paying Off in Visitors," *Printers' Ink*, August 11, 1950, 80; "Travel Ads Increase, Tourist Business Expands," *Printers' Ink*, January 14, 1952, 10; "Washington State Expands Campaign to Midwest and Southwest," *Advertising Age*, May 11, 1953, 3; "Hawaii Beckons," *Business Week*, November 19, 1949, 62.

15. Thomas, "All-Year Club Seeks to Break Summer Vacation Habit," 108. Similarly, Ottawa tourist authorities called the province's attractions the "tourist plant." Karen Dubinsky, "Everybody Likes Canadians: Canadians, Americans, and the Post–World War II Travel Boom," in Baranowski and Furlough, *Being Elsewhere*, 326.

16. "States and Cities Seek Tourists, Industries," *Advertising and Selling*, January 1947, 45; "Battle between the States," *Advertising Age*, May 6, 1946, 12.

17. "All-Year Club Gets More Coupons from Informative Newspaper Copy," *Advertising Age*,

March 16, 1953, 84; "This Is New Mexico," *Holiday*, December 1948, 74; "Now . . . Plan Your Vacation in France," *Holiday*, December 1948, 123.

18. "Rosser Reeves," in *The Art of Writing Advertising: Conversations with Masters of the Craft* (1965; Lincolnwood, IL: NTC Business Books, 1986), 108. On Reeves as the ultimate embodiment of postwar technocracy on Madison Avenue, see Thomas Frank, *The Conquest of Cool: Business Culture, Counterculture, and the Rise of Hip Consumerism* (Chicago: University of Chicago Press, 1997), 38–50. Frank characterizes Ogilvy in similar fashion. I argue below that Ogilvy was much more of a transitional figure, who greatly valued the enigmatic selling power of fantasy and archetypal imagery.

19. Margaret Mead, "The Pattern of Leisure in Contemporary American Culture," *Annals of the American Academy of Political and Social Science* 313 (September 1957): 11.

20. "All-Year Club Sets $800,000 Budget to Push Southern California," *Advertising Age*, November 12, 1956, 6.

21. "The Great American Travel Adventure," *Holiday*, December 1954, 12–13.

22. Ibid.; "All-Year Club Gets More Coupons from Informative Newspaper Copy," 84; "All-Year Club Finds Hard Facts Lure Tourists," *Sales Management*, September 1, 1952, 138.

23. "All-Year Club Sets $800,000 Budget to Push Southern California," 3, 6; "Where Else Can You See So Much So Easily?" *Holiday*, February 1959, 15. "Choose a new kind of vacation fun everyday" tagline quoted in "All-Year Club Sets $750,000 3-Media Drive," *Advertising Age*, December 12, 1960, 12. Also see "Southern California All-Year Club Ads Use Economy Theme," *Advertising Age*, November 8, 1965, 92.

24. Bernard DeVoto, "Heavy, Heavy, What Hangs Over?" *Holiday*, March 1956, 37.

25. "New Mexico's Motivational Research Revises Ad Campaign," *Printers' Ink*, April 1, 1955, 102; "New Mexico the Land of Enchantment," *Holiday*, April 1957, 4.

26. Hal K. Rothman, "Selling the Meaning of Place: Entrepreneurship, Tourism, and Community Transformation in the Twentieth-Century American West," *Pacific Historical Review* 65, no. 4 (November 1996): 532–36; "New Mexico the Land of Enchantment," *Holiday*, March 1957, 31.

27. Michael Berkowitz, "A 'New Deal' for Leisure: Making Mass Tourism during the Great Depression," in Baranowski and Furlough, *Being Elsewhere*, 199.

28. "Uncle Henry Took the Hint," *Holiday*, December 1948, 133.

29. "A Preview of Your Thrilling Vacation in San Francisco and Its Wonderland," *Holiday*, May 1946, 37; Richard K. Popp, "Domesticating Vacations: Gender, Travel, and Consumption in Post-War Magazines," *Journalism History* 36, no. 3 (Fall 2010): 126–37; Elaine Tyler May, *Homeward Bound: American Families in the Cold War Era*, rev. ed. (New York: Basic Books, 1999).

30. "Ad Drive Boosts Travel to Germany," *Advertising Age*, July 28, 1952, 40; "Goerl Shop's $375 Motive Study Keys German Tourism Ads," *Advertising Age*, February 16, 1959, 2.

31. "Ad Drive Boosts Travel to Germany," 41; Horace Sutton, "Return to the Reich," *Saturday Review*, March 10, 1951, 36.

32. "Advertising Agencies Pick Their Best of 1954," *Advertising Age*, March 14, 1955, 48.

33. On the Holocaust and postwar memory, see Barbie Zelizer, *Remembering to Forget: Holocaust Memory through the Camera's Eye* (Chicago: University of Chicago Press, 1998), 163–69. On American GIs' largely favorable view of Germany during postwar occupation, see Levenstein, *We'll Always Have Paris*, 63–64, 88–89.

34. Horace Sutton, "SRO for Serenity," *Sports Illustrated*, February 29, 1960, 60; Dennis Merrill, "Negotiating Cold War Paradise: U.S. Tourism, Economic Planning, and Cultural Modernity in Twentieth-Century Puerto Rico," *Diplomatic History* 25, no. 2 (Spring 2001):

179–214, 186; "Puerto Rico Tourist Bureau Makes a Discovery: It Pays to Advertise," *Advertising Age*, November 10, 1952, 2.

35. "Spend a Cool Summer Vacation in Puerto Rico, U.S.A.," *Holiday*, June 1954, 69.

36. David Ogilvy, "Address to New York Chapter Public Relations Society of America," January 1, 1959, 4–6, box 78, folder Speeches 1957–1959, DO; David Ogilvy to Ted Moscoso, March 15, 1956, 2, box 58, folder PRC 1956, DO.

37. Ogilvy quotes from this letter in his *Confessions of an Advertising Man* (New York: Ballantine, 1963), 44–45.

38. "Girl by a Gate in San Juan" and "Pablo Casals Is Coming Home—to Puerto Rico," Puerto Rico Visitors' Bureau ads dating from 1957 and 1958, reproduced in David Ogilvy, *Ogilvy on Advertising* (New York: Crown Publishing, 1983), 133, 207. Excerpt from "Girl by a Gate in San Juan."

39. Reynolds Girdler, "The Big Black Fiddle of Pablo Casals," *Saturday Review*, April 14, 1962, 69. The campaign earned OBM a string of accolades, and Elliott Erwitt's cello photograph was selected in 1960 as the only commercial image in the New York Metropolitan Museum of Art's contemporary photography exhibit. Inge Bondi to David Ogilvy, May 16, 1960, box 59, folder PRC 1960–1961, DO.

40. Ogilvy, *Confessions of an Advertising Man*, 1–2. Hewitt soon left, and Ogilvy took full control in 1952. Stephen Fox, *The Mirror Makers: A History of American Advertising and Its Creators* (New York: William Morrow & Co., 1984), 227–32. Anderson F. Hewitt to Carter Burgess, December 10, 1948, box 36, folder General Aniline & Film Corp., DO; "One-Eyed Flattery," *Time*, June 23, 1952, 88.

41. Spencer Klaw, "Is Ogilvy a Genius?" *Fortune*, April 1965, 143; "How to Succeed, Trying," *Time*, November 1, 1963, 98.

42. "Wrangle, 65, Dies," *Advertising Age*, June 16, 1969, 26; Thomas Whiteside, "Ogilvy the Ineffable Ad Man," *Harper's*, May 1955, 55.

43. Ogilvy, *Confessions of an Advertising Man*, 58, 107.

44. David Ogilvy, *Blood, Brains and Beer: The Autobiography of David Ogilvy* (New York: Atheneum, 1978), 127.

45. Ogilvy, *Ogilvy on Advertising*, 127.

46. Robert Glatzer, *The New Advertising: The Great Campaigns from Avis to Volkswagen* (New York: Citadel Press, 1970), 104. The other industry figures named were Boeing president William M. Allen, aviation executives D. W. Douglas Sr. and D. W. Douglas Jr., resort maven Laurence Rockefeller, and Polaroid inventor Edwin H. Land. Homer Bigart, "The Men Who Made the World Move," *Saturday Review*, April 22, 1967, 59. Later, when *Advertising Age* polled experts for a 1976 retrospective titled "Best Ads I've Ever Seen," the only tourism campaigns mentioned were OBM's work for the BTA and for Puerto Rico. Editors of Advertising Age, *How It Was in Advertising: 1776–1976* (Chicago: Crain Books, 1976) 61, 46–48. From the mid-1950s through the 1960s, dozens of advertisers ranging from Kodak to the San Diego tourist board would imitate the layout and tone OBM pioneered. For examples of other businesses and boosters that adopted the BTA format in ads appearing in just one magazine (*Holiday*), see "Viyella's Little Lambs—From England," *Holiday*, December 1955, 135; "Father Wore This Viyella Shirt at Mafeking in 1899," *Holiday*, January 1956, 73; "Her Charms and Grace Are Made of Many Things," *Holiday*, March 1956, 80; "Relax Longer . . . Go by Train or Plane . . . Rent a Hertz Car There," *Holiday*, April 1956, 138; "Announcing a Great New Selection of Kodak Home-Movie Cameras," *Holiday*, May 1956, 91; "Now You Can Call Great Britain by Transatlantic Cable," *Holiday*, February 1957, 32; "A Resort That's a Way of Life . . . ," *Holiday*, June 1958, 26; "The Lady Brings Him Luck,"

Holiday, June 1958, 114; and "How to Train an Airline Hostess," *Holiday*, February 1960, 34. When OBM developed a multipictured format for the BTA in the mid-1950s, other agencies imitated that, too. For examples, see "7 Course Meal—1600 Miles Long," *Holiday*, April 1960, 23, and "Take the Connoisseur's Road from Paris to Nice and Know France," *Holiday*, May 1960, 195.

47. David Ogilvy to William Stephenson, April 4, 1951, box 44, folder BTA 1948–1952, DO; Peter Greer to David Ogilvy, May 11, 1951, box 44, folder BTA 1948–1952, DO; Victor W. Turner and Edith Turner, *Image and Pilgrimage in Christian Culture* (New York: Columbia University Press, 1978).

48. On tourism and the consumption of experience, see Hal K. Rothman, *Devil's Bargains: Tourism in the Twentieth-Century American West* (Lawrence: University Press of Kansas, 1998), 17–21; Fairfax Mastick Cone, "High Readership and Low-Cost Coupon," in *100 Top Copy Writers and Their Favorite Ads* (New York: Printers' Ink Publishing Co., 1954), 162.

49. "The Development of Tourist Traffic," *Economist*, June 30, 1945, 902; "British Group Plans New Tourist Drive," *Advertising Age*, October 1, 1945, 13; "$40,000 to Boost Britain in U.S.," *Printers' Ink*, March 8, 1946, 113; "England Wants Tourists," *Business Week*, November 16, 1946, 109; "The International Outlook," *Business Week*, June 15, 1946, 96; "Tourist Dollars," *Business Week*, November 1, 1947, 49; Cyril Ray, "Planning to Visit England," *Harper's*, April 1947, 364; Horace Sutton, "Beelines to Britain," *Saturday Review*, April 17, 1948, 54; Buzard, "Culture for Export," 302.

50. David Ogilvy to William Stephenson, April 4, 1951, box 44, folder BTA 1948–1952, DO; David Ogilvy to Peter Green, July 5, 1951, box 44, folder BTA 1948–1952, DO; Peter Greer to David Ogilvy, July 31, 1951, box 44, folder BTA 1948–1952, DO. The Hathaway format was suggested by agency worker Peter Greer. There is good evidence to suggest that Greer's idea differed remarkably from what Ogilvy had in mind. When Greer outlined the BTA template, he also referred to Ogilvy's initial ideas as "grotesquely labored." He appeared to be offering his ideas as an alternative. Peter Greer to David Ogilvy, May 11, 1951, box 44, folder BTA 1948–1952, DO.

51. The ad drew kudos throughout the trade and earned copywriter Clifford Field an American Association of Advertising Agencies (AAAA) award for institutional copywriting in 1959. "Writing Unafraid to Be Great," *Advertising Age*, February 16, 1959, 68; Hal Stebbins, "Repeat, Repeat, Repeat," *Printers' Ink*, January 29, 1960, 52.

52. "It's a Short Lane That Has No Hollyhock," *Holiday*, April 1955, 141. Another depicted the "ageless pageantry" of the Life Guards streaming in procession past Wellington Arch. "All heads turn as the cavalry troop sweeps by with a brave jingle," the copy explained. "London's heart beats faster. Yours will, too." "London's Heart Beats Faster" reproduced in Ogilvy, *Ogilvy on Advertising*, 130.

53. Ogilvy, *Confessions of an Advertising Man*, 122; David Ogilvy to Norman Robbins, October 17, 1952, box 44, folder BTA 1948–1952, DO. On the importance of metonymic icons in tourism, see Dean MacCannell, *The Tourist: A New Theory of the Leisure Class* (1976; Berkeley: University of California Press, 1999), 109–33.

54. "General Campaign Format," 2, box 45, folder BTA 1957, DO.

55. On "Italianicity," see Roland Barthes, "The Rhetoric of the Image," in *Classic Essays on Photography*, ed. Alan Trachtenberg (New Haven: Leete's Island Books, 1980), 271, 270–73.

56. Ogilvy, *Confessions of an Advertising Man*, 121; Creative Department to G. F. Sorgatz, April 8, 1952, box 44, folder BTA 1948–1952, DO.

57. "General Campaign Format," 12, 5, box 45, folder BTA 1957, DO; "Tourist's Guide to British Money," *Holiday*, February 1957, 2; David Ogilvy to James Turbayne, July 5, 1955, box 44, folder June 1955–July 1955, DO.

58. Stanley Donen, *The Grass Is Greener* (London: Grandon Productions, 1960).

59. David Ogilvy to Roger Lloyd, August 18, 1954, 44, folder BTA 1953–1954, DO.

60. David Ogilvy to Anderson Hewitt, December 17, 1952, box 44, folder BTA 1948–1952, DO; David Ogilvy to Roger Lloyd, September 2, 1955, box 44, folder BTA August 1955–December 1956, DO; "General Campaign Format," 2, box 45, folder BTA 1957, DO.

61. "The Grand Tour Revisited," *Fortune*, December 1958, 62; "Come to Britain," *Economist*, September 7, 1957, 750; "Tourist Industry in United Kingdom Becomes Leading Dollar Source," *Foreign Commerce Weekly*, June 16, 1958, 26.

62. David Ogilvy to Roger Lloyd, July 18, 1956; David Ogilvy to James Rooke, July 18, 1956; Ian Kerr to *Manchester Guardian*, July 17, 1956, all three in box 44, folder BTA August 1955–December 1956, DO. David Ogilvy to Leonard Lickorish, May 21, 1957, box 45, folder BTA 1957, DO; William Mabane, "One Image of Britain," *Times* (London), April 14, 1961, 15.

63. Ogilvy, *Confessions of an Advertising Man*, 122–23; David Ogilvy to Louis Heren, December 14, 1961, box 45, folder BTA September–December 1961, DO; "Holidayland," *Economist*, October 20, 1962, 214–15; "The Grand Tour Revisited," *Fortune*, December 1958, 62; "Come to Britain," *Economist*, September 7, 1957, 750.

64. David Ogilvy, "How the New Tourism Can Be Sold," box 78, folder Speeches 1963–1968, 5, DO; "General Campaign Format," box 45, folder BTA 1957, DO.

65. Jack Mawson to David Ogilvy, August 5, 1955, box 44, folder BTA August 1955–December 1956, DO.

66. The request stemmed in part from a desire to show as many regions of Great Britain as possible. As a national body, the BTA had to promote all of Britain—from the busy streets of London to the Scottish Highlands. While sympathetic to this mandate, Ogilvy was vehement that the agency had found the perfect lure in large, color photos that showcased one particular sight. "General Campaign Format," box 45, folder BTA 1957, DO; David Ogilvy to Jack Mawson, March 25, 1958, box 45, folder BTA 1958–1960, DO. The quality of photographs became an issue of contention as well. Ogilvy insisted that the campaign needed a first-rate photographer and over the course of the 1950s recommended, to no avail, Henri Cartier-Bresson, Tom Hollyman, Eliot Elisofon, Marc Riboud, and others. David Ogilvy to Norman Robbins, October 7, 1952, box 44, folder BTA 1948–1952, DO; David Ogilvy to John Mawson, September 24, 1954, box 44, folder BTA 1953–1954, DO; David Ogilvy to John Mawson, May 28, 1957, box 54, folder BTA 1957, DO; David Ogilvy to Roger Lloyd, August 29, 1957, box 54, folder BTA 1957, DO.

67. Johnston, *Real Fantasies*.

68. Ogilvy, *Confessions of an Advertising Man*, 122; Genevieve Smith, "How Editorial-Style Ads in Full Color Help Double Britain's Tourist Trade," *Printers' Ink*, March 30, 1956, 46; Ogilvy, "How the New Tourism Can Be Sold," 5. Also see Clifford Field to David Ogilvy, New Puerto Rican Commonwealth Campaign Photographs—A Guide for Tom Hollyman, October 10, 1960, 1–2, box 59, folder PRC 1960–1961, DO.

69. Roland Barthes, *Camera Lucida: Reflections on Photography* (New York: Hill and Wang, 1981), 26, 47, 77. Susan Sontag made a similar argument about the "material vestige" embedded in every photograph. *On Photography* (New York: Farrar, Straus and Giroux, 1977), 154.

70. Hal Stebbins, "You Begin at the End," *Printers' Ink*, January 25, 1957, 50.

71. "General Campaign Format," 2, box 45, folder BTA 1957, DO. This maxim was echoed in an *Advertising Age* guide to effective travel copy in 1965. "The empathy or vicarious delight to be derived from either a travel article or a travel ad," the author observed, "is easier to achieve without the barrier of having to watch other people enjoying what the reader wants to imagine himself enjoying." Johanna T. Rock, "What Makes Your Ads More Memorable," *Advertising Age*, February 1, 1965, 78.

72. Ogilvy, *Confessions of an Advertising Man*, 122.

73. Myron Clement, "French Government Tourist Office Overcomes Misconceptions by Citing Facts with Tact," *Public Relations Journal*, October 1961, 34.

74. Hal Stebbins, "You Can't Beat Realism," *Printers' Ink*, June 16, 1961, 34.

75. Ibid.

76. Myron J. Helfgott, "Increasing Advertising Effectiveness through Copy Testing," October 28, 1956, 19, 21, box 78, folder Speeches 1954–1956, DO.

77. David Ogilvy to Ronald Tree, June 7, 1954, box 44, folder BTA 1953–1954, DO; Creative Department to George F. Sorgatz, April 8, 1952, box 44, folder BTA 1948–1952, DO. After three years of pleading with the association to commission a top-rank photographer, Ogilvy was finally able to send Magnum's Cornell Capa on an expensive shoot in 1954. The trip, however, was plagued by gray skies, and Ogilvy responded by scrapping the entire portfolio. W. Lone to David Ogilvy, September 17, 1954, and David Ogilvy to W. Lone, September 22, 1954, both in box 44, folder BTA 1953–1954, DO. Also see David Ogilvy to Ronald Tree, June 7, 1954, box 44, folder BTA 1953–1954, DO.

78. David Ogilvy to Roger Lloyd, August 18, 1954, box 44, folder BTA 1953–1954, DO. Also see the discussion of French and British food in Levenstein, *We'll Always Have Paris*, 190–91.

79. Social Research, Inc., *P&O-Orient Lines in California: A Research Report* (August 1964), 41, box 57, folder P&O 1964, DO.

80. "The Roast Beef of Old England Is Back," *Holiday*, May 1954, 12–13; Anthony Bailey, "Of Puddings (Yorks.)," *New Yorker*, May 28, 1960, 112–13; "Now You Can Eat Like a King—in Britain," *Holiday*, June 1956, 13; "Traveler's Guide to Good Food in Britain," *Holiday*, April 1958, 2; David Ogilvy to Cliff Field, June 17, 1957, box 45, folder BTA 1957, DO.

81. David Ogilvy to Norman Robbins, October 7, 1952, box 44, folder BTA 1948–1952, DO; David Ogilvy to Anderson Hewitt, December 17, box 44, folder BTA 1948–1952, DO; "English Spoken Here," *Holiday*, November 1953, 132.

82. "These Friendly People Invite You to Visit Britain 1954," box 44, folder BTA 1953–1954, DO; Ogilvy, *Ogilvy on Advertising*, 135.

83. "Recommendations for the British Travel Association's Advertising in America during Fiscal Year 1952–1953," box 44, folder BTA 1948–1952, DO; "Media" (n.d.), 17, box 44, folder BTA August 1955–December 1956, DO.

84. Ed Berrol to Paul Biklen, n.d., box 45, folder BTA June 1961–August 1961, DO; Bill Blair, "Comments on 'Potential Travel Market for Europe in the U.S.A.'" (n.d.), box 45, folder BTA 1958–1960, DO. Ogilvy made a similar recommendation in a speech to travel industry leaders five years later. "The biggest barrier to trans-Atlantic travel is the cost," he argued, continuing: "Your advertising should help people rationalize their extravagance by selling cultural and status overtones." Ogilvy, "How the New Tourism Can Be Sold," 5. On vacations, upward mobility, and middle-class whiteness, see Bryant Simon, *Boardwalk of Dreams: Atlantic City and the Fate of Urban America* (New York: Oxford University Press, 2004).

85. Bailey, "Of Puddings (Yorks.)," 112–13.

86. Opinion Research Corporation, *Pleasure Travel to Europe*, vol. 1 (Princeton, NJ: Opinion Research Corporation, January 1962), 3; Social Research, Inc., *P&O-Orient Lines in California*, 17, 37.

87. David Ogilvy to Roger Lloyd, October 16, 1957, box 45, folder BTA 1957, DO.

88. Ogilvy, *Confessions of an Advertising Man*, 58, 107; Whiteside, "Ogilvy the Ineffable Ad Man," 52.

89. *New Yorker* cartoon described in Horace Sutton's *Sports Illustrated* article "SRO for Serenity," 60; *Puerto Rico/Time* booklet (1962), box 59, folder PRC 1962, DO.

90. David Ogilvy to John I. Snyder, January 17, 1955, 4, box 58, folder PRC 1954–1955, DO.

91. Daniel J. Boorstin, *The Image: A Guide to Psuedo-Events in America* (1961; New York: Atheneum, 1971), 77–117, 102; Hans Magnus Enzensberger, "A Theory of Tourism" (1958), *New German Critique* 68 (1996): 126. Enzensberger's article originally appeared in the German magazine *Merkur* in August 1958. Bernard DeVoto, "Outdoor Metropolis," *Harper's*, October 1955, 12.

92. Lawrence P. Lessing, "State of Florida," *Fortune*, February 1948, 68; "A Place in the Sun," *Time*, December 19, 1955, 20. On mass culture see, Dwight W. Macdonald, "A Theory of Mass Culture," in *Mass Culture: The Popular Arts in America*, ed. Bernard Rosenberg and David Manning White (Glencoe, IL: Free Press, 1957), 61, 63–64, 66.

93. Ogilvy, "Address to New York Chapter," 8; David Ogilvy to Rafael Durand, June 19, 1957, box 58, folder PRC 1957, DO.

94. David Ogilvy to William Mabane, June 1, 1961, box 45, folder BTA January–August 1961, DO; David Ogilvy to Jack Mawson, December 22, 1961, box 45, folder BTA September–December 1961, DO.

95. Ogilvy, "How the New Tourism Can Be Sold," 3; "Extending a Print Campaign," *Printers' Ink*, April 17, 1964, 34; "Travel Turns to TV," *Sponsor*, October 26, 1964, 33–40; "Radio-TV Gets 31% of Travel Firms' Budget," *Broadcasting*, November 29, 1965, 34–35; "French Tourism Drive Uses B&W Print, TV Color," *Advertising Age*, February 6, 1967, 104; "Jamaica Eschews Elite Approach," *Advertising Age*, February 22, 1965, 10.

96. Paul Bowles, "The Challenge to Identity," *Nation*, April 26, 1958, 360. On tourism communities transforming into reflections of tourists, see Rothman, *Devil's Bargains*, 368–70.

CHAPTER SIX

1. Russell Lynes, "How Do You Rate in the New Leisure," *Life*, December 28, 1959, 85, 87.

2. "Beyond the Horizon," *Time*, May 19, 1961, 70; "Summertime '61: Vacations Off the Beaten Track," *Newsweek*, July 3, 1961, cover; "Vacation Spots Off the Beaten Track," *Newsweek*, July 3, 1961, 45; "Tourism's New Twist," *Printers' Ink*, April 12, 1963, 5.

3. "The Grand Tour Revisited," *Fortune*, December 1958, 62; "Where Vacation Money Is Going," *Business Week*, June 17, 1961, 28; "Footloose Americans Are Trooping Abroad," *Business Week*, April 7, 1956, 29; Mitchell Goodman, "Europe in the Off Season," *Atlantic Monthly*, June 1955, 94; Bernard DeVoto, "Outdoor Metropolis," *Harper's*, October 1955, 12. On the move toward off-the-beaten-track locales and highly specialized tours, also see "Off the Track," *Newsweek*, June 3, 1957, 61, and "West to the East," *Newsweek*, May 26, 1958, 91.

4. Editorial quoted in "Blast at the Blossoms," *Newsweek*, April 18, 1955, 30.

5. "Americans Touring Europe in 1956 Will Travel off the Beaten Path," *Business Week*, March 10, 1956, 134; "Footloose Americans Are Trooping Abroad," 29; Christopher Endy, *Cold War Holidays: American Tourism in France* (Chapel Hill: University of North Carolina Press, 2004), 135–36; "Europe Leads but Loses Ground," *Business Week*, October 17, 1959, 64; "Vacationers Take to Backwoods," *Business Week*, September 17, 1960, 30; "The Caribbean: A Travel Boom," *Printers' Ink*, July 10, 1964, 53; Dennis Merrill, "Negotiating Cold War Paradise: U.S. Tourism, Economic Planning, and Cultural Modernity in Twentieth-Century Puerto Rico," *Diplomatic History* 25, no. 2 (2001): 196–97, 203–10.

6. "Winter Comes; the Boss Goes Far Away," *Business Week*, December 26, 1959, 27; Laurence Lafore, "The Tourist's Persia," *Harper's*, June 1957, 51.

7. Ira Wolfert, "Walt Disney's Magic Kingdom," *Reader's Digest*, April 1960, 144; Karal Ann Marling, *As Seen on TV: The Visual Culture of Everyday Life in the 1950s* (Cambridge, MA: Harvard

University Press, 1994), 106–26; Eric Avila, *Popular Culture in the Age of White Flight: Fear and Fantasy in Suburban Los Angeles* (Berkeley: University of California Press, 2004), 106–44; Neil Gabler, *Walt Disney: The Triumph of the American Imagination* (New York: Vintage, 2007), 604–11.

8. Hal K. Rothman, *Devil's Bargains: Tourism in the Twentieth-Century American West* (Lawrence: University Press of Kansas, 1998), 230–32, 237; Annie Gilbert Coleman, *Ski Style: Sport and Culture in the Rockies* (Lawrence: University Press of Kansas, 2004); Ellen Furlough, "Packaging Pleasures: Club Méditerranée and French Consumer Culture," *French Historical Studies* 18, no. 1 (Spring 1993): 65–81; "Shoestring Vacations with a Midas Touch," *Business Week*, September 9, 1967, 42; Louis Turner and John Ash, *The Golden Hordes: International Tourism and the Pleasure Periphery* (Constable: London, 1975), 107–12; "Producing Vacations," *Time*, May 27, 1966, 94.

9. "For More and More Americans: Offbeat Europe," *Newsweek*, May 11, 1959, 103; "Winter Comes," 28; "Where Vacation Money Is Going," *Business Week*, June 17, 1961, 28; Horace Sutton, "Under the Fractured Frangipani Sky," *Sports Illustrated*, July 11, 1960, 66; "A Far Cry from Gauguin," *Sports Illustrated*, March 27, 1961, 11; Lynes, "How Do You Rate in the New Leisure?" 87.

10. Somerset Maugham, *The Razor's Edge, a Novel* (Garden City, NY: Doubleday, Doran & Co., 1944); Paul Bowles, *The Sheltering Sky* (1949; New York: Vintage, 1990); "Latest Boom in Travel," *U. S. News and World Report*, October 9, 1967, 92.

11. "Latest Boom in Travel," 91; "Selling the 747," *Marketing/Communication*, April 1970, 32.

12. Hans Magnus Enzensberger, "A Theory of Tourism" (1958), *New German Critique* 68 (1996): 117–35; Daniel J. Boorstin, *The Image: A Guide to Pseudo-Events in America* (New York: see Atheneum, 1961). On tourism as a quest for authenticity, see Dean MacCannell, *The Tourist: A New Theory of the Leisure Class* (1976; Berkeley: University of California Press, 1999), and Donald Horne, *The Great Museum: The Re-presentation of History* (see London: Pluto Press, 1984). On the therapeutic aspects of vacation travel, see Victor W. Turner and Edith Turner, *Image and Pilgrimage in Christian Culture* (New York: Columbia University Press, 1978). On the emerging professional class's search for authenticity in the postwar city, see Suleiman Osman, *The Invention of Brownstone Brooklyn: Gentrification and the Search for Authenticity in Postwar New York* (New York: Oxford University Press, 2011). Tuner and Ash, *Golden Hordes*, 15.

13. "Africa," *Holiday*, April 1959, 49; "Holiday Handbook of African Travel," *Holiday*, April 1959, 143; "The South Seas: A New Legend," *Holiday*, October 1960, 50.

14. "Beyond the Horizon," 75. John Urry has characterized this shift as the move from the "collective gaze" toward the "romantic gaze." John Urry, *The Tourist Gaze* (London: Sage, 1990), 59–73.

15. "Draft," May 31, 1961, box 45, folder BTA January 1961–August 1961, DO.

16. David Ogilvy to Jack Mawson, September 28, 1960, box 45, folder BTA 1958–1960, DO. He added that the "leg shows in London are just as provocative as the leg shows in Paris, and the girls are 'nuder.'" On enlisting citizens into tourism industry initiatives, see James Buzard, "Culture for Export: Tourism and Autoethnography in Postwar Britain," in *Being Elsewhere: Tourism, Consumer Culture, and Identity in Modern Europe and North America*, ed. Shelley Baranowski and Ellen Furlough (Ann Arbor: University of Michigan Press, 2001), 304–5, and Karen Dubinsky, "Everybody Likes Canadians: Canadians, Americans, and the Post–World War II Travel Boom," in Baranowski and Furlough, *Being Elsewhere*, 338–42.

17. Ogilvy, "How the New Tourism Can Be Sold," 4, November 3, 1966, box 78, folder Speeches 1963–1967, DO; David Ogilvy to Francis Ogilvy, May 24, 1961, box 45, folder BTA January–August 1961, DO.

18. David Ogilvy to William Mabane, June 1, 1961, box 45, folder BTA January–August

1961, DO; David Ogilvy to Jack Mawson, December 22, 1961, folder BTA September–December 1961, DO.

19. David Ogilvy to W. S. Blair, March 14, 1955, box 44, folder BTA January–July 1955, DO; Bill Blair, "Comments on 'Potential Travel Market for Europe in the U.S.A.'" (n.d.), 7, 11, box 45, folder BTA 1958–1960, DO; David Ogilvy to Roger Lloyd, August 31, 1959, box 45, folder 1958–1960, DO.

20. David Ogilvy to William Mabane, June 1, 1961, box 45, folder BTA January–August 1961, DO; David Ogilvy to Jack Mawson, December 22, 1961, folder BTA September–December 1961, DO; Creative Policy for the American Advertising, draft, n.d., box 45, folder BTA September–December 1961, DO.

21. Ellen Furlough, "Making Mass Vacations: Tourism and Consumer Culture in France, 1930s to 1970s," *Comparative Studies in Society and History* 40, no. 2 (April 1998): 282–83; Rothman, *Devil's Bargains*, 17–21; "Travel Ads Are Outmoded, Boring Van Brunt Says," *Advertising Age*, October 5, 1964, 167. On the therapeutic ethos, see T. J. Jackson Lears, "From Salvation to Self-Realization: Advertising and the Therapeutic Roots of the Consumer Culture, 1880–1930," in *The Culture of Consumption: Critical Essays in American History, 1880–1980*, ed. Richard Wightman Fox and T. J. Jackson Lears (New York: Pantheon, 1983), 1–38. On nonconformity and antiestablishment stances as advertising theme, see Thomas Frank, *The Conquest of Cool: Business Culture, Counterculture, and the Rise of Hip Consumerism* (Chicago: University of Chicago Press, 1997), 136–52.

22. "Take the Connoisseur's Road from Paris to Nice and Know France," *Holiday*, May 1960, 195; "Greece's National Tourist Ads Win Top International Award," *Printers' Ink*, June 7, 1963, 6.

23. Alfred Mayor, "Club Méditerranée," *Holiday*, August 1967, 62; "Club Mediterranee's Exotic Retreat Appeals to Pentup Crusoe Instincts," *Advertising Age*, February 10, 1969, 8; "Low-Cost High-Old-Time," *Life*, February 24, 1966, 82; Furlough, "Making Mass Vacations." On the Crusoe narrative, see Orvar Löfgren, *On Holiday: A History of Vacationing* (Berkeley: University of California Press, 1999), 9.

24. "Only One Person in a Hundred Should Vacation in Australia," *Holiday*, December 1961, 148; "Lovely. Everyone Knows," *Harper's*, January 1965, cover II; "Four South American Countries Sell Selves as 'Difficult' to Travel In," *Advertising Age*, July 5, 1965, 3; Hal Stebbins, "Selling the Hard Way," *Printers' Ink*, September 24, 1965, 74. Later the group rebranded the region as "Uncommon Places." See "Difficult Lands, Now 'Uncommon Places,'" *Advertising Age*, November 21, 1966, 47.

25. "Adventure Trips to Far Outposts," *Life*, September 8, 1967, 79; Paul Theroux, *The Great Railway Bazaar: By Train through Asia* (Boston: Houghton Mifflin, 1975), 72; Ray Moseley, "U.S. Warns Young Travelers of Drug Laws Abroad," *Philadelphia Evening Bulletin*, May 18, 1972; Alan Parker, *Midnight Express* (Hollywood: Casablanca Filmworks/Columbia Pictures, 1978).

26. Don Murray, "We Spent Our Vacation Down at the Farm," *Saturday Evening Post*, August 3, 1957, 42; "Covered-Wagon Days—1958," *Look*, October 28, 1958, 28, 33. Also see Paul Schubert, "Can You Survive Your Two Weeks with Pay," *Saturday Evening Post*, June 18, 1960, 32, and John Masters, "We Take Our Holidays on Foot," *Reader's Digest*, May 1961, 102.

27. "Looking for Yourself?" *Travel and Leisure*, December–January 1971/1972, 13. On antimodernism, see T. J. Jackson Lears, *No Place of Grace: Antimodernism and the Transformation of American Culture, 1880–1920* (Chicago: University of Chicago Press, 1981), and Marguerite S. Shaffer, *See America First: Tourism and National Identity, 1880–1940* (Washington, DC: Smithsonian Institution Press, 2001), 86–91.

28. "Tourist Trap at Docks," *Business Week*, September 2, 1961, 96.

29. David Halberstam, "Federal Travel Service Launched," *New York Times*, June 25, 1961, XX1.

30. "A Bid for Travelers," *Business Week*, February 18, 1961, 122; Halberstam, "Federal Travel Service Launched," XX1; "Ah, Oui. Oui! Exotic U.S.A. Beckons Visitors," *Advertising Age*, March 19, 1962, 12.

31. Shaffer, *See America First*, 312–13; "Tourists Change Course," *Business Week*, February 10, 1968, 21; "More Lures Are Out for the Foreign Tourist," *Business Week*, May 4, 1968, 35.

32. "Sightseeing in the Sixties," *Saturday Review*, January 9, 1960, 30, 65; George A. W. Boehn, "The SST: Next Step to Instant Travel," *Fortune*, June 1961, 161.

33. Marilyn Bender and Selig Altschul, *The Chosen Instrument: Pan Am, Juan Trippe, the Rise and Fall of an American Entrepreneur* (New York: Simon and Schuster, 1982), 500–501; Horace Sutton, *Travelers: The American Tourist from Stagecoach to Space Shuttle* (New York: William Morrow and Co., 1980), 272–77; Alan Cowell, "Nostalgia Abounds as the Concorde's End Is Set," *New York Times*, April 11, 2003, W1; "Farewell to Supersonic Travel," *New York Times*, October 24, 2003, A22.

34. Larry Gelbart, "The Future Is Past," *New York Times*, April 26, 2003, A19; John Schwartz, "Russia Leads Way in Space Tourism with Paid Trips into Orbit," *New York Times*, October 8, 2008, nytimes.com/2008/10/11/science/space/11space.html.

35. "The Expanding Vacation," *Fortune*, September 1961, 195, 198; Mary A. Holman, "A National Time-Budget for the Year 2000," *Sociology and Social Research* 46 (October 1961): 25; "12-Month Vacation Is Firm's Policy," *Philadelphia Evening Bulletin*, July 11, 1947; "Motor Company to Give One-Year Paid Vacations," *Philadelphia Evening Bulletin*, October 15, 1947; "Year's Rest in Every 5 or 7 Urged to Cut Labor Toll," *Philadelphia Evening Bulletin*, April 11, 1959.

36. Bureau of Labor Statistics, "Table 36: Paid Vacations: Number of Annual Days by Service Requirement, Private Industry Workers, National Compensation Survey, March 2010," in *Employee Benefits Survey: Holiday, Vacation, Sick and Other Leave Benefits* (Washington, DC: U.S. Department of Labor), bls.gov/ncs/ebs/benefits/2010/benefits_leave.htm.

37. "An Open Letter to Ted Patrick from 12 of Holiday's 3,263,000 Readers," *New York Times*, January 20, 1964, 88.

38. Matthew J. Culligan, *The Curtis-Culligan Story: From Cyrus to Horace to Joe: The Inside Story of the Decline of the Curtis Publishing Company* (New York: Crown, 1970), 163, 110–11, 122.

39. David Ogilvy to Ted Patrick, September 24, 1962, box 11, folder Holiday, DO; Ted Patrick to David Ogilvy, October 1, 1962, box 11, folder Holiday, DO; David Ogilvy to Howard Clark, December 19, 1962, box 20, folder Ted Patrick, DO; Howard Clark to David Ogilvy, December 27, 1962, box 43, folder American Express, DO.

40. Lewis Nichols, "In and Out of Books," *New York Times*, March 29, 1964, BR8; "Mrs. Ted Patrick," *New York Times*, October 4, 1963, 33; Kathryn News, "Edwin Hill ('Ted') Patrick," in *American Magazine Journalists, 1900–1960*, 2nd ser., ed. Sam G. Riley (Detroit: Gale Research, 1994), 223; "Ted Patrick Dies," *New York Times*, March 12, 1964, 35.

41. Robert E. Bedingfield, "4 Editors Resign from Curtis Jobs," *New York Times*, December 4, 1964, 55; Robert Bedingfield, "Prominent Contributors Praise Four Who Resigned at Holiday," *New York Times*, December 10, 1964, 75; "Four Special Men," *New York Times*, December 10, 1964, 52.

42. Culligan, *Curtis-Culligan Story*, 187; Martin S. Ackerman, *The Curtis Affair* (Los Angeles: Nash, 1970), 123; Dorothy Herrman, *S. J. Perelman: A Life* (New York: G. P. Putnam's Sons, 1986), 250.

43. Ackerman sold *Ladies' Home Journal* and *American Home* outright and sold half-ownership stakes in *Holiday, Saturday Evening Post,* and the rest of the Curtis magazines. The original *Saturday Evening Post* published its last issue in 1968. James Playsted Wood, *The Curtis Magazines* (New York: Ronald Press, 1971), 272–81; "Curtis Sustained $11.1 Million Loss in '69 Operations," *Wall Street Journal,* April 24, 1970; "Holiday Plans to Reduce Number of Issues, Size and Circulation Base," *Wall Street Journal,* June 1, 1970, 9.

44. "Curtis Names SerVaas Publishing Unit Head," *Wall Street Journal,* May 6, 1970, 31; "Curtis Sells Holiday to Publisher on L.I.," *New York Times,* July 9, 1977, 36; "New Owner to Merge 'HOLIDAY' into 'TRAVEL,'" *Philadelphia Evening Bulletin,* July 10, 1977; John Tebbel and Mary Ellen Zuckerman, *The Magazine in America, 1741–1990* (New York: Oxford University Press, 1991), 253; "Week in Review," *Crain's New York Business,* April 28, 2003, 46.

45. "Cowles Plans to Fold Venture Magazine," *Wall Street Journal,* May 28, 1971, 6; Herrman, S. J. Perelman, 274; Philip H. Dougherty, "Advertising: Revamping Travel and Leisure," *New York Times,* July 26, 1971, 33.

46. "Stinnet to Get Editor's Post at Travel Magazine," *Philadelphia Evening Bulletin,* January 26, 1971; Tebbel and Zuckerman, *Magazine in America,* 291, 302–3; Alex Kuczynski, "A Champion of the Tourist Class," *New York Times,* April 12, 1999, C8.

47. James L. Baughman, *The Republic of Mass Culture: Journalism, Filmmaking, and Broadcasting in America since 1941* (Baltimore: Johns Hopkins University Press, 1992), 126–128, 189–91, 220–21; Lawrence R. Samuel, *Brought to You By: Postwar Television Advertising and the American Dream* (Austin: University of Texas Press, 2001), 192–94.

48. Peter B. B. Andrews, "Coming Boom in Top-Class Market," *Printers' Ink,* November 17, 1953, 33.

49. On the move toward specialized markets, see Lizabeth Cohen, *A Consumers' Republic: The Politics of Mass Consumption in Postwar America* (New York: Vintage, 2003), 292–344; Andrew Hurley, *Diners, Bowling Alleys, and Trailer Parks: Chasing the American Dream in Postwar Consumer Culture* (New York: Basic Books, 2001), 290–326; Joseph Turow, *Breaking Up America: Advertisers and the New Media World* (Chicago: University of Chicago Press, 1997), 31; David Abrahamson, *Magazine-Made America: The Cultural Transformation of the Postwar Periodical* (Cresskill, NJ: Hampton Press, 1996). On life-stylization see Pierre Bourdieu, *Distinction: A Social Critique of the Judgment of Taste,* trans. Richard Nice (Cambridge, MA: Harvard University Press, 1984), 174–75, 310–11.

50. "The Marketing Pattern: Room for Diversity," *Business Week,* June 6, 1959, 134.

51. "Top Management and Advertising Heads Look Ahead at the '70s," *Advertising Age,* January 19, 1970, 52.

52. Martin Stone, "The Age of Specialization," *MediaScope,* October 1969, 58; E. B. Weiss, "Today's Consumer (and Tomorrow's) Gets a New Look in Our Society," *Advertising Age,* February 8, 1971, 35. On the "new class," see Daniel T. Rodgers, *Age of Fracture* (Cambridge, MA: Harvard University Press, Belknap Press, 2011), 82–85.

53. "Individualism Is Ad Trend of '70s, Predicts O'Toole," *Advertising Age,* June 14, 1971, 18; "'Hedonism' Will Orient Ads to Pleasure, Sex, Says Ayer's Bach," *Advertising Age,* February, 3, 1969, 104; James H. Myers and Jonathan Gutman, "Life Style: The Essence of Social Class," in *Life Style and Psychographics,* ed. William D. Wells (Chicago: American Marketing Association, 1974), 235–56. For a contemporary critique of the turn inward in American society, see Christopher Lasch, *The Culture of Narcissism: American Life in an Age of Diminishing Expectations* (New York: W. W. Norton, 1979).

54. Alan R. Nelson, "New Psychographics: Action Creating Ideas, Not Lifeless Statistics," *Advertising Age,* June 28, 1971, 1; E. B. Weiss, *Marketing to the New Society* (Chicago: Crain Communications, 1973), 81.

55. "A Discreet Marriage of East and West," *Holiday,* November 1957, cover II; "Holiday Arsonists, Arise!" *Holiday,* December 1957, 204. On Americans' limited interest in foreign and gourmet food prior to the mid-1960s, see Harvey Levenstein, *Paradox of Plenty: A Social History of Eating in Modern America,* rev. ed. (Berkeley: University of California Press, 2003), 213–26.

56. Joan Shelley Rubin, *The Making of Middlebrow Culture* (Chapel Hill: University of North Carolina, 1992); Janice A. Radway, *A Feeling for Books: The Book-of-the-Month Club, Literary Taste, and Middle-Class Desire* (Chapel Hill: University of North Carolina Press, 1997).

57. Culligan, *Curtis-Culligan Story,* 164.

58. "Wish You Were Here," *Printers' Ink,* August 19, 1955, 83–84.

59. Meg Jacobs, *Pocketbook Politics: Economic Citizenship in Twentieth-Century America* (Princeton, NJ: Princeton University Press, 2005); Cohen, *Consumers' Republic.*

60. On the move toward therapeutic notions of vacationing in 1960s France, see Furlough, "Making Mass Vacations," 247–86. On early twentieth-century therapeutic tourism, see Shaffer, *See America First,* 248–49, 263–64, 305–9.

EPILOGUE

1. On the restructuring of the global economy in the 1970s, see Manuel Castels, *The Rise of the Network Society,* 2nd ed. (Oxford: Blackwell, 2000), and David Harvey, *The Condition of Postmodernity: An Enquiry into the Origins of Cultural Change* (Oxford: Blackwell, 1990). On post-1970s fragmentation in American culture and society, see Daniel T. Rodgers, *Age of Fracture* (Cambridge, MA: Harvard University Press, Belknap Press, 2011); William Graebner, *Patty's Got a Gun: Patricia Hearst in 1970s America* (Chicago: University of Chicago Press, 2008), 117–80; Jefferson Cowie, *Stayin' Alive: The 1970s and the Last Days of the Working Class* (New York: Free Press, 2010).

2. Richard L. Neale, "Marketing a New Magazine," address to American Marketing Association, November 5, 1956, quoted in Roland E. Wolseley, *Understanding Magazines* (Ames: Iowa State University Press, 1965), 414.

3. On the reemergence of conservative, free market ideology, see Kim Phillips-Fein, *Invisible Hands: The Businessmen's Crusade against the New Deal* (New York: W. W. Norton, 2009). On free market ideology and the service sector, see Bethany Moreton, *To Serve God and Wal-Mart: The Making of Christian Free Enterprise* (Cambridge, MA: Harvard University Press, 2009). On the ratcheting back of vacation time, see Juliet B. Schor, *The Overworked American: The Unexpected Decline of Leisure* (New York: Basic Books, 1993), 32–35.

4. Figures derived from U.S. Bureau of Labor Statistics, *The Employment Situation, March 2010,* Table B-1 (Washington, DC: U.S. Department of Labor), 28–30, bls.gov/schedule/archives/empsit_nr.htm#2010, and U.S. Bureau of Labor Statistics, "Table 32: Leave Benefits: Access, private industry workers, National Compensation Survey, March 2010," in *Employee Benefits Survey: Holiday, Vacation, Sick and Other Leave Benefits* (Washington, DC: U.S. Department of Labor), bls.gov/ncs/ebs/benefits/2010/benefits_leave.htm.

5. International figures from 2007 study by the Mercer human resources consulting firm, cited in Jeanne Sehadi, "Who Gets the Most (and Least) Vacation," CNNMoney.com, June 14, 2007, money.cnn.com/2007/06/12/pf/vacation_days_worldwide/#table; U.S. Bureau of Labor Statistics, "Table 36: Paid Vacations: Number of Annual Days by Service Requirement, Private

Industry Workers, National Compensation Survey, March 2010," in *Employee Benefits Survey: Holiday, Vacation, Sick and Other Leave Benefits* (Washington, DC: U.S. Department of Labor), bls.gov/ncs/ebs/benefits/2010/benefits_leave.htm.

6. Sidney W. Mintz, *Sweetness and Power: The Place of Sugar in Modern History* (New York: Penguin, 1985), 204.

7. Amar C. Bakshi, "Why More Americans Don't Travel Abroad," *CNN World: Global Public Square*, March 4, 2011, globalpublicsquare.blogs.cnn.com/2011/03/04/why-more-americans-dont-travel-abroad/; John Ibbitson, "A Little Parochialism Goes a Long Way in Breeding Intolerance," *Toronto Globe and Mail*, June 27, 2007, A19.

8. Helene Cooper, "An Unwritten Rule of Political Vacations: Think Domestic," *New York Times*, August 14, 2010, 11; The controversy surrounding Michelle Obama's summer 2010 vacation in Spain offers a powerful example. Peter Baker, "Obama Tries to Shake Tag as Elitist," *International Herald Tribune*, November 1, 2010, 4.

9. John Steinbeck, "The Yank in Europe," *Holiday*, January 1956, 25.

INDEX

A. C. Nielsen Co., 34
A. H. Robins Company, 65
AAA (American Automobile Association), 15, 73
Abrahamson, David, 53
Ackerman, Martin S., 139, 190n43
Adler, Judith, 175n5
Adorno, Theodor, 5
advertising: affecting market changes, 142; British Travel Association, 116–21; building future desires for travel, 19; color in travel ads, 84, 86, 140; contemporary culture themes, 105; Depression-era, 19–20; destination advertising (see community advertising); effective travel copy, 185n71; evolution of, 104–5; experiential nature of tourism and, 126–27; as geographic pedagogy, 104; lure advertising, 105, 108; market research and, 34; patriotic language in wartime ads, 22; pipedreams and, 62; sex appeal and hedonism in, 133–34; shift from magazines into television, 50–51; tourism market definition, 38; tourist travel promotion, 19
Advertising Age (magazine), 103, 106–7, 112, 185n71
Advertising Classification Analysis (Curtis Publishing), 36, 162n21
Advertising Council, 65, 66, 170n25
Advertising and Selling (magazine), 106
African Americans: foreign travel by, 79; ski resorts open to, 80; tourism and second-class status of, 60, 78–81, 143; YMCA camps welcoming, 79
Air Transport Association, 27
air travel: interwar period, 16–17, 156n20; as liberation, 4; planning for postwar travel boom, 25, 159n62; supersonic transport, 136–37; utopian possibilities of, 75–76
Alderson, Wroe, 40
All-Year Club (Southern California): ads targeting consumers, 108; tourism advertising, 19, 104, 106; on travel as good investment, 109–10
American Automobile Association (AAA), 15, 73
American culture: and media industry, 142

American economic system: paid vacation time representing, 65, 170n23, 170n25; as "People's Capitalism," 66–67, 147
American Express, 18, 139
American Guides (WPA), 20–21
American Marketing Association (AMA), 35, 37
American Mercury (magazine), 21
American national identity: contrasting open societies with totalitarianism, 71; freedom to play and, 73; land of leisure narrative, 3–4; technological liberation of mobility, 44, 151n16; travel boom and, 3–4; travel without borders, 74; wanderlust narrative, 3, 72–73
American System, 63–64, 65, 73, 170n25
Amerika Illustrated (magazine), 68
amusement industry: growth of, 11
Andrews, Peter B. B., 140
Angell, Roger, 74
Anglo-American Caribbean Commission, 25
anti-tourism in travel advertising, 129, 131, 133–34
Arizona Highways (magazine), 88–89
Aron, Cindy, 13
Ash, John, 131
Ashton, Horace D., 88
Atwood, William, 76–77
Australian National Travel Association, 134
authenticity: attraction of, 131–32
authoritarianism: border crossing restrictions as, 74
automobiles: affordability of auto tourism, 18; driving as depression-proof, 15; driving as leisure activity, 14–15; ownership as status symbol, 14

Baby and Child Care (Spock), 97
Balcom, Margaret, 24
Bartlett, Tommy, 61
Baum, Arthur W., 72
Bauman, Zygmunt, 8
Bay View Magazine, 87
Beaman, J. Frank: on armchair tourists, 46; as *Holiday* editor, 28, 43, 48, 166n74
Berkowitz, Michael, 19–20, 111

Berlin Wall, 77
Berman, Marshall, 101
Bernard, Tom, 61
Better Homes and Gardens, 26, 28
Biemiller, Carl, 63
Blue Ridge Parkway, 21
Bogart, Leo, 51, 53–54
Bok, Edward, 32
Book-of-the-Month Club, 46
Boorstein, Daniel, 130–31
Boston and Maine Railroad, 105
Bowles, Chester, 28
Bowles, Paul, 126–27, 131
Brenner, Anita, 82, 90–91, 92
British Travel Association (BTA): Ogilvy advertising campaign, 69, 116–21, 183n46; postwar tourism planning, 25; targeting American vacationers, 117
Bruner, Edward, 93
Buck, Tom, 135
Budget Travel (magazine), 139
Buelna, Alejandro, 82, 90–91
Burnett, Leo: on *Holiday*, 138
Business Week: on changing media landscape, 51; on economic impact of tourism, 68; on market specialization, 140; on paid vacations, 13; on specialized magazines, 52; on tourism advertising, 20; on travel industry in 1939, 12
Butler, Ralph Starr, 33

cable television: psychographic marketing, 40
Cameron Anne, 15
Capa, Cornell, 186n77
Capa, Robert, 50
Capote, Truman, 99
capriciousness: mobility and, 73
Carnegie, Dale, 41
Cartier-Bresson, Henri, 101
Casals, Pablo: image of cello, 115–16, 183n39
Charles Coolidge Parlin Memorial Lecture, 39
Cherry Blossom Festival (Washington, D.C.), 129
Civilian Conservation Corps (CCC), 21
Clark, Evans, 65
class stratification, 54
classlessness: as postwar ideal, 47, 66, 70; tourism dissolving class lines, 62–63
Clawson, Marion, 37
Club Med (Club Méditerranée), 130, 134
Cochran, Eddie, 63
Cold War: diplomatic aspects of international tourism, 144, 147; German tourism and, 112; magazine revenues and, 50; tourism showcasing American standard of living, 2; U.S. political culture in, 59
Coleman, Prentis & Varley International, 133
Coli, Francois, 177n29
Collier's (magazine), 51, 84
color: in travel advertising, 84, 86, 140
Commager, Henry Steele, 77
Commander Whitehead (Schweppes ad campaign), 116, 125
Commonwealth of Puerto Rico Visitors Bureau, 113
community advertising: archetypal imagery in, 117–18; booster groups and, 106–7; "climate prejudice" and, 106–7, 122–23, 181n15, 186n77; cognitive dissonance of vacations, 111–12; consumers targeted by, 108; European governments and, 106; evolution of, 104–5; experiential, 127; France and, 121–22; German image problem in, 112–13; Great Britain and, 116–21, 122–25; lures in, 108; motivational research and, 110–11; negative perceptions addressed by, 111; New Mexico and, 111; overcoming fear of the unknown, 122–23; Puerto Rico and, 113–15, 125–26; railroads promoting vacation destinations, 105; "reason why" ads, 108–9; sophistication in, 122; status and segmentation in, 122–27; traffic control function, 107; uniformity of, 103–4. See also destination profiles
Concorde (airplane), 137
Cone, Fairfax, 116–17
Confessions of an Advertising Man (Ogilvy), 115, 119
consumer society: advertising and (*see* advertising); affluence and mobility as hallmarks of, 55; consumer behavior, 38–40, 147, 150n4; consumer spending and standard of living, 9, 67; consumer-research of Census Bureau, 34; culture of control in, 47; industrial modernism and, 8; lifestyle profiling, 8–9, 54, 140–41; predictability of consumers, 48; psychographic marketing, 40, 53–54; travel and (*see* leisure; tourism); vacations as symbol of consumer-driven economy, 1–2, 144; World War II as fight for consumerism, 26. See also Keynesian economy; market research; market segmentation
Cook, James, 8
Corwin, Norman, 75
Cosmopolitan (magazine), 32
cosmopolitanism: middlebrow culture and, 83, 102; taste and, 141

Cowles Communications, 50
Crowell-Collier publications, 50
cultural capital: authenticity in travel and, 130–31; magazine reading and, 89–91
cultural hierarchy, 128, 130–31
cultural production, 7, 8
culture of control, 47, 57
Cunard Line, 18
Curtis, Cyrus, 32–33
Curtis, Louisa Knapp, 32
Curtis Publishing Company: capitalizing on travel boom, 5, 31–32; cost-cutting measures, 166n86; Development Division, 43; emotion in advertising, 38; envisioning culture of mass mobility, 37; financial crisis of 1960s, 139, 190n43; "Magazine X" project, 49; magazines published by, 32; market research division, 32–33; psychographic approach of, 31, 40; reader response testing methods, 43–44; Research Department, 35. *See also Holiday* (magazine); *Saturday Evening Post*

Daniels, Draper, 49
DeAlton, E., 24
Death of a Salesman (Miller), 71
democracy and renewal, 71
Department of Commerce, U.S., 34, 37–38
destination profiles: archetypal figures and mythologies in, 94; cultural tension in, 95–96; fictionalized elements, 94–95; high-modern sensibility of, 102; pedagogical function of, 101–2; as promotional genre, 82; psychosocial themes, 97; tourism advertising and, 84, 85; as touristic representations of place, 83; transforming geographic space into narratives of place, 86. *See also* community advertising
DeVoto, Bernard, 110, 126, 129
Dichter, Ernest, 53–54
"Difficult Countries" tourism, 134
Disneyland, 130
Donen, Stanley, 117
Dos Passos, John, 17–18
Douglass, Paul F., 3
Doyle Dane Bernbach (DDB), 121–22, 126
Dulles, Foster Rhea, 11, 72

Early Times (distiller), 85
Eastman, Joseph B., 24
Ebony: on discrimination against African American travelers, 78–81; profiles of racially tolerant locations, 79–80; as specialized magazine, 52
Edman, Irwin, 39
Efron, Edith, 3
Eisenhower, Dwight D., 136
Elder, Robert F., 39
Elisofon, Eliot, 84
Eloise (Thompson), 143
Endy, Christopher, 68, 171n38
Erwitt, Elliott, 115, 183n39
Europe on $5 a Day (Frommer), 129
European Travel Commission, 2
Evans, Walker, 76
experiential appeal of tourism, 116–17, 121–22, 126–27, 147

"The Face of Europe" (Cartier-Bresson), 101
Fadiman, Clifton, 89
Farm Security Administration (FSA), photo file, 21
farm vacations, 135
Farthest Reach (Wilson), 92
Faulkner, William, 50, 90–91
Fawcett-Dearing (printer), 85–86, 105
fear of the unknown, 123
femininity, 42
Field, Clifford, 117, 123, 184n50
Field, Richard, 91, 92
Fielding, Temple, 76
financing of vacations, 18–19
Flair (magazine), 50
Fleischer, Ari, 148
Florida: mass tourism and, 126
Florida Special (film), 17
Flying Down to Rio (film), 17
Fones-Wolf, Elizabeth, 170n25
Foote, Cone & Belding (advertising agency), 108
Foote, Nelson, 54
forced migrations, 74
Fortune (magazine): on automobile-related economy, 15; on employer-sponsored vacations, 64–65; on Florida mass tourism, 126; on tourism trade, 37; travel guides in, 17
France: TV tourism advertising, 126; worker vacation initiatives in, 21
Fratterigo, Elizabeth, 169n5
free time. *See* leisure; paid vacations
French National Tourist Office, 108, 121–22
From Here to Eternity (Jones), 93
Fromm, Erich, 97
Frommer, Arthur, 129
FSA (Farm Security Administration): photo file, 21

INDEX 197

Fuller, Ethel Romig, 14
Fuller, Walter D., 49–50
fun and American culture, 3, 42
fun morality: American values and, 108; emergence of, 4, 42
Furlough, Ellen, 133

Gallagher, Bernard, 52
gasoline and tire rationing, 24, 28
gated communities, 9
Gelbart, Larry, 137
Gelhorn, Martha, 4
gender: and fun morality, 42
General Motors Corp., 34–35
geographic curiosity, 12, 147. *See also* wanderlust, American
German Democratic Republic, 76
German Tourist Association, 112–13
Germany: Nazi era tourism promotion, 21; postwar tourism marketing, 106, 112–13
Glacier Park, 105
Glatzer, Robert, 116
Glessman, Louis R., 98
Glinn, Burt, 99
globalization, tourism, 148. *See also* international tourism
The Globe Trotter (magazine), 87
The Golden Opportunity (Curtis Publishing), 36
Goodbye to a River (Graves), 94–95
Grand Central Station (radio program), 17
Grant, Cary, 1, 117, 118
The Grass is Greener (Donen), 117
gratification, delayed, 61
Graves, John: destination profiles of, 94–97
Great Britain: ads recasting as fun destination, 132–33; OBM campaign promoting, 116–21, 183n46; segmentation of advertising, 122–25; tourism as trade export, 117
Great Depression, 13, 19–20
Greece, 133–34
Green, Peter, 184n50
Greene, Jerome, 54
Gutheim, Frederick, 20
Guthrie, A. B., Jr., 96–97, 178n60

Harper, Marion, Jr., 54
Harper's Magazine, 128
Harpers Monthly (magazine), 19
Harrison, Richard Edes, 17
Hathaway Man, 115–16, 125
Hayes, Helen, 100
hedonism and sex: in travel advertising, 133–34

Helbing, Hans, 130
Helfgott, Myron J., 122
Hemingway, Ernest, 85
"Here Is New York" (White), 50, 98
The Hidden Persuaders (Packard), 54, 97
hierarchy of needs, cultural, 3
Hildred, William P., 74
Hines, Duncan, 30
Hitchcock, Alfred, 1
Hobart, Donald M.: doubts about mass market, 52; on dynamic marketing, 36; on market research, 34, 45; on predictability of consumers, 48; scientific media-research methods, 35–36, 162nn20–21; on size of travel market, 37
Hofstadter, Richard, 97
Holiday (magazine)
—accepting alcohol advertisements, 42–43
—attention to symbolic value, 90
—audience: framed in terms of "mood," 41, 164n43; identification of, 44–46, 147, 165n60; marketing to niche audience, 6; as people of leisure, 42
—as bridge to specialized publications, 139–40
—contributors, 50, 90–91, 92–94
—destination profiles, 86–87, 92–94; beatnik New York, 99–100; commercially instrumental purposes of, 102; cultural tensions in, 95–97; Mexico, 82; New York City, 98–101; Paris, 101; Wales, 92–93
—didactic tone of, 46
—editorial control of creative process, 98
—fictional elements in articles, 94, 95
—launch of, 37–43
—market research using mock-ups, 43–48
—middlebrow flavor of, 46, 89–90, 92, 98, 142–43, 177n35
—mixed reviews of first issues, 48, 166n73
—name of, 163n29
—niche marketing and, 141–42
—Patrick as editor, 49–50
—photo use in, 99–101
—on postwar travel, 28, 30
—psychosocial themes in articles, 97
—as research instrument, 48
—reshaping identity of, 49–50
—revisionist perspective of the West, 95–96
—selling powers of, 138
—on South African tourism, 77
—as specialized magazine, 52
—themed issues, 98
—on tourism as force for peace, 74

—transformation in 1960s, 138–39
—travel boom and, 5, 31–32, 71
—on travel restrictions, 77
—travelogues as short stories, 94–96
Hopkins, Harry, 20
Hot Rod, 53
How American Buying Habits Change (U.S. Department of Labor), 66
How Green Was My Valley (Llewellyn), 92–93
How to Win Friends and Influence People (Carnegie), 41
Huizinga, Johann, 47

Ickes, Harold, 28
Independent Woman (magazine), 25
Indian Tourist Office, 134
individualist ethos, 133–35, 141. *See also* therapeutic ethos
industrial modernism, 5
International (magazine), 87
International Air Transport Association, 74
International Brotherhood of Electrical Workers, 64
international tourism: by country, 9–10; as indirect foreign aid, 2; isolationism and, 148; showcasing American standard of living, 2
internationalism, 5–6, 74–75
Isham, Warren and W. Parsons (printers), 87
isolationism, resurgent, 148
It Happened One Night (film), 17

J. Walter Thompson (advertising agency), 34
Jacobs, Meg, 29
Jamaica, 106–7, 126
Joans, Ted, 99
Johnson, Philip C., 99
Jones, James, 93
Journeys Beautiful (magazine), 87, 88

Kelly, Hubert, 61
Kerouac, Jack, 50, 72, 91
Kerr, Deborah, 117, 118
Keynesian economy, 1, 67–68, 145
Kitty Kat Klub, 58, 61, 74
Knowles, Malcolm S., 47
Kouwenhoven, John A., 71
Kyrk, Hazel, 23

labor movement: paid vacations and, 13
Ladies' Home Journal, 5, 32, 42
Lagemann, John Kord, 72
land of leisure, American, 3–4

Larsen, Roy, 66
Laughlin, Clara E., 88–89
Lazarsfeld, Paul, 39
Lears, Jackson, 8, 47
leisure: America as land of, 3–4; apparel and, 73; automobile driving and, 14–15; changing face of, 128–29; classlessness and, 65–67; democratized, 11, 66–67; dominance in adult lives, 42; egalitarian mass leisure, 5; scarcity of free time, 147; as state of mind, 39–40, 163n34; U.S. standard of living and leisure travel, 13, 143–44
leisure class: and elite travel, 88
Lhamon, W. T., 78
Life (magazine): on capriciousness in travel, 73; on changes in American leisure, 128; on Club Med, 134; on culture of mass mobility, 11; destination profiles, 84; on employer-sponsored vacations, 65; on travel boom of 1946, 28
lifestyle profiling, 8–9, 140–41; psychographic marketing, 40, 53–54
Linen, James A., 84–85
Llewellyn, Richard, 92–93, 94
Look (magazine), 28, 72, 84
Lorelei legend, 105
Lorimer, George Horace, 32
Ludeke, Herbert C., 43–44
Lundberg, George A., 39–40, 163n34
lure advertising, 105, 108
Lynd, Helen Merrell, 14–15
Lynd, Robert, 14–15
Lynes, Russell, 128

MacCannell, Dean, 83, 99
MacPherrin, James, 72
Magazine of Travel, 87, 88
magazines: destination profiles, 84–85; ignoring Jim Crow discrimination against African Americans, 78; interwar representations of New Mobility, 17; linking editorial content and travel advertising, 84–85; as lorelei of media, 85–86, 105, 143, 181n8; marketing travel and tourism, 4–5; mass marketing function of, 51–52, 140; for middle-class travel market, 88–89, 177n35; "plus factor" in travel articles, 86–94; postwar media landscape, 48–52; reading as symbolic act, 40; research and content specialization, 56–57; segmented nature since 1970s, 139; specialization of, 52–57, 140–41; television impact on, 50–51; tourism promotion by,

INDEX 199

magazines *(continued)* 8; travel magazines, 87–89; visual nature of, 140

The Manchurian Candidate, 97

Marchand, Roland, 34

Margaux, Mimi, 100

market research: Curtis Publishing and, 32–33; expansion of, 33–34; motivational research and, 54, 110–11; Parlin and, 33; psychological traits in, 54; qualitative methods in, 53–55; reader response testing methods, 43–44; as service for advertisers, 45; slow adoption by businesses in 1940s, 35; social stratification in, 38–39

market segmentation: American isolationism reflecting, 148; lifestyle profiling and, 8–9, 145; social transformation and, 140; solidifying, 52–57; steps in, 141

Martineau, Pierre, 54

masculinity, 42, 87–88, 96–97

mass leisure: egalitarianism of, 5, 143–44; masculinity and, 87–88, 96–97

mass media: promoting classless society, 66

mass mobility: capriciousness and, 73; as physical and mental phenomenon, 11; postwar vision of, 26–27; travel boom as, 71

mass tourism: American classlessness and, 47; culture of, 8, 11; diminishing free time, 9; early efforts in mass marketing, 18–22; economies of scale and affordability of, 60; escaping standardized aesthetics of, 130–31; foundations of, 12–13; global consciousness and, 144; international travel as egalitarian leisure, 62; rhetoric vs. actual travel practices, 70–71; travel boom reflecting egalitarian assumptions, 143

Maugham, Somerset, 131

Mauldin, Bill, 30

Maxwell, James, 24

May, Don, 45

McCann-Erickson (advertising agency), 111

McClure's (magazine), 32

McCullers, Carson, 92, 178n60

McGovern, Charles, 26

McPherrin, John W., 84–85

Mead, Margaret, 108

media companies: as market research promoters, 34

media specialization, 141

Mercier, Louis F. V., 101

Merrill, Dennis, 113

Mexico, 79, 82

middle class: magazine reading, 4–5; as prototypical tourist, 88–89; sightseeing sensibility, 83, 143; travel anxieties, 123–24

middlebrow culture: cosmopolitanism and, 83, 102; *Holiday* audience and, 46, 89–90, 92, 98, 142–43, 177n35; OBM campaigns appealing to, 114, 125; travel articles focusing on, 5

middle-income masses: as travel market, 123, 125, 146–47

migrations, forced, 74

Miller, Arthur, 71, 99

Mills, C. Wright, 97

Mintz, Sidney, 147

The Miracle of America (booklet), 65

"Mississippi" (Faulkner), 90

Mitchum, Robert, 119

mobility: Communist restrictions on, 76–77; decline of mobility culture, 135–44; easy mobility, 6, 131; as mastery of physical environment, 4; New Mobility as height of, 15–16, 17; ritualized, vacations as, 12; sense of individual freedom and, 71; U.S. travel restrictions, 77–78. *See also* mass mobility

modernism, industrial, 5

modernity, 151n16

Molyneux, Edward, 73

Moscoso, Ted, 114

Moses, Robert, 100–101

Motherwell, Hiram, 19

motivational research, 54, 110–11

Munsey's (magazine), 32

Nation (magazine), 77

National Association of Manufacturers, 35

National Geographic (magazine), 17, 87

National Geographic Traveler (magazine), 139

National Industrial Conference Board, 63

National Park Service, U.S., 20, 105

national parks, 20, 105

Nazism: as image problem for German tourism, 113

Neale, Richard L., 56, 145

New Class: as desirable market, 140–41

New Deal, 20–21

New England Council, 19, 25, 106

New Mexico, 108

New Mexico State Tourist Bureau, 111

New Mobility, 15–16, 17. *See also* mass mobility

New York City: beatnik New York, 99–100; *Holiday* profiles of, 98–101; Robert Moses as metaphor for, 100–101

New Zealand Government Tourist Office, 135

Newill, Philip, 46
Newill, Phyllis, 46
Newman, Arnold, 50, 100
Newsweek (magazine): destination profiles, 84; on economic impact of tourism, 68; on "off-the-beaten-path" vacations, 129; on travel boom of 1946, 28
niche marketing. *See* market segmentation
Nichols, John, 73
Nielsen (A. C.) Co., 34
Nomad (magazine), 87, 88
North American Travel Organization, 25
North by Northwest (Hitchcock), 1, 143
Nye, David, 75–76

obsolescence, planned, 42
ocean liners, 4
O'Connor, Edward, 129–30
Office of Defense Transportation (ODT), 22
Office of Price Administration (OPA), 22
Office of War Information (OWI), 24
"off-the-beaten-path" vacations, 128–35
Ogilvy, Benson & Mather (OBM): archetypal imagery in "cordially English" campaign, 117–18, 184nn50–52; Hathaway Man, 115–16, 125; photography function in ads, 120, 185n66; present tense in ad copy, 120–21; Puerto Rico advertising campaign, 114–15, 125–26, 183n39; recasting Britain as fun destination, 132–33; Schweppes campaign, 116; tourism campaign for U.S., 136; tourism clients of, 116
Ogilvy, David: allusions in ads to famous books and films, 119; on American travel to Europe, 70; archetypes in campaigns, 115–16; career of, 115; on criticism of BTA campaign, 119; focus on fantasies and desires of tourists, 116; on *Holiday*, 138; impact on advertising industry, 116, 183n46; middlebrow sensibility and, 125; on selling of trans-Atlantic travel, 186n84; on selling travel, 8; snobbery of, 126; on tourists collecting clichés, 117
On the Road (Kerouac), 72
One World (Wilkie), 75
One World philosophy, 75–76
opinion leaders: influence of, 56
Opinion Research Corporation, 124
Otham, Frederick C., 30
O'Toole, John, 141

Packard, Vance, 54

paid vacations: contraction of, 146; economic benefits of, 2; as expectation for workers, 2; labor movement and expansion of, 13; as norm of American life, 5; prevalence of, 150n3; stabilized at 1960s level, 137–38; "two weeks" as period of personal autonomy, 13–14, 63–64; as welfare capitalism, 64–65; World War II and, 23
Pan American Airways, 16–17
"Paris! City of Types" (Cartier-Bresson), 101
Parker, Sanford S., 67
Parlin, Charles Coolidge, 33
Partridge, Nell, 24
Patrick, Ted, 66; antiwar movements and, 74; career of, 49; on fictional elements in *Holiday* articles, 94; *Holiday* changes affecting, 138; as *Holiday* editor, 49–50, 83
Patten, Simon N., 32–33
Patterson, William D., 71
"People's Capitalism": U.S. economy as, 66–67, 147
"Pepsi Generation" marketing campaign, 40
Perelman, S. J., 50, 139
Peterson, Robert, 53
Philadelphia Evening Bulletin (newspaper), 24
Phillips, H. H. S., Jr., 55, 56
photographic seeing, 99
photographs: FSA Historical Section photo file, 21; in *Holiday*, 99–101; in OBM ad campaigns, 120, 185n66
pipedreams about travel, 61–64, 68–70
planned obsolescence, 42
play, benefits of, 47
Playboy (magazine), 52, 169n5
Polking, Kirk, 90
Pons, Lily, 108
Popular Photography (magazine), 53
Potter, David, 51, 66
"Prayer for the Vacations of Young Office Workers" (Fuller), 14
Pringle, Henry, 24
Printers' Ink: on community advertising, 103; Fawcett-Dearing ad in, 85–86; on financing vacations, 18–19; on market research, 34; on market specialization, 140; on mass tourism, 71; on paid vacations as American System, 65; on specialty publications, 53
psychographic marketing, 40, 53–54
psychological traits, 54
Puerto Rico: changing mainland perceptions of, 113–15; OBM advertising campaign, 114–15, 125–26

Pullman Car Company, 25

Queen for a Day (radio program), 61
Quick (magazine), 50

railroads: mobility and, 4, 16; promoting vacation travel, 105
Ranieri, Mary, 64
rationing, gasoline and tire, 24, 28
reader response research, 44
Reader's Digest (magazine), 76
Reck, F. M., 26, 27
recreation, 23–24, 47
Reed, Virgil D., 34
Reese-Davis, W. R., 132
Reeves, Rosser, 108
Reisman, David, 41, 97
"Return to the Reich" (Sutton), 112
roadmaps, 76
Robeson, Paul, 77
Robin, Toni, 73
Robins (A. H.) Company, 65
Rocky Mountain National Park, 28
Roosevelt, Eleanor, 23
Roosevelt, Franklin D., 23
Roper, Elmo, 38
Ross, Nancy Wilson, 92, 97
Rubicam, Raymond, 138

S. S. *Booker T. Washington*, 79
S. S. *United States*, 4
sabbatical plans, 64, 137
Said, Edward, 7, 86
Sales Management (magazine), 39
Saturday Evening Post: on automobile driving, 15; as Curtis Publishing publication, 5; death and restructuring of, 139, 190n43; history of, 32; on postwar tourist travel, 25; redefinition of audience, 42, 43
Saturday Review of Literature, 20, 74
Saunders, Dero A., 67
Schanche, Don A., 138
Schlesinger, Arthur, Jr., 97
Schnor, Juliet B., 153n30
Schweppes advertising campaign, 116
self-realization and travel, 133–35. *See also* therapeutic ethos
SerVaas, Beurt R., 139
service economy, 22, 140–41, 146
sex and hedonism: in travel advertising, 133–34
Shaw, Irwin, 62
sightseeing: as modern sensibility, 83, 133,

175n5; recreational tourism vs., 6, 152n19; redefinition of, 147
Sinnot, Edmund W., 66
Sions, Harry, 90, 92, 93, 98–99
Sloan, Alfred P., Jr., 34
Social Research, Inc. (SRI), 123, 125
social stratification, 38–39
socioeconomic groups, 38
Sontag, Susan, 99, 102
Soule, George, 63
South Africa, 77
Spain, 77
Sparkes, Boyden, 25, 26
Spillane, Mickey, 97
Spock, Benjamin, 97
Sports Illustrated: affirming culture of control, 57, 168n118; *Holiday* as model for, 55; marketing to niche audience, 6; research, development, and marketing of, 55–56; sports as selling theme, 55
sportswear, American, 73
standard of living, U.S.: buying power vs. personal time, 9, 153n30; consumer spending and, 67; as fruit of free enterprise, 65; leisure travel as component of, 13, 143–44 (*see also* leisure); postwar, 59; producing classless society, 66; redefinition of, 146
Starch, Daniel, 40
status anxiety, 124, 186n84
Stebbins, Hal, 121–22
Steinbeck, John, 50, 61, 72, 148
Steinhauser, Bert, 85
Stephen Goerl Associates (advertising agency), 113
stereotypes: as marketing problem, 111
Stevenson, Robert Louis, 71
Stinnett, Caskie, 138
Stryker, Roy, 21
suburban development, postwar, 59
Sunset (magazine), 89
supersonic transport (SST), 136–37
Sutton, Horace, 10, 77, 112
"Swinging London," 132

Taft-Hartley Act, 59
Tahiti, 130–31
Tarascon, Paul, 177n29
Ted Bates & Company, 108
Tedlow, Richard, 40
television: cable television and psychographic marketing, 40; impact on magazine readership, 51, 140; tourism advertising, 50–51, 126

theme parks, 130
therapeutic ethos, 121–22, 126–27, 133–35, 141
Theroux, Paul, 134
Thomas, Don, 18, 39, 106, 110
Thomas, Lowell, 46
Thompson, Kay, 143
Tide (trade journal), 31, 55, 87
Time (magazine), 49, 54, 84–85
Time, Inc., 55–56
tourism (tourist travel)
—American travel tastes and, 129–30
—antitourist sentiment in, 130–31
—authenticity concerns, 131–32
—characteristics: affirming individuality, 147; as delayed gratification, 61; as democratic experience, 6; dissolving class lines, 62–63; as expectation of American life, 23; as force for peace, 74–75; geographic curiosity, 12; as major industry, 21; modernist longing for totality, 99; as social and economic good, 20
—cultural production and, 7
—democratization of leisure, 11
—discrimination against African Americans, 78–81
—experiential appeal of, 116–17, 121–22, 126–27, 147
—foreign travel: disincentivizing, 135–36; fear of the unknown, 123–24; globalization and, 148; internationalist ethos of, 74–75; operationalizing One World philosophy, 76; political borders restricting travel freedom, 73–74; prestige of, 124–25; status anxiety and, 124, 186n84; structural adjustments to global economy and, 145
—geography of, 7
—mass affluence and, 59–60
—mobility culture decline and, 135–44
—narratives of: economic benefits, 67–68; "off-the-beaten-path," 130–31, 134–35; self-fulfillment, 133–35; social reality vs., 60; transformation, 6, 58, 147
—sightseeing vs. recreational, 6, 152n19
—Soviet, restrictions on, 76–77
—state of mind and, 39
—travel boom: celebrating social fluidity and reinvention, 71; narratives vs. social reality, 60; postwar vacation rush, 28–29; reflecting egalitarian assumptions, 143
—travel practices vs. pipedreams, 68–70
—travel surveys, 68–69
—wanderlust and vacation travel, 72
—World War II impact on, 22–27, 159n57

—*See also* mass tourism; travel industry
traffic control: tourism advertising and, 107
transatlantic voyages, 16
Travel (magazine), 89
travel advertising. *See* advertising
"Travel America Year" (1940), 21
Travel and Leisure (magazine), 139
travel fantasies as pipedreams, 61–64, 68–70
travel industry: contraction of vacation time and, 145–46; Depression-era advertising, 19; government support for, 21–22; mass mobility rhetoric vs. reality of travel, 70–71; mass-merchandising travel, 18–22; measuring vacation spending, 37–38; New Deal interventions in, 21; patriotic language in wartime advertising, 22; planning for postwar development of, 25, 159n62; postwar marketing practices, 6–7; postwar price gouging, 29; selling vacations as American System, 64–71; structural changes in, 130; tourism as "cash crop," 12
travel profiles. *See* destination profiles
Traveler (magazine), 139, 166n74
Travel-Holiday (magazine), 139
Travels with Charley (Steinbeck), 50
Trigano, Gilbert, 130
Trippe, Juan, 62, 71
Turner, Louis, 131
"two weeks" vacation. *See* paid vacations

U.S. News and World Report, 29
U.S.A. trilogy (Dos Passos), 17–18
unique selling proposition (USP), 108
United Airlines, 25, 175n8
United States: barriers to travel, 77–78; Department of Commerce, 34, 37–38; disincentivizing foreign travel, 135–36; economy as American System, 64; economy as "People's Capitalism," 66–67, 147; political culture in postwar era, 59; State Department travel restrictions, 77; "Visit U.S.A." campaigns, 136. *See also* standard of living, U.S.
United States Information Agency (USIA), 68
United States Travel Bureau (USTB), 21
United States Travel Service, 136

vacations: association with idleness, 19; close to home, in World War II, 24; cognitive dissonance of, 111; as consumer entitlements, 144; democratization of, 11, 13, 61–63; employer-sponsored, 64–65, 170n23; extension of, 63–64; functionalist view of,

INDEX 203

vacations *(continued)*
110; mass mobility rhetoric vs. reality of travel, 70–71; "off-the-beaten-path," 128–35; personal autonomy and, 63–64; pipedreams and, 61–62, 68–70; sabbaticals, 64, 137; savings and credit plans for, 18–19; selling as American System, 64–71; as symbol of consumer-driven economy, 1–2; time disparity, U.S. vs. other countries, 9, 146, 153n30; travel as ritualized mobility, 12; types of vacationers, 128. *See also* paid vacations; tourism (tourist travel)
Vail, Colorado, 130
Venture (magazine), 139
Wales, James Albert, 14
"Wales" (Llewellyn), 92–93
Wallace, Henry, 74
Walsh, Henry Collins, 87–88
Walt Disney World, 130
Wanamaker's Department Store: American Express travel desk, 18; employee vacations, 63–64
wanderlust, American: dampening of, 147; as national identity, 3, 11, 72–73; sportswear reflecting, 73; travel and, 15
Ward, Douglas, 32–33
Warner, W. Lloyd, 38, 54
Weaver, John D., 95
Weaver, Sylvester "Pat," 66
Weber, Max, 3
Wechsberg, Joseph, 10
Weidman, Jerome, 89, 90
Weiss, E. B., 140, 141
Welcome Travelers (radio program), 61
welfare capitalism: paid vacations as, 64–65

Wendell Wilkie Foundation, 75
West Side Story (play), 114
White, E. B., 50, 98
White, Marion, 25
Whitman, Walt, 75
Wilkie, Wendell, 75
Williams, Raymond, 86
Wilson, Charles, 81
Wolfenstein, Martha, 42
working class: leisure habits, 66–67; paid vacations, 13
Works Progress Administration (WPA), 20–21
workweek, shortening of, 11
World Traveler (magazine), 87, 88, 177n29
World War II: campaign against unnecessary travel, 22, 24, 159n57; discourse of war as fight for consumerism, 26; discretionary spending on recreation, 23–24; impact on tourism, 12, 22–27; Japanese surrender, 28; postwar tourism planning, 24; postwar vacation rush, 28; postwar vision of mass mobility, 26–27; rationing and travel restrictions, 27–28; recreation centered around home, 24; U.S. spared devastation of, 59; vacations as patriotic duty, 23
World's Fair of 1939 (New York), 17
Wrangle, George, 115

YMCA camps: integration of, 79
Young, Robert R., 70–71

Zachary, Frank, 100
Zagray, Ida, 58
Zagray, Walt, 58